MOON OF POPPING TREES

Rex Alan Smith

∧∧∧∧∧∧∧∧∧∧∧∧∧∧∧∧∧

READER'S DIGEST PRESS

DISTRIBUTED BY
THOMAS Y. CROWELL COMPANY
NEW YORK
1975

Designed by Nancy Dale Muldoon
Manufactured in the United States of America

Library of Congress Cataloging in Publication Data
Smith, Rex Alan.
    Moon of Popping Trees.
    1. Wounded Knee Creek, Battle of, 1890.   I. Title.
E83.89.S58   978.3′66′02   75-12854
ISBN 0-88349-075-7
ISBN 0-88349-076-5 (pbk.)

1 2 3 4 5 6 7 8 9 10

Contents

Preface

DURING THE 1973 occupation of the Indian community of Wounded Knee by other Indians, many people asked me what happened at Wounded Knee "the first time." They knew it was something bad, but they weren't quite sure what it was. And that's how *Moon of Popping Trees* began. Originally it was intended only as an article telling the story of the Wounded Knee tragedy of 1890. Had the project stopped there, *Popping Trees* would no doubt have been just the basic story of that event, and probably no more enlightening than a hundred previous ones on the same subject. But then I was given a Reader's Digest assignment to investigate and report on the Indian problems of today. And the more I traveled, studied, and interviewed in researching the so-called Indian problem, the more I realized that all of its elements—racial attitudes, cultural conflicts, interpretation of treaties, congressional actions, impact of the press,—are directly tied to and influenced by those same elements as they existed on the frontier nearly a century ago. Then I began seeing *Moon of Popping Trees* as much more than the simple story of a fight. It began to emerge as a potential vehicle for giving Indians and non-Indians alike a better understanding of the Indian problems of today through a more accurate understanding of their background and development.

At that point the Popping Trees project shifted from article to book. And even though I already had a comprehensive background in its subject material, I suddenly found myself buried under a burden of research far heavier than anything I had expected. The reason is that key word, "accurate." For in no area of American history is true accuracy harder to achieve, nor has more inaccurate nonsense been written, than in that pertaining to the American Indian. There are several reasons.

vii

One is that, having no written language, the Indians of earlier times could not record events and impressions as they occurred. Thus, their history was written by non-Indians who, more often than not, knew little about Indians, and who had to depend to a considerable extent on the Indians' stories. As might be expected, however, as those stories were handed down they tended to change in the retelling to the extent that Indian oral history is very undependable. (A good example of this is the Indian accounts of the destruction of Custer's force at the Little Big Horn. Dozens of Indian accounts of that fight are in existence. And yet, historians still cannot agree on just what happened there because the Indian accounts are so fragmented and contradictory that no reasonably consistent story can be constructed from them.)

Also, of course, all of the "Indian" fiction of the past was written by non-Indians. And for the romantic novelists the Indians were a bonanza. They didn't have to know anything about the realities of Indians to write about them because their readers wouldn't know the difference anyway. Moreover, that same unknown quality allowed the novelists to indulge in extravagant flights of fancy which, as it turned out, hid the real Indians behind a romantic curtain from which they have not yet fully emerged.

In most of those Victorian literary disasters Indians were depicted either as totally good or totally bad. Usually—especially in the dime novels—it was the latter. The pure-hearted, stalwart settler defending his family against a horde of shrieking savages was a popular theme. Actually, that same sort of writing is still going on, only with the roles reversed. Now the story is usually one of an Indian, noble and speaking with a straight tongue, defending himself against brutal oppression by greedy, racist whites.

Obviously, both of these approaches are preposterous oversimplifications. And yet, because we have had such long exposure to them in literature and films, there can be little doubt that they have gradually conditioned a great many of us to automatically think of difficulties between Indians and non-Indians as simple morality plays in which pure good is pitted against pure evil. And it is this sort of absurd polarization that must be eliminated if we are ever to resolve our Indian problems fairly, and with justice to Indians and non-Indians alike.

Thus, the present-day writer in Indian affairs bears a heavy responsibility. He must not load his literary dice by selecting only those facts that fit his own emotional, racial, or political bias and thereby "prove" his preconceived opinions. Rather, he must diligently seek to accumulate all of the facts, whether or not personally pleasing, and form his conclusions from what he sees as their truth.

That is the approach I have attempted to take in this book—that of allowing the facts to dictate the conclusions—and I will confess that as the assembled facts were fitted together, the resulting picture held some surprises and overturned some of my previously held opinions. And because these facts contradict some of our most popularly held notions about the conflict between whites and Indians during the American westward movement, perhaps they will upset some of yours also. For, once we penetrate the romantic curtain and also get behind the "good versus evil" accounts of those who are grinding some personal ax, the old stereotyped images are shattered, and the "good guys" and "bad guys" quickly disappear and are replaced simply with "different guys." We soon discover that although the Indians and whites were poles apart in their cultural codes, they were identical in their common humanity, and that each race contained about the same mix of virtue and vice as the other. In their struggles on the frontier there was little deliberate wrongdoing by either side. Rather, those of each side performed as their own beliefs and cultural conditioning dictated that they had to perform, and each side was generally in the right according to its own understanding of right.

Moreover, these things are as true today as they were yesterday. And the better both Indians and non-Indians understand that, the easier it will be for us to walk in each other's moccasins, and to see ourselves as *people* first, and as Indians or non-Indians second. Only in that sort of understanding will we ever find just answers to our complex Indian problems. And it is, hopefully, as some small contribution to that understanding that *Moon of Popping Trees* was written.

Rex Alan Smith

Foreword

THE WRITING OF any history—and particularly the history of the American Indian—in such a way that its true realities are always transmitted to the reader without distortion is an almost impossible challenge. If for no other reason, this is true because the conversion of living persons and events into mere marks on paper is, in itself, a distortion. History that is presented only as ink-embalmed data is as a flower pressed in a book. Although the dry petals still hold all the elements of the original flower, they cannot show us how it looked blooming in the field. The color and fragrance—and thus the true reality—of the flower are gone.

In *Moon of Popping Trees* I have striven earnestly to preserve the story of the struggle of the Sioux with the white man not as a dried flower, but in the colorful reality in which it was lived. Thus—even as the artist must make certain deviations from nature if he is to achieve reality in a three-dimensional scene painted on a two-dimensional canvas—in the interest of historical accuracy in its fullest sense, I have found it necessary to make certain deviations from the approach of the conventional history book. They are as follows:

VERBATIM QUOTATIONS OF INDIAN STATEMENTS

It would be preposterous to believe the Indians of the past century expressed themselves in ornate Victorian phrases, the "governmentese" of civil servants, or in the complex sentences of professors. And yet, it is often in these forms—in stilted "verbatim" quotes that are obvious misquotes—that history has preserved their comments.

The reason is simple. The Indians' statements were not recorded by the Indians themselves but by white men listening through interpreters, and often from memory at a substantially later date. Generally, these reporters had no reason to be interested in the Indians' actual words, but only in what they thought they would have said had they been able to speak "good English."

Unfortunately the use of these quotations exactly as they are recorded in the primary research sources—placing the sentences of, say, an English professor in the mouth of a tribal Indian—injects a jarring note of unbelievability into an Indian history. And so long as the Indians' original meaning is kept intact, there seems no reason to perpetuate historical inaccuracy by keeping their words forever frozen in sentences that were never theirs anyway. Therefore—taking the greatest care to preserve the meaning—I have removed such statements from words which the Indians would not have said and have put them into words which the Indians might very well have said, for that is where they belong.

INDIAN LETTERS

By the late 1800s a number of the Sioux could write, and some of their letters are quoted in this book. So as to preserve their flavor I have changed them as little as possible. But because they were written in what has been called "Carlisle English," which is almost unintelligible to anyone unfamiliar with it, I have rephrased them sufficiently to make sense to the reader.

RECONSTRUCTION OF THOUGHTS

In the development of some sequences certain pertinent material is presented in the form of thoughts running through the minds of those involved. This is done for realism, and to allow characters to assume flesh-and-blood humanity.

Naturally, we cannot *know* if they were actually thinking those particular thoughts (or any others, for that matter) at those particular times. Even so, from their known attitudes, statements, and actions we can surmise; and by using facts that they would have both possessed and been influenced by, and opinions that substantial evidence shows them to have held, we should be able to fairly accurately reconstruct things that they *must* have been thinking at some time during a particular occurrence. And if we can, then the only potential deviation from history lies in whether they thought them at a particular moment.

MOON OF
POPPING TREES
∧∧∧∧∧∧∧

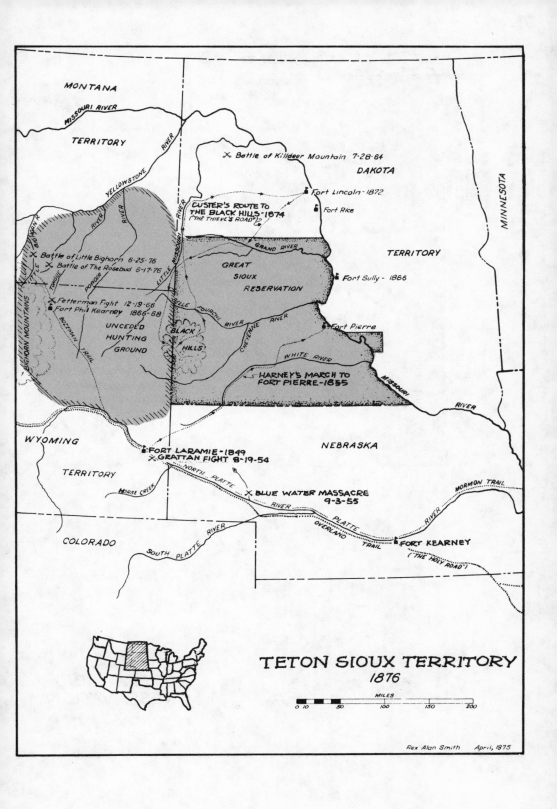

MONTANA

Missouri River

TERRITORY

X *Battle of Killdeer Mountain 7-28-64*

DAKOTA

■ *Fort Lincoln - 1872*

YELLOWSTONE

CUSTER'S ROUTE TO
THE BLACK HILLS - 1874
("THE THIEVE'S ROAD")

Fort Rice

GRAND RIVER

TERRITORY

X *Battle of Little Bighorn 6-25-76*
X *Battle of The Rosebud 6-17-76*

GREAT
SIOUX
RESERVATION

Fort Sully - 1866

X *Fetterman Fight 12-19-66*
■ *Fort Phil Kearney 1866-68*

UNCEDED
HUNTING
GROUND

BLACK
HILLS

BELLE FOURCHE RIVER

CHEYENNE RIVER

■ *Fort Pierre*

BIGHORN MOUNTAINS

WHITE RIVER

HARNEY'S MARCH TO
FORT PIERRE - 1855

MISSOURI

MINNESOTA

WYOMING

NEBRASKA

TERRITORY

■ *FORT LARAMIE - 1849*
X *GRATTAN FIGHT 8-19-54*

RIVER

NORTH   PLATTE

HORSE CREEK

X *BLUE WATER MASSACRE*
9-3-55

MORMON TRAIL

RIVER

PLATTE

OVERLAND   TRAIL

■ *FORT KEARNEY*

COLORADO

SOUTH   PLATTE   RIVER

("THE HOLY ROAD")

TETON SIOUX TERRITORY
1876

MILES
0 10   50   100   150   200

Rex Alan Smith   April, 1975

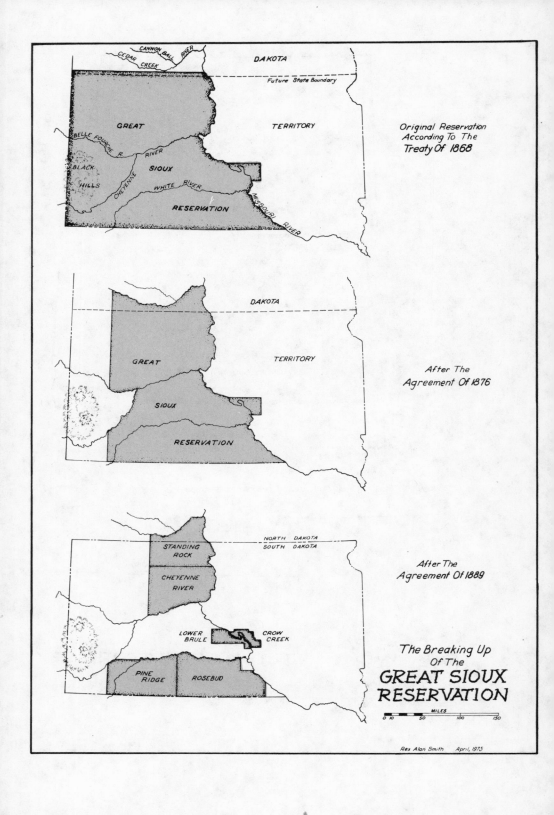

Original Reservation
According To The
Treaty Of 1868

After The
Agreement Of 1876

After The
Agreement Of 1889

The Breaking Up
Of The
GREAT SIOUX
RESERVATION

Rex Alan Smith   April, 1975

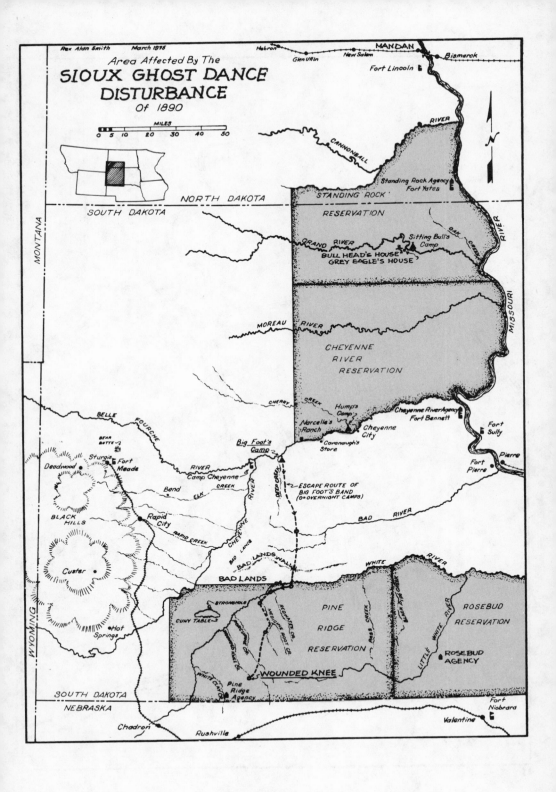

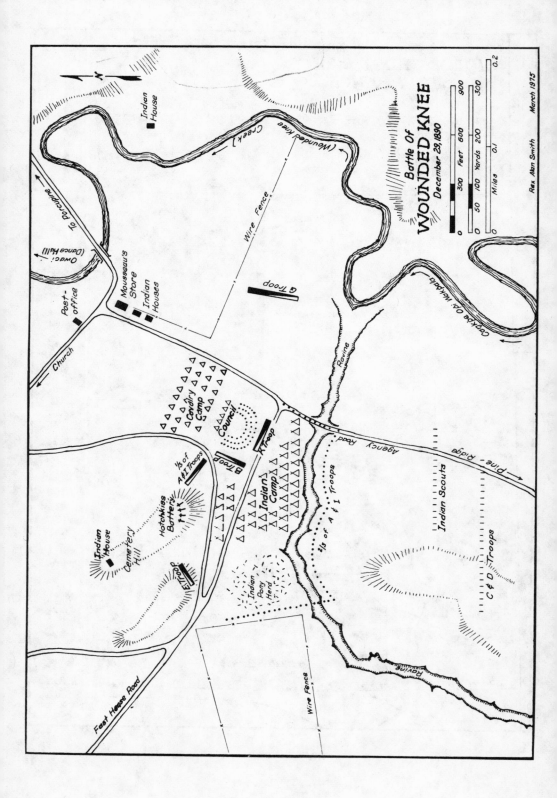

Battle of
WOUNDED KNEE
December 29, 1890

Rex Alan Smith   March 1975

CHAPTER
1
ΛΛΛΛΛΛΛ

In the Moon of Popping Trees

THE LAST SIGNIFICANT BATTLE between the American Indian and the white man took place on December 29, 1890, on the banks of Wounded Knee Creek in South Dakota. It has been called both a "battle" and a "massacre"—the term used depending on the bias of the speaker. Actually, it was mostly a battle, partly a massacre, and entirely a tragic blunder. Of the three hundred and fifty Indians present, two-thirds were women and children. When the smoke cleared, eighty-four Lakotah (Teton Sioux) men and sixty-two women and children lay dead, their bodies scattered along a stretch of more than a mile where they had been trying to flee. Of some five hundred soldiers and scouts, twenty-five were dead—some, possibly, from the crossfire of their own guns.

Involved in the affair, either centrally or peripherally, was a diverse cast of personalities. There were the great Sioux chiefs, Sitting Bull and Red Cloud. There was Wovoka, a Paiute Indian who may have thought he was the Wanikiye—the Christ—returned to earth, and whose followers were sure he was. There was Buffalo Bill Cody. There was General Nelson Miles, who would later assume supreme command of the United States Army. Accompanying the general was Frederic Remington, an artist famous for his paintings of the West. Helping to treat the wounded after the battle was a young German private in the Red Cross, the Baron Erwin von Luittwitz; later he would become Defense Minister of Germany and, as a general, would lead the Kaiser's forces into Belgium. There was a young officer in General Miles's command who would later defeat those forces, Second

1

Lieutenant John J. Pershing. And also—or so it had been said—there was the ghost of Lieutenant Colonel George Armstrong Custer.

Yet the tragedy that occurred at Wounded Knee was the result of neither individual personalities nor intentions. That it occurred where it did was an accident. That it would occur somewhere was almost predestined. It was the result of one of those inevitable tides of history that dictate change; for the long road to Wounded Knee actually began at the door of the first factory of the Industrial Age—an age that was to be the doom of nomadic hunting cultures everywhere. It ended with a final confrontation of two cultures separated by thousands of years of development, and so different that mutual understanding was improbable and coexistence impossible. It was the death spasm of the stone age hunter—vanquished by the industrial age farmer.

The frontier farmer, or settler, of the late 1800s, for instance, saw himself as sober, God-fearing, and industrious; and generally he was. He saw the Indian as an ignorant savage, uncouth, unsanitary, and unpredictable. He was convinced that in bringing "civilization" to the red man he was doing him an immense favor. And he couldn't understand why the Indian was so stubbornly and irritatingly ungrateful. Nor did he feel wrong in seizing the land. On the contrary, he felt right about it. In his opinion the land belonged to no one, certainly not to any scattered bands of nomadic Indians. They didn't take care of it, and they didn't use it. They neither plowed, nor planted, nor tended flocks. Like children, he thought, they simply regarded it as a vast playground on which to hunt and fight and loaf. He saw a clear duty to make the land productive and, if possible, to make the Indian "productive" too.

On the other hand, the Indian saw himself as generous, God-fearing, honest, and self-respecting. Generally he was, and he thought the white men were uncivilized. They were like greedy, undisciplined children. They wanted to own everything and to shut it up where it couldn't get away—even the grass. They were crazy-wild for the maza skaze, that yellow metal that was too soft to be used for arrowheads or axes or any useful thing. They were so harsh to their little ones that sometimes they even struck them. And they had wantonly wasted the buffalo that was the food of life. They had killed it for merely the hide or just for the head and horns to hang in their lodges, and they had left the good meat to rot on the prairie. The Indians had done the same thing, it is true, once they found they could trade the hides for the white-man goods. However, the white man had done it so much more efficiently that it was his fault the buffalo now were gone. But worst of all, the white men were liars, and with each of their broken promises the Indians'

land had shrunk until it, too, was gone. Now the once-proud Lakotahs could
live only on barren reservations and on the white man's charity.

Then, unexpectedly, when it seemed that everything had been taken away
and the old life was gone forever, the prophet Wovoka gave the Indian a new
dream and a new hope—and the course was set for the final bloody collision
at Wounded Knee.

Late in the Moon of Popping Trees (December 28, 1890) icy air had
been lying for days like a frozen blanket over the long gray hills of
southwestern South Dakota. Suddenly it disappeared—pushed aside by
a day so sparkling it seemed the Great Holy had borrowed it from spring
to give the suffering frostbitten land a rest. So now the thin-clad hills,
their grass stunted by the past summer's drought, slept like grateful old
dogs in the warming sun. From the distant Bad Lands ridges to the north
a soft breeze searched its way up the snow-dappled draws of Porcupine
Creek coaxing cold rivulets of melt-water from under the drifted banks,
and whispering through the scattered pines and junipers standing green
against the barren hillsides; it carried their fragrance across American
Horse road to a band of travelers who were winding their way
southwestward up the slope of Porcupine valley.

It was a large band—maybe three hundred and fifty people—some
men, but mostly women and children. A few of them were dressed in
white-man clothing, and a few were in Indian dress, but most wore a
combination of the two, and all of them were shabby. Some were riding
winter-gaunt horses, some were in old gray-weathered wagons, and many
were walking. In the bed of the lead wagon, huddled in blankets despite
the warm day and so ill with pneumonia he was spitting blood, lay a
middle-aged man made old by hardship and sickness . . . Chief Big
Foot. For five days now, ever since escaping from the soldiers who had
come to take them away from their Cheyenne River homes and into
confinement at the soldier post at Fort Meade, the sick chief had been
leading these Minneconjou Sioux across the windswept miles away from
the searching soldiers and toward Red Cloud's people at Pine Ridge. It
was said that even though there were soldiers at Pine Ridge also—many
soldiers—they would be safe there and not have to go away to Fort
Meade. And maybe they could even continue to do the Ghost Dance for
the second coming of the Wanikiye—the Son of God—who, they were
told, was soon to return to earth and throw away the white men who had
crucified Him and give the world to the Indian people.

It had been a bitter trek. They were always hiding, usually cold, and there had been barely enough food. Bitter, too, was the fact that now, with the hard trip almost over and Pine Ridge maybe only seven hours away, they were going to have to surrender after all. They were, that is, if the four Indian army scouts they had captured at noon on Porcupine Creek spoke true. According to these scouts, the soldiers were now directly in their path in a big camp on Wounded Knee Creek, just over the next divide. However, the scouts had also said that these were not the soldiers seeking to take the Minneconjous to Fort Meade, but were the ones from Pine Ridge. They had further reported that the soldier chief, Major Whitside, had a good heart for Indian people and meant them no harm. In fact, they said, all the major wanted of Big Foot's people was for them to allow his troops to escort them peaceably on into Pine Ridge agency. Ah-h-h. These were good words, if true, and they seemed reasonable. Maybe, too, this beautiful day—after all the bad weather— was an omen of good. And finally, there was little choice anyhow. Therefore, although knowing his decision would doubtless anger some of his young men who didn't know what it was like to fight white soldiers, the chief told two of the scouts to remain with him and the other two to ride to the soldier chief and tell him that the Minneconjous of Big Foot were coming to his camp in peace.

Meanwhile, Major Samuel Whitside, Seventh Cavalry, United States Army, and camped at Wounded Knee Creek, had been in the field since Friday morning. General Miles in Rapid City had ordered General Brooke at Pine Ridge, and he in turn had ordered Major Whitside, to find Big Foot and his people (known to be on the loose and, according to General Miles, "very cunning and very bad") and to disarm them and bring them in. Now it was early Sunday afternoon on December 28, and despite intensive searching by the scouts—searching spurred by a reward of more than three months' pay offered, half by the army and half by the newspaper correspondents, to the one who found Big Foot—the long hours of riding had produced nothing but saddle sores, chilblains, and one empty draw after another. Then, as Whitside and his officers were lingering over a late lunch, Old Hand and another scout came galloping in with Big Foot's message and to report that his band was no more than six miles away—just over the divide to the northeast. Despite Big Foot's word that he was coming peacefully and directly to Whitside's camp, the major immediately ordered four troops of cavalry to saddle up, and he prepared to move out to intercept him. At this point, level-headed John

Shangreau, the mixed-blood chief of scouts, suggested that the wisest course might be to merely stay in place and allow the Indians to come in as promised. Whitside disagreed. He pointed out that even now the troops of Major Henry's Ninth Cavalry were sweeping southward from Iron Spring in the Bad Lands, also looking for Big Foot. And if these soldiers, not knowing that the Minneconjous' intentions were peaceful, found them first there could be a fight. Thus, Whitside reasoned, it would be best for all, and particularly for the Indians, if the Seventh got to them as soon as possible. (And, although he didn't mention it, Whitside was also probably recalling that only five days before, Big Foot had made the same promise to the commander of the army's camp on Cheyenne River and had then broken it and had taken his people and run away.)

At about two o'clock, as Whitside was leading his command over the ridge west of Pine Creek—a dry wash between the valleys of Wounded Knee and Porcupine—two distant horsemen were seen racing toward them from the far slope. Upon arrival, they turned out to be the two scouts that Big Foot had detained (and now released) when he sent the other two to Whitside with his message. John Shangreau asked them about the attitude of the Minneconjous. "Pretty tough," replied the one called Little Bat (Baptiste Garnier). "We are liable to catch it today." Then, as the troops moved down through the sun-fragrant pine glades of the creek bottom and out onto the open slope beyond, the head of the Indian column topped the ridge a mile or so ahead. As it did, Whitside could see that Little Bat had been right about the Indian mood. Warriors, some waving rifles, were fanning out in a skirmish line ahead of the Indian wagons. Not only that, they were galloping their horses back and forth to get them their second winds, as was the old custom before a battle; and through the field glasses he could see that the ponies' tails had been tied up, which was also the old way before a fight. Whitside forthwith ordered, "Dismount!" and he, too, spread his troops into a skirmish line. Next he had his two small Hotchkiss cannon brought to the front, where the Indians couldn't miss seeing them, and began a slow advance. Now, as the two sides moved warily toward each other, tension building because neither trusted the other, there followed one of those danger-hushed times—brief, but seemingly endless—when people who are excited and frightened on the inside are extra calm on the outside, and when all movement is slow and deliberate because the least false step can touch off a fight that neither side wants. Suddenly, through the warrior line two men came walking, followed by a wagon with a white flag fluttering from a pole tied to its box. Whitside halted the army line. The tension was broken. Now Shangreau strode out to meet the two Indians. Shaking hands with both, he asked, "Si'tanka tokiyaya who?" (Where is Big Foot?) "Here," said one, "in this wagon."

Shangreau moved to the side of the wagon box and greeted the huddled figure of the chief, "Hau Kola!" (Hello, friend!) He then shook Big Foot's hand and said, "Partner, come with me to see the soldier chief." Big Foot, weak and coughing in his bloodstained blankets, motioned his driver forward. At the same time, Major Whitside was coming forward. Upon meeting the wagon he, too, shook hands with the chief and, through Shangreau, asked him where he was going. "To Pine Ridge agency," Big Foot whispered hoarsely. Whitside then told him that he had been informed that Big Foot was hostile, but now that he saw him could see this was not so and that the people who said it must have lied. Big Foot agreed. In fact, he said, he was a peacemaker on a peacemaking mission. The chiefs at Pine Ridge agency were squabbling among themselves and with the white chiefs, also, until there seemed no end to it. Therefore, offering a hundred ponies if Big Foot could make peace among them, they had invited him to come to Pine Ridge, and that was where he was going. "I'm glad you speak frankly with me," Whitside responded. "However, Big Foot, I want you to come to the camp with me." "All right," said the chief, "I was going there anyway." Recalling now his orders from General Brooke, Whitside said to Shangreau, "John, tell them I want their horses and guns." But Shangreau, well aware that not all of the nervously milling warriors were feeling as cooperative as their sick chief, frowned and hesitated. Then he said, "Look here, Major. If you do that there is liable to be a fight here, and all you will do is kill some women and children and the men will get away from you." Whitside reminded Shangreau that the general's orders specifically stated that they were to disarm and dismount the Indians as soon as they had found them. Well, the general might know about orders, but Shangreau —being Sioux himself—knew about Indians. He stood his ground, saying that any disarming and dismounting that was done had better be done after the Indians were in the cavalry camp. Whitside, having had a good deal of experience with another tribe fully as warlike as the Sioux (the Apache), saw the wisdom of Shangreau's words and withdrew the order. Turning back to Big Foot, the major said, "I see you are in a hard wagon. I want you to ride to our camp in an easier one." He ordered the ambulance brought up, and Big Foot transferred into it. Once more

Whitside shook Big Foot's hand. Then he had the column formed up for marching and motioned "Forward!" So now, enclosed between two troops of blue-coated soldiers ahead and another two with two cannon behind, and with wagons creaking and hoofs and wheels clucking and clattering on the prairie sod, Big Foot's people started moving southwestward toward the sunset that now flamed red over the ridges of Wounded Knee.

Their surrender to the cavalry that day and the tragedy that would overtake them on the following morning at Wounded Knee were not precipitated by military orders or actions per se, however, but by the final movement of the Industrial Age avalanche which had overrun American Indians everywhere . . . simply because they were in its path. Like the mountain avalanche, which is slow in building and yet is made inevitable the moment snow begins to gather on an unstable mountain slope, and which when it is ready may be touched off by the footfall of a wandering rabbit, the white avalanche that overran the seven tribes of the Lakotah—the Teton Sioux—was made inevitable the moment the first white man started westward. Once released, it ground over the Sioux for thirty-six years before finally coming to rest on the banks of a creek called Wounded Knee. And when it was set off, it was not by a rabbit, but by a wandering Mormon cow.

CHAPTER

2

⋀⋀⋀⋀⋀⋀

The Holy Road

AT ABOUT THE TIME the American colonists acquired their independence from Great Britain and began to build an empire, the Teton Sioux, who called themselves Lakotah, acquired the horse, and with this new weapon they began to build an empire, also. They defeated the Mandans and the Arikara at the Missouri River and took their lands. Whooping westward they defeated the Crows and the Cheyenne and took their lands. From the Kiowa they seized the Black Hills, which became the sacred mountains of the Sioux and a place so holy that they soon forgot they had taken it from the Kiowa and, instead, came to believe they had received it directly from the Great Holy, Himself. Of the seven tribes or council fires of the Lakotah, the larger tribes were the Oglala, Hunkpapa, Brulé, and Minneconjou, and the smaller ones were the Sans Arc, Two Kettle, and Blackfeet. By the early 1800s, the newly conquered lands of these seven tribes stretched from the Missouri River of Dakota to the Big Horn Mountains of Wyoming, and from the North Platte River of Nebraska and Wyoming to the Cannon Ball River of North Dakota. As a result, a mere twenty-five thousand or so people were occupying and controlling a territory larger than New York and Pennsylvania combined.

It was at this time that the first white men came among the Lakotah. They were traders seeking the hides of beaver and buffalo, and they got along with the Indians fairly well. This was not because the two liked each other—generally they did not. Although the traders usually treated the Indians with dignity and courtesy, it was mostly because there were

8

few traders and many Indians, and they would have been afraid to do otherwise. Privately they tended to regard the Indians as treacherous savages. And since the Indians sometimes cooked and ate the washed-out entrails of the buffalo, the white men occasionally called them "gut-eaters" behind their backs.

The name the Lakotah gave the white men was a somewhat better one. They called them Wasicun, which was what they also called their sacred medicine bundles and meant "bearer of a sacred power." It therefore sounded as if it were an honoring name, but in the case of the white men it was not. True, the white people must have had some sacred power that helped them to make such magic things as sugar and coffee and tobacco as well as good steel knives and fine-woven blankets and booming sticks that killed from far away. But this did not mean to the Lakotah that the white men were their superiors, or even their equals. They could not be, for as every Lakotah knew, the Sioux were The People—the only true children of Wakan Tanka, the Great Holy—and all others, white and Indian alike, were their inferiors. So behind their hands they made scornful fun of these pale men, calling them "dog-face" because of their beards, "crooked-feet" because of their toes-out walk, and "flop ears." In fact, even those traders who took Sioux wives and honored them and stayed with them and their people and did not run away after a while and never come back (as did most white men who married Sioux women)—even these were seldom fully accepted, for they were from a strange people, and in those days the Sioux word for "stranger" and for "enemy" was the same.

Nonetheless, the Indians wanted the white-man things—the coffee and sugar and blankets and guns—and they could get them only so long as they treated the traders well enough to keep them coming back. Thus, not because they liked each other, but because they needed each other, the Lakotah and these early white men kept their differences and their true feelings buried and, thereby, got along in peace.

Their feelings and differences were still there, however, even though they were covered up, much like the winter river is still there though it runs hidden and silent beneath the ice; so the peace was fragile. It could last only so long as the white men in Sioux country were too few and weak either to take anything that was the Lakotah's or to threaten their way of life. But it stayed this way for a long time, because the Lakotah country lay deep in the so-called Great American Desert, and was popularly supposed to consist mainly of sand, snakes, and savages. It was often said that "a buzzard couldn't cross it alive unless he carried provisions," and traders and a few adventurers were about the only people who ever found any reason to go there. But suddenly in the 1840s, all that changed. Although the white men still didn't want to go *to* the Great American Desert, they now wanted to go *through* it, to California and Oregon. And when they finally discovered that it could be crossed by wagons, they went through by the thousands. With their wagon wheels they ground out a two-thousand-mile set of ruts that tied the towns of the Missouri River to the settlements of the Pacific coast, and they called it the Overland Trail. For the United States, the Overland Trail was the beginning of a transcontinental nation. For the Sioux, it was the beginning of the end.

As far back as the Lewis and Clark expedition of 1804, there had been some travel across the continent to the Pacific. Most of it, however, had been accomplished by a few horseback adventurers wandering wherever curiosity and dreams of fortune carried them, and except for the routes they explored and the stories they brought back, their meanderings had little impact upon either the United States or upon the Indians whose lands they crossed. Then, on a sunny May morning in 1841, a little column of ten or so white-topped wagons rocked out onto the untracked prairies west of St. Joseph, Missouri, some bound for Oregon and others for California. It was a daring experiment. There was no evidence the continent could be crossed by wagon, and there was a great deal of evidence it could not. Nevertheless, sixty-nine undaunted men, women, and children in the wagons were betting their lives that the evidence was wrong, and in spite of considerable hardship, five months later all had arrived safely at their destinations. As word of their success was carried back to the United States, others rushed to follow. In the summer of 1843, a thousand people went west in two hundred wagons, and in the year after that more went, until the trickle of westward emigrants became a stream and the stream a flood. And the Overland Trail, the road pioneered by that first handful of wagons, continued to be the road for all.

About three weeks out of St. Joseph, at the forks of the Platte River, the wagons entered the territory of the Lakotah. Following the North Platte River, they remained in it for the following two weeks, passing first through the southern hunting grounds of the Brulés, and then of the Oglalas and their allies, the Cheyenne.

When the wagon trains first began passing through Sioux country the

Indians watched them from the bluffs. Saw them creeping up the North Platte valley like slow white worms eating their way along—eating up the grass and the game and the firewood, and leaving a bare, dusty track behind them. When the wagons stopped for resting at the hide trader's fort above Horse Creek, the Indians could see what they carried. They saw that, unlike those who had come before, these wagon people were neither traders nor wandering adventurers. They were family people and carried with them the things for plowing and fencing and building, which meant they were looking for land to claim and settle upon. And though it was said the land they were planning to take lay far to the west, even beyond the land of the Fish-eaters, it seemed that sometimes, out of the sides of their eyes, these land hunters were also looking at the good grass bottoms of the North Platte. These were disturbing things. The wagon people themselves were disturbing, also. If the traders had occasionally been hard to like, these people were impossible. They were greedy and stingy both. They traveled the Lakotah land and took the grass and wood and used the good camping places, but they gave no gifts in return. In fact, if an Indian should approach them and make the signs for eating or smoking, thereby trying to beg a little food or tobacco, they would hurry on, pretending not to see him. Or they would shame him by driving him away with shouting and guns, and whenever they actually did give an Indian something, they always wanted him to pay for it.

Considering these things and the fact that (unlike the traders) the emigrants brought nothing useful to the Indians, even though they used his land and grass, it is hard to understand why the Sioux didn't make trouble on the Overland Trail from its very beginning. Perhaps it was because the annual traffic season was so very short. The trains had only a narrow "window" of time in which to leave St. Joseph—late enough for spring grass, yet early enough to be across the mountains before snow closed the passes. Thus, at any given point the trail would be traveled for perhaps six weeks, and the rest of the year it would be deserted. For whatever the reason, the early emigrants on the trail had little to fear from the Sioux.

In 1846, Oregon became a part of the United States. In 1847, the Mormons began their migration to Utah. In 1848, gold was discovered in California. Now the face of America was turned fully westward, and the migratory flood became a torrent. In the summer of 1850, fifty-five thousand people—one of every four hundred Americans—traveled west in wagons, and sixty-five thousand head of emigrant livestock ate their way up the valley of the Platte. On peak days as many as five hundred wagons would pass a given point between daylight and dark. During that summer the North Platte valley became a great dusty ditch with wagons always in sight, and with the grass and wood all used up, and with the Indians' favorite camping and wintering places ruined. Moreover, as the game grew scarce, emigrant hunters began ranging out as far as twenty miles or more on either side of the valley, making a strip of disturbance through the Lakotah country that was fifty miles wide and three hundred miles long.

Worse than the destruction of the valley were the sicknesses these wagon people brought. First there was the Asian cholera, a disease so strong that even the tea of juniper leaves was powerless against it, and many people died. Then came smallpox and measles. These, too, were strong sicknesses against which the Indians had no resistance. Their good medicines such as the tea of juniper leaves and chokecherry bark, as well as the juice of the blazing star, were useless against them also, and more people died.

Now, the Lakotah looked at the empty places in their lodges and looked again at their ruined valley, so trampled by men and animals that it truly was—as the white men called it—Nablaska, which means "flattened out by the foot," and were peaceful no longer. They began to threaten the wagon trains—galloping their horses around them, staying just out of rifle range but yelling and shooting, trying to frighten the people into turning back. When they found a very small train or an isolated wagon, they often attacked, sometimes killing the people and taking their animals and goods.

At the same time, the white men were also becoming more threatening. To have traveled the Overland Trail was such an accomplishment that those who had done it could often talk of little else, and they naturally enough tended to dwell on the dangers they had faced. Although the Indians were probably the least danger during the first several years of the trail—certainly a far smaller one than thirst or sickness—they were by far, however, the most dramatic. Consequently, as the stories grew in the telling, an Indian spoken to was apt to become an Indian fought and then to become an Indian raid. As these overblown tales grew, so did the caution of the emigrants, and more and more they traveled with rifles at the ready and a philosophy of "When in doubt, shoot!"

By early 1851, tensions had reached the point where war between the whites and the southern Lakotah and the Cheyenne threatened to break out at any moment. To head it off, the president sent messages to all tribes in the affected area inviting them to meet with his representatives in a big council for making peace.

The council was held on Horse Creek near Fort Laramie, Wyoming, and opened on August 31, 1851. Present were not only the Brulés and southern Oglalas together with their Cheyenne allies, but also some of their enemies such as Crows, Shoshonis, and others. Because of this mixture, there was so much jealous wrangling over seating and over which tribes should have the places of honor that the council almost fell to pieces before it began. However, after the government representatives had given the Indians many days of feasting, and many presents as well, the mood was mellowed enough to allow talking to begin.

At the council, Commissioner Mitchell showed the Indians more wagonloads of tempting presents—knives and blankets and copper pots and all those things they had learned from the traders to need. For the chiefs he had blue uniforms and long shiny swords. Not only would the White Father give the Indians these things, the commissioner told them, but he would give them many more—$50,000 worth—every year for the next ten years, and he would also have the white soldiers protect the Indians from the whites, but only if the Indians would agree to certain things. Because the White Father wanted peace on the frontier, he wanted each tribe to promise to stay within certain boundaries. Furthermore, he wanted each tribe to promise not to molest either whites or other Indians. Also, he wanted permission to put roads and soldier forts on Indian lands. And finally, of course, he wanted the Indians to promise not to bother travelers on the Overland Trail.

After much talk and many more feasts, the chiefs finally agreed, and on September 17, 1851, the Treaty of Horse Creek was signed. Then the chiefs who had come to the council looking regal and dignified went away looking foolish and uncomfortable in their awkwardly misbuttoned uniforms with their swords flopping and banging around their legs. Commissioner Mitchell, however, went away euphoric. He grandly announced that he had so changed the hearts of the Indians that "all previously warring tribes are now behaving toward each other like brothers," and "nothing but mismanagement . . . can ever break it." This proved only that the commissioner didn't know very much about Indians. For it was not only the white men who remembered only those parts of the treaties that they wanted to remember and conveniently forgot the rest; it was the Indians also. Nor could the Lakotah give up fighting with other tribes, for war was the very centerpost of their culture. It was in war that men proved their bravery and brought honor on their families. And it was in war that young men won coup feathers and horses and the hearts of maidens. In asking the Lakotah to give up war, the foolish white men had asked an impossible thing, and no one could be expected to keep impossible promises. Thus, the Oglalas and Brulés went on fighting with their neighbors as before. They knew, however, they would receive no more annuities if they made trouble on the Overland Trail, so they left it alone. In fact, they named it the Holy Road, presumably because it was the source of many rich presents and was, therefore, a thing to be honored.

CHAPTER
3
∧∧∧∧∧∧

The Mormon Cow

DEPENDING ON whether one was a Brulé or an Oglala, it was the summer after the Winter When Mean Bear Died, or else the Winter When Deer Dung Broke His Neck (the white men called it 1854) that the Brulé and the Oglala returned to Fort Laramie on the North Platte to receive their third year of presents for not molesting travelers on the Holy Road. They came in the Moon of Cherries Ripening (August) and finding that the agent who gave the presents was away for a few days, they moved down the river about four miles and camped . . . and waited. For such a large camp—perhaps five thousand people in the six hundred lodges that stretched for three miles along the river—it was a bad place for waiting, there by the Holy Road. True, it was late enough in the season that about the only traffic was an occasional group of Mormons who could start later than the other emigrants because they were going only as far as Utah instead of clear to Oregon or California. Even so, the animals of those who had already passed had used up the grass so that it was hard to find pasture for the pony herds, and all the easy-to-gather firewood was gone from the cottonwood groves, making much extra work for the women. Worst of all, however, was the fine, sandy dust that the hot August wind whipped out of the wagon ruts and sifted through the lodges, where it coated everything with a dull, tan powder. At such a time, waiting in the heat with the skin always gritty from the drifting dust, tempers are apt to grow short and judgment to grow bad. And that may be part of the reason why Straight Foretop shot the Mormon's cow, and why there was such bad trouble over it.

15

On August 17—one of the waiting days, hot and the people quiet around the lodges and hoping that maybe the fleecy afternoon thunderheads would grow and blacken until they brought a cool breeze and a rain shower—a few Mormon wagons came along the Holy Road with a little herd of cows trailing behind them. The heat seemed to be pressing down on these travelers, too; their slow-plodding oxen were dull-eyed from much travel, and the people were the same, drawn into themselves and looking ahead at nothing and just enduring until they could reach the resting place at the fort. And so, possibly, that is why the herder didn't notice a bony cow had strayed from the herd until she was already wandering into the Brulé camp of Chief Conquering Bear.

Once inside the tipi circle the cow meandered on until she came to the lodges of a few Minneconjou Lakotah guests who were down visiting their Brulé relatives. And there, a Minneconjou named Straight Foretop shot her. It was done because the camping and waiting in this place of scarce game had made the people hungry for meat. Even so, it was a bad thing, this shooting a cow without knowing the owner. It could make trouble. And the trouble started immediately. Pursuing the cow, her owner arrived at the edge of the camp just in time to hear the shot and to see her go down. Fearing to go any farther, he stood outside the tipi circle shouting his wrath and then continued shouting as he stomped back to the wagons.

A little farther on—between the Brulé camp and that of the Oglalas—stood the weathered stone buildings of a French trader, James Bordeaux. There, the wagons stopped again, and the man poured out his angry story to the trader. These Indians were "a nest of snakes," he declared, and he was going to see to it that the army "cleaned them out." To Bordeaux's ears this was bad talk. It was the kind of thing that could easily get out of hand and lead to much anger and even fighting, which would be very bad for the trade. It could also be very bad for him, even though it was true that he had a Brulé wife and that Conquering Bear's people were his in-laws. For in times of anger, when the carefully buried feelings grew hot and burned through their covering, the Indians were prone to treat white brothers-in-law as any other white men and sometimes even worse. Worried, Bordeaux said calming things to the man and offered him ten dollars—more, probably, than the trail-thin cow had been worth—to forget the whole thing. But the man would not be pacified by mere money. He was determined to see that the cow's killer be arrested and properly punished, so spurning the trader's offer, he fumed on toward the fort.

The moment the Mormon wagons creaked into the dusty, adobe-walled compound that was Fort Laramie, the owner of the cow sought out the commanding officer, a Lieutenant Fleming. Again he poured out his grievance, and again he demanded action against "that band of snakes." Fleming heard him out, agreeing with the obvious fact that the man had been done a wrong and had suffered a loss. Then he pointed out that according to the Treaty of Horse Creek, it was the chiefs who were responsible for making restitution in cases like this, and it was also the chiefs who were supposed to arrest the perpetrators. Therefore, in the morning he would send for Conquering Bear and they would council about this thing. Meanwhile, the best thing for the man to do was to have supper and get some rest.

As soon as the wagons had left the trading post, Bordeaux hurried to the lodges of the Brulés to smoke with Conquering Bear and tell him what the man of the cow was saying. For Conquering Bear these were heavy words. Ah-h-h. These wild Minneconjous from the north! This was not the first time they had made trouble. Last summer, also, they had come visiting while the Brulés had been at Laramie getting their annuities. Maybe they did it that way thinking their relatives would be generous in sharing their presents. Anyhow, that time one of the Minneconjous had shot at a soldier in a boat (because the soldier refused to ferry him across the river, some said). The soldier went after more soldiers, who then came to the camp to arrest the Minneconjou. As they approached, some foolish person shot at them, also. The soldiers shot back, and when the smoke had blown away, five good Lakotah were dead on the grass. And now there was this thing about the cow, and it could be even worse. It was known that the white people placed great importance on everything they owned. Thus, to shoot at one of their cows and kill her might very well be worse than to shoot at one of their soldiers and miss. Tomorrow he would go to the fort and see what he could do about keeping the peace.

Next morning the sun was no more than three hand-widths above the horizon and the last of the night cool still lingered on the shaded sides of the draws when Conquering Bear saddled a horse and set out for the fort. Passing the Oglala camp, he was joined by Man Afraid. Man Afraid's full name was Man of Whose Very Horses the Enemy Is Afraid, but that was pretty long. The white men had shortened it to Man Afraid of His Horses, but that was long, also, and besides, it changed the meaning. Man Afraid was better. And he was a good one to have along in a time like this. First of all, he was a big man and impressive to look at—six feet four inches tall and straight as the *wazicun,* the Black Hills pine. He was big in another way too—he was a famous traditional chief from a family that one writer would later refer to as "the Adams family of the Sioux." But best of all, Man Afraid was a level-headed, tactful negotiator.

When the two chiefs arrived at the commanding officer's office, Lieutenant Fleming gave them a warm greeting and some food and coffee and tobacco. Then he let them know that he thought this matter of the cow had grown into entirely too much of a gravy-stirring for such a small thing. Conquering Bear agreed. Through the interpreter, Wayuse, he also agreed that a wrong thing had been done and that he understood why the owner of the cow was angry. He explained that it was one of the guests and not one of his people who had done this thing, but as chief he still accepted the responsibility. To make things right he would give the man the finest horse in his herd, and the man himself could make the choice. Surely one fine horse for an old cow so worn out she might not have lived to get to Utah anyway should be more than fair. The lieutenant thought so, too—but not the Mormon. In fact, he wouldn't have it. He wanted the killer of the cow arrested, and that was that. Then the two chiefs pointed out that this was the kind of problem that the agent was supposed to settle (which was true) and that it should be allowed to sleep until he returned. Now it was the lieutenant who could not agree and for a pretty good reason. Whatever else the Indians might be, they were not angels. And if the young men, especially, saw a thing like this seeming to pass unnoticed, some of them were likely to think the army was like a dog with no teeth and be tempted to do something that would really start a fight.

And so the conversation went. At least, that is the way it *seemed* it went; no one could be really sure. The trouble lay in the mixed-blood Iowa interpreter, Wayuse. He was both a troublemaker and a drunk. Though married to a Lakotah woman, he spoke the Lakotah tongue poorly—which is a bad thing in an interpreter. Moreover, Wayuse didn't like the Lakotah very much, and it was said that he often twisted their words just to make them trouble. Anyhow, as the matter was left, Conquering Bear was to return to his camp and try to persuade Straight Foretop to give himself up to the soldiers.

It may have been that Lieutenant Fleming thought Conquering Bear could either order Straight Foretop to come into the fort or have him seized and carried in if necessary; for the white men, used to the idea of kings and presidents and armies and organized police forces, usually thought like that. Few of them realized that most Indian societies—and certainly those of the Lakotah—were the next thing to anarchy and remained orderly to the extent they did only because of social pressures and customs and the desire for prestige. That was the only real power of a chief—his prestige. It was the power to persuade rather than the power to order. And even so, a chief had to use it carefully or he would lose it.

Remembering the five dead Lakotahs of last year, Conquering Bear used all the persuasion at his command when he talked to Straight Foretop. But the Minneconjou would not be convinced. Arrested Indians, he contended, were always found guilty and were always killed. Actually, this was not true. The fact was that whereas arrested Indians *were* found guilty most times, they were killed very seldom. Usually they were merely locked up in the iron-house for a little while and then sent home. Straight Foretop, however, was certain that to surrender was to die, and he would have none of it. He was a hot-blooded Minneconjou who, if he must die, would die fighting.

Back at the fort, meanwhile, another young hot-blood was also talking of fighting. Second Lieutenant J. L. Grattan was a feisty little Irishman who had come to Laramie fresh from West Point itching to "crack it to the Sioux." Both visibly and vocally disappointed at not having found Fort Laramie's tiny garrison actively at war with the Sioux nation, Grattan had somehow badgered Lieutenant Fleming into a promise that if an expedition to the Sioux camps ever became necessary, he could lead it. Now, determined to turn the trail of the cow into a path of glory, Grattan was in Fleming's office reminding him of his promise.

Fleming wasn't finding the cow problem nearly so delightful as Grattan was. In fact, it was giving him a very hard day. The thing to do, of course, was to shift it to the shoulders of the agent, where it properly belonged, but he couldn't do that because the agent hadn't come back. Also, he had been hoping that Conquering Bear would resolve the matter by bringing in the guilty Indian, but Conquering Bear hadn't come back either, and it was beginning to look as if he wasn't going to. Grattan kept reminding him of that and reminding him, also, that it was dangerous to let these savages think they were getting away with anything, and he was pressing for permission to take a detail of soldiers to seize the

Minneconjou by force. Also present in Fleming's office—with blood in his eye and demanding both restitution and retribution—was the fool emigrant who didn't have sense enough to accept a good horse in exchange for a bad cow. Man Afraid was there too, and he seemed to be counseling patience, although you could never tell what an Indian was thinking, nor, with an interpreter like Wayuse, what he was saying either. And so it went, the voices droning on like the flies that buzzed and bumbled against the dusty windowpanes until Fleming, like Pilate, finally washed his hands of the matter and told Grattan he had permission to go after the Indian. He did, however, instruct the young hothead that he was to be tactful about it and that whatever else he did, he was not to start a fight.

The jubilant Grattan immediately issued a call for volunteers for "dangerous duty" and set about organizing his expedition. When he finally got it assembled in the fort compound, it consisted of twenty-nine men, which was three-fourths of the entire Fort Laramie garrison, plus Wayuse, the interpreter, who was half drunk. There were also wagons for transporting the troops, two cannon, and Man Afraid, who was going along to see if he could head off the fight that this fiery young officer seemed to be looking for and which, Man Afraid suspected, some of the fiery young Indians were looking for, too. The expedition was doomed from the start. Not because of its small size, although sending a handful of troops among hundreds of truculent warriors was always a chancy thing and in this case the soldiers would be outnumbered by more than forty to one, but because of the attitude and inexperience of its commanding officer. For while most Indians had no love for the soldiers and (except for fear of the consequences) would happily kill them whenever and wherever they could, the chiefs and headmen knew well that killing a few white soldiers only brought more soldiers until finally it was the Indians themselves who were killed. Therefore, in such confrontations as the one developing here, they usually managed to control even their young hot-bloods to the point that it took extreme provocation to start a fight. Unfortunately, Grattan was one to provide such provocation.

He made his first mistake even before the detachment left the fort. When he inspected his troops for field readiness, he failed to inspect the most essential member of this kind of operation—the interpreter. Had he done so, and the man's condition clearly indicated that he should have, he would have found that Wayuse's canteen contained not water, but whiskey. Unaware of this crucial oversight, however, Grattan grandly announced to his men that they were going forth "to conquer or to die" and led them out of the gates and eastward down the emigrant trail.

An hour later the command was rolling through the first of the Indian camps. There, among the lodges of the Oglalas, it sowed the seeds of the battle that would shortly destroy it. The problem, of course, was Wayuse. During the hot, dusty ride he had found much occasion to quench his thirst from the uninspected canteen and was now thoroughly drunk. Passing the first of the lodges, he went roaring out of control. These were the lodges of the Oglala, whom he hated, as he did all the Lakotah, because they looked down on him as an Iowa and a mixed-blood. So he began shouting insults at these Oglalas and pelting them with horse dung, and then shouting threats of what the soldiers were planning to do to them. The Oglalas probably wouldn't have paid much attention to the insults or even the horse dung—some of their own people acted the same way or worse when they had too much whiskey. Besides, this was merely Wayuse and everybody knew what *he* was. But the threats were another thing. They could see the soldiers in their camp, and they could see the cannon. Yes, there might be something to the threats. So the warriors sent the boys out to the horse herds for war ponies, which soon came streaming in from the hills. An experienced man would have recognized the horse gathering as a bad sign, but Grattan, not being equipped to read it, continued to lead his men deeper into the Indian nest.

At the Bordeaux buildings he halted the wagons and went inside to talk to the trader. Fleming, aware of the incompetence of Wayuse, had instructed Grattan to take Bordeaux as interpreter when he went to the Brulé camp. Unfortunately, Bordeaux wasn't interested. Too dangerous. He could feel big trouble coming and he wanted no part of it. The best he could do for Grattan was to give him two pieces of advice. First, it would be disaster to attempt to capture Straight Foretop by force. Conquering Bear and Man Afraid must be allowed to handle it. Second, for heaven's sake, Grattan must do something about Wayuse. The fool was out there now, giving war whoops and racing his horse up and down the road as if to second-wind it for a fight and shouting to the Brulés across the way that he was going to have them all killed and would be eating their hearts before sundown. It would not be at all unreasonable for the Brulés to read such a performance as meaning the soldiers had come to make war.

From the trading post to the Brulé camp was only a short distance, and the army wagons covered it quickly. Immediately upon their arrival and even as Conquering Bear was coming out to greet him, Grattan deployed his troops in a skirmish line and ordered the cannon loaded and so positioned that they could rake the lodges with shotgun blasts of grapeshot. At the same time—and with little commotion so as not to attract attention—the Indians began filtering out of the threatened camp. Perhaps again it was because of Grattan's inexperience, but he seemed not to notice that while the women and children were going to the trees by the river, the warriors with bows and guns were quietly slipping into the nearby gullies. At any rate, he then turned to Conquering Bear and demanded that he surrender Straight Foretop. The chief replied that unfortunately it was not possible, for the man still refused to be surrendered. However, if Conquering Bear were to give *two* horses, perhaps the soldiers would forget the matter and go away. Curtly, Grattan responded that he had come for the Minneconjou, and the Minneconjou he would have. There could be no other settlement. Then, surprisingly, considering Grattan's shortening patience and the fact that all this conversation was taking place through the drunken Wayuse, Conquering Bear and Man Afraid persuaded the officer to wait while they had another council with Straight Foretop. The two chiefs may have had some hope of success, or they may have been just buying time. But whichever it was, the talk was long—long enough for the women and children to get well away and for the warriors to become well deployed in the gullies. Finally the chiefs returned. The Minneconjou would not surrender, they reported; he sent word that if he must die, he would die fighting the soldiers. And even as they said it, the Minneconjou gave truth to their words by standing before his lodge with his rifle in hand and shouting his angry defiance. "However," added the chiefs, "if only the white people would accept *five* horses for that bony old cow, the gathering trouble might still be avoided." At least, that is the gist of what they said to Wayuse. What Wayuse told the lieutenant is not known. But whatever it was, Grattan became furious and shouted, "Fire!" In the first crashing volley, Straight Foretop died. Conquering Bear, leaping forward and shouting "Stop shooting!," fell mortally wounded in the second. Seeing this, the leaders in the gullies cried out, "Hopo! Hopo!" and the hidden Indians fired a return volley, killing Grattan and all the men working the cannon. Next the enraged Indians boiled out of their hiding places attacking with everything they had—guns, bows, hatchets, war clubs—anything that was a weapon. Leaderless and disorganized, the soldiers fled in panic back up the Holy Road . . . just in time to meet a charge of war-whooping Oglalas coming down. The waves of Brulé and Oglala flowed together. When they receded, Grattan's expedition was finished. His men had not conquered, but they had died.

Conquering Bear, still alive but dying, had been carried to Bordeaux's. The Lakotah warriors went to Bordeaux's, also, as soon as they had finished with the soldiers—scalping them and slashing and mutilating their stripped bodies so the men would go to the afterlife as hopeless cripples and, thereby, be punished forever for this day. It was full night now, and by the light of smoking torches they milled around the yard. Angry and confused, the growing mob seethed with crosscurrents like a boiling kettle. Some were for immediately striking their lodges and running for the far places where punishing soldiers might not find them. Others were for breaking open the warehouses and taking the presents which the agent had still not returned to give them. Others (particularly the young men) were for war and their talk curled around—heavy and biting as gunsmoke. They talked of a great war party that would range up and down the Holy Road killing travelers and traders and keepers of way stations and any other whites that could be found. And especially they talked of wiping out Fort Laramie and of doing it this very night. It would be easy. There were no more soldiers left now than the fingers of both hands, and their cannon were gone, standing burned in the camp of the Brulé. Yes, it would be easy and it would show these white men the power of The People, the Lakotah, and it might even scare them so much they would not come to Lakotah country anymore. So, as the night wore on and the heat lightning flickered and flared along the summer horizon, the war talk grew, and the power of the Lakotah kept sounding bigger until only the words of the chiefs were holding them back. And there were some big men there. Such chiefs as Man Afraid, High Backbone, Little Thunder, Swift Bear, and Spotted Tail all knew what the white armies might do to the Indians if the Indians ran over one of their forts. But even with much talking by them it was hard to hold the wild young men back, Bordeaux was there, too, talking with the chiefs, which was dangerous since Bordeaux was a white man himself. When he talked for not killing whites, there were many who thought he was on that side. Yet in the end, it was Bordeaux more than the chiefs who saved the fort and the white people along the Holy Road. For whenever the hotheads seemed about to break away from the chiefs, Bordeaux would give out some more of his goods as presents, and the bloodthirsty men would stay a little longer to receive them and to eat the food Bordeaux also put out. As morning approached, the trader had given away almost everything he had and was well-nigh destitute. But the crisis was past.

As the day wore on, the Lakotah broke open the warehouses and took the annuity goods (after all, they were theirs anyhow). Then the great Brulé and Oglala camps broke up into small bands and scattered north and west away from the Holy Road. But they did not go in peace; from that time until the Lakotah were totally subjugated by the whites, there was to be fighting between them. It would not be steady fighting, but rather sporadic outbursts of whites attacking the Indians or—just as often—Indians attacking the whites. Most of the attacks, whether by whites or by Indians, would be unnecessary and senseless. Yet, they would continue—with no Lakotah band fighting the whites all of the time, but with every band fighting them some of the time—until the avalanche released by the Mormon cow would finally stop at Wounded Knee.

CHAPTER
4

ᐱᐧᐱᐧᐱᐧᐱᐧᐱ

Growing Conflict

News of the Grattan affair echoed through the posts and stations of the North Platte valley like a cry of "Fire!" shouted in the night. Every breeze carried fresh rumors of raids and atrocities, and the whites braced themselves for the worst. Yet for a while nothing happened, and when something did happen, it was far less than expected.

The reason for the quiet was the time of year. It was now September, the Moon of Leaves Turning Brown, and if the Sioux were not to have a hungry winter, it was time for making meat. So for the next two months they followed the buffalo—the men hunting and skinning, and the women drying the meat into thin black strips of *papasaka* to be folded into the parfleches for keeping, pounding some of it together with chokecherries to make the *wasna*, and fleshing and curing the great hides for robes and lodge covers. Perhaps all this hard work cooled the tempers of the young men, for when the parfleches were full and there was again time for fighting, only one small war party went out, and it made but two raids.

It was a five-man party from the Brulé camp of the slain Conquering Bear and was gotten up by Long Chin. Although there were two men in the group, Spotted Tail and Red Leaf, who were rising young chiefs and bigger men than Long Chin, it was the way of a war party that the one who got it up was also the leader. So Long Chin led them—south to the North Platte and the Holy Road. There, a few miles above Fort Laramie, they struck the trading post of Ward & Guerrier. They did little damage

25

and nobody was hurt, but it did remind the whites that the Lakotah were angry.

The second raid was more serious. Only a few miles below the place where Grattan and Conquering Bear were killed, the war party struck a mail wagon, killing its two drivers and a passenger. Furthermore, when the army troops found the wagon later, there was $20,000 missing from its mail bags. It is said that no one ever knew whether the Indians took the money or what happened to it, but if they did take it, they spent it in such a way that it was never obvious. Still, it might be noted that whereas the Oglalas named 1854 the Year They Killed Thirty White Men, the Brulés named it the Year of Much Money.

Following the raid on the mail coach in November, things were quiet for the rest of the winter. That is to say, they *seemed* quiet. Actually, beneath the calm surface there were forces of agitation at work. One of these forces—as was ever true in the Indian wars—was the press. The publishers knew, as they have ever known, that sensationalism sells newspapers. And what could be more sensational than battles with the Indians? To the news-buying public, the Indians were wild, mysterious savages who lived in distant romantic places; they were barbarian butchers standing in the path of that Advancing Civilization of which the soldiers and settlers were the stouthearted banner carriers. Thus, every Indian raid or armed encounter provided the newspapers with grist from which they ground days of stories of heroism and pathos and glory and gore. And the public loved it. Furthermore, not only was there high drama in "Indian" stories, but also two other great advantages. One was that they were "safe" copy—to the readers the distinction between the "good guys" and the "bad guys" in an Indian fight was so clear-cut and unanimous that the papers never needed to fear accusations of one-sided reporting. The other was that the readers had so little true knowledge of Indians that the writers were not inconvenienced by the need for accuracy. Hence it is not surprising to find that whenever an Indian war flamed up, it was often the press that supplied the kindling, and always the press that helped stoke the war fires once they were burning. Accordingly, when the newspapers received word of the Grattan fight, they responded true to form. The headlines screamed MASSACRE! and during the following months inflammatory columns demanded retaliation against the "primitive brutes" who committed it.

While the newspapers were thus working at agitating the whites during the winter of 1854, the Brulés of Conquering Bear were working at agitating the Indians. The Indians were in their winter camps now with nothing much to do but talk and think. So the Brulés began carrying the war pipe across the vast, wind-chilled plains to one and then another of the small clusters of tipis that nestled under the sheltering bluffs of rivers and creeks. There they would sit by pine and cottonwood warming fires in the snug lodges, smoking with the headmen, and talking of war.

The war pipe traveled far that winter. Not only was it circulated among the Brulés and the Oglalas, but it was also carried north to the Minneconjous in the Belle Fourche River country, and then still farther north to the Hunkpapas on Grand River and on the Cannon Ball. Everywhere the carriers found agreement that the killing of Conquering Bear had been a bad thing, and everywhere they found strong, bitter talk against the way the white men were pressing in. This was especially true among the Hunkpapas—where Four Horns was a big man and whose nephew, Sitting Bull, was gaining a strong name also. However, the Hunkpapas were little concerned with problems on the North Platte— they never went there anyhow. What they were worried about was encroachment by the whites in the north. With the Minneconjous it was much the same. The North Platte was not their country; their difficulties were with whites along the Missouri. Even among the Oglalas and the Brulés themselves, opinions were divided. Some thought the white men had been punished enough. Some were afraid that raiding would bring so many soldiers and cannon that it would be the Indians who were punished instead of the whites. Others were strong with words, but noncommittal about action. The result of all this was that, although the Brulés caused much talk of war, they accomplished little in the way of starting one.

In view of the Sioux way of war, this was not surprising. The problem the Brulés faced was the same one that would always prevent the Lakotah from making the kind of powerful resistance to the whites that they could have made had they been organized. They were almost completely disorganized, however, and in a way which—from the standpoint of making war—gave them two insurmountable problems. First, the so-called Great Sioux Nation was not a nation at all. On the contrary, it was simply a large number of intermarried and interrelated small bands that shared a common religion, language, and culture. Consequently, the individual bands were concerned primarily with their own interests and welfare and only secondarily with those of the overall "nation." Second, the Sioux had no chains of command, no centralized authority, nor actually much of any kind of authority except social pressures. Thus, no one chief could order another chief to join him in making war, or tell him how or where to fight if he did join. Neither could a chief "order" his own men to make war; he could only invite or persuade them to. Therefore, the only way the Lakotah could ever assemble a substantial battle force at any given time or place was as a result of a direct, obvious, and immediate threat to several bands simultaneously. Rarely did this happen. And clearly, since the Grattan attack and the killing of Conquering Bear involved only the Brulés and the Oglalas, it was not seen as such a threat.

Because of the Brulés' failure with the war pipe, the summer of 1855 began peacefully enough along the North Platte—at least on the surface. By the time the grass was green and the cottonwoods were in leaf, trains of Russell, Majors & Waddell freight wagons came creeping heavily up the Overland Trail, and the annual flood of emigrant wagons came soon after. And because the Holy Road had always had some sort of hypnotic fascination for the Brulé and the southern Oglala, many of them were back in the valley, also. But, despite all the winter's talk, they were not raiding.

So to an outsider it might have appeared that things were the same as they had always been since the trail began. But they were not the same. Among both Indians and whites there was a feeling of ominous waiting—a feeling of dark things from the past summer hanging over like clouds gathering for a sudden storm. The Indians were generally sullen from the beginning, and as the summer wore on, some of them became openly defiant and hostile. The whites were hostile as well, and theirs was the hostility of tension and fear. They thought (probably correctly) that unless the Indians were taught some sort of lesson and shown that there were penalties attached to such things as killing soldiers and raiding mail wagons, no white along the North Platte could feel entirely safe.

Nevertheless, despite these growing pressures—from the whites along the trail, the press, and the Russell, Majors & Waddell freight line— nothing was done to impose any such penalties until August 10. Then a new agent, a Major Thomas Twiss (all Indian agents were called "major"), took over at Fort Laramie. And with the major came a plan for disciplining the Indians. It was designed to apply only to "hostile" Indians, but the problem was: how do you identify the "hostiles"? Twiss's solution was simple: let them identify themselves. So in order to do it, he promptly sent runners to all the camps with the message that all friendly Indians were to move immediately to the south side of the river and then to report to him for orders.

In three weeks' time nearly all the Indians had decided that they were, indeed, friendly and had assembled in great camps near Fort Laramie. At that point General W. S. "Whitebeard" Harney, leading a mixed force of cavalry and infantry, started marching up the north side of the North Platte, and the rest of the plan was unfolded. His was a punitive expedition. The Indians had been ordered to move to the south side of the river if they were friendly; therefore, any Indians Whitebeard found on the north side would be considered hostile and dealt with accordingly. On September 2 his scouts found the camp of the Brulé, Little Thunder.

Why Little Thunder had remained on the north side of the river has never been satisfactorily explained. He had never shown himself to be hostile, and testimony taken at the investigation of the Grattan disaster revealed that he had been one of the chiefs who had labored through the night to prevent the young men from attacking Fort Laramie. On the other hand, there is no question of his not receiving the message from Major Twiss. Nonetheless, he was there—camped on the Blue Water, which runs down to the North Platte from the lake country of the Sand Hills. And because the camp was only a few miles up the Blue Water from the river and was near the heavily used campground at Ash Hollow, the Indians obviously were not trying to hide. Whatever Little Thunder's feeling and intentions, they were of no consequence anyhow, because Harney didn't know whose camp he had found. He knew only that he had found *a* camp and that its occupants were presumably hostile and in need of chastisement.

The valley of the Blue Water where Little Thunder was camped is a trough, flat-bottomed and bluff-sided. Realizing that if he simply marched his army up the creek that the Indians would flee ahead of him and probably escape, the general decided to dam the trough. Acting accordingly—and undetected by the Indians, who were as yet unaware of his presence—he moved his cavalry during the night into a blocking position above their camp.

In the gray stillness of the following dawn, Harney's infantry tramped through the dew-damp grass of the Blue Water bottoms to make the attack. While they were yet some distance off they were seen by a startled, early-rising Brulé who began crying the alarm, "Soldiers coming! Soldiers coming!" As the frightened Indians sprang from their sleeping robes, preparing to flee, Little Thunder burst from his tipi and ran toward the troops, all the while signaling for a counseling. Whitebeard, however, had not come to talk, and the troops never stopped. Nearing the lodges, they commenced firing, whereupon the Indians stampeded up the creek only to find the cavalry coming down it. Now they were between the hammer and the anvil, and their flight became a rout. Like frightened prairie chickens, they scattered, leaving everything behind. They ran to the side—to the draws that led up the bluffs and away from the now deadly valley.

When the shooting stopped and quiet returned, eighty-six Indians lay dead in the grass—some of them women and children. Seventy women and children were captives, and all the Indians' lodges and personal possessions had been captured, searched, and then destroyed. The search revealed not only some of the things taken from the captured mail coach, but also two fresh white men's scalps—white women's scalps, according to Harney. Clearly, at least some of Little Thunder's people were, after all, hostile. Even so, the slaughter at Little Thunder's camp was a tragic, senseless massacre. Harney, himself, later came to that realization. Now, however, accompanied by his captives, he marched his army on up to Fort Laramie.

News of the destruction of Little Thunder's camp had run ahead of Whitebeard, causing such fearful stirring in the camps of the friendly Indians assembled near Fort Laramie that by the time he arrived they were trembling on the brink of flight—afraid to stay and even more afraid to run. Harney's first act upon his arrival was to demand the surrender of the men who had attacked the mail coach, and as soon as the five men heard of the demand, such was their fear that they immediately decided to give themselves up in the hope of saving the rest of their people from Whitebeard's deadly wrath. Still, if they were going to surrender, they would surrender like men. So they dressed themselves in their best buckskins (with the fine porcupine quilling designs worked in) and painted their faces; then they mounted their finest war ponies and came riding into Fort Laramie proudly, as brave men should. As they rode in through the gates of the adobe walls, they sang their death songs, for they knew that if Whitebeard would kill people simply because they were on one side of the river instead of the other, surely he would kill the confessed slayers of the three white men on the mail coach. Whitebeard, however, had no intention of killing them. Instead, he sent them down the river to spend two years as prisoners at Fort Kearney, where they were never so much as locked up, and not only did they have the run of the fort, but sometimes even rode with the soldiers on scouting expeditions. In fact, it actually turned out to be a good thing for them in view of all the things they learned. They discovered that there were both good and bad people among the whites, the same as among the Indians. They learned to understand the white man's language and some of his ways of thinking and how to use his tools. Thus, what was intended to be a punishment turned out to be a valuable learning experience—especially for Spotted Tail, who was to become one of the most effective of all the chiefs in dealing with the whites.

As for Harney, now that he had swept the North Platte clear of "hostiles" and had arrested the raiders of the mail coach, the punitive part of his expedition was finished. What remained now was to see that the point he had made was not lost on the Indians and to convince them that the army had the power to operate freely in their territory whenever it was deemed necessary. Consequently (as a challenging show of force) he now marched his troops out of Fort Laramie and straight through the Lakotah country to Fort Pierre on the Missouri River. And as they marched, his soldiers sang:

> *We did not make a blunder*
> *We rubbed out Little Thunder,*
> *And we sent him to the other side of Jordan.*

When they arrived at Fort Pierre, however, and saw the barren outpost that was to be their home until the following summer, they changed their tune. Now they sang:

> *Oh, we do not mind the marching*
> *Nor the fighting do we fear*
> *But we'll never forgive old Harney*
> *For bringing us to Pierre.*

Meanwhile, among the Indians, the sound of the Little Thunder disaster was reverberating through the tribes like gunshot echoing in a canyon. Never in anyone's memory, or even in the oldest stories, had so many Sioux died in a single fight. And never since the Lakotah had left the forests of Minnesota to become the unconquerable power of the plains had an enemy actually captured and destroyed one of their camps. Their pride was badly hurt and their sense of security was shaken. Further, it is quite possible that because the shock of the Little Thunder disaster was so severe no war pipes were sent around during the following winter—the winter of the year that the Brulé named White-beard Seizes the Sioux. Instead, the people sat by the warming lodge fires in their winter camps and soberly pondered the meaning of the slaughter of the Brulés on the Blue Water.

After the snow-melting time of the following spring, Whitebeard Harney invited headmen from all the tribes to meet with him at a council on the Missouri River. Many came, and when the council was finally assembled, all the tribes were represented. Whitebeard began the talking by saying he was sorry for what he had done to Little Thunder's people, and he now wanted to make an agreement whereby the Sioux and the whites could keep peace with each other. After much more talking, such a treaty was prepared and the chiefs touched the pen. It was wasted work, however, for two reasons. First, the signing chiefs were not the ones the Indians had chosen to speak for them, but the ones whom Harney (like other white men were always doing at councils) had appointed, himself. And second, the United States Senate later failed to ratify the treaty, anyway. But for the Indians the conference was far from a failure. It gave the chiefs of the various bands an opportunity to consult with each other and resulted in the decision to hold a Great Council of all the Lakotah in the following summer of 1857.

When the next summer came and the Great Council met, it was at the time of the Sun Dance, which was a sacred time. They assembled on the northeastern edge of the Black Hills at the foot of a sacred mountain—a great, blue-shadowed hump with a smaller hump at one end, like the body and head of a sleeping bear—which the Sioux called Mato Paha, meaning Bear Mountain, and which the white men called Bear Butte.

No one knows how many people followed the council pipe to the sacred mountain that summer, but it is known that it was the first—and also the last—time that all the Lakotah were gathered together in one place at one time. As the chiefs stood on the slopes of Mato Paha and saw the miles of white cowskin lodges and saw the pony herds spread like great ragged robes clear to the horizon, they realized (maybe for the first time) the power that could be the Lakotah's if only they would stand together.

Following the four holy days of the Sun Dance, the chiefs convened the council. First they spoke of how they were becoming as an island in a river of white men and of the danger that the white river would begin to wash away the edges of the Lakotah island and make it steadily smaller.

Then they spoke of the strength they had seen when they were looking from the mountain and how, together, the Lakotah had the power to prevent the whites from shrinking their island. Finally, they made a pledge wherein they promised to stand together at resisting the white man wherever he threatened.

Then they went home as they had come, no more organized than before and each band no less willfully independent than before. Despite all the good words and the promises, that is how it would remain—simply because that is how it had always been. Nothing had been accomplished or changed. But they *had* had a good visiting time.

For the next several years following the Great Council, the Indians' failure to organize made no difference, for (contrary to the Indians' expectations) the whites made no attempt to encroach on the "Lakotah island"—they merely continued to flow past it on their way to the far west. So these were years of relative peace between Indians and whites in Teton Sioux country. The war fires were not extinguished, however; the pressure of the American westward movement was such that they could not be. But for a time they smoldered low, with only an occasional whiff of smoke from a border incident revealing their presence.

Consequently, these were good years for the Lakotah—possibly better than they had known before and certainly better than they would ever know again. At the agencies they collected their annuities of white-man goods. The interior of their land, as yet undisturbed by the white man, was as it had always been. The buffalo still roamed over it in great shaggy herds, and although they were fewer of them than in the past, there were still more than enough to make the robes and lodge covers and to fill the parfleches for winter. Thus, for a time the Lakotah not only had all the old things they had always possessed and could live the old life as usual, they also had the annuities from the white men, and therefore enjoyed the best of both worlds.

It was obvious, though, that these fat times of the Lakotah could not last. The line of white settlement was pressing relentlessly westward from Minnesota and Iowa into eastern Nebraska and Dakota. Immediately ahead of it, by now, was the "Lakotah island," a territory so vast, but with the number of Indians occupying it so small, that by white standards it was the same as uninhabited. Also, by white standards, the few Indians who *did* live on it didn't even *use* it, but merely drifted across it like the shadows of scattered clouds. They didn't hoe, or plow, or plant. They merely hunted and danced and loafed and enjoyed a sort of perpetual picnic. To all eastern whites the Indians' "slothfulness" was a sin against God. To the land-hungry and the poor their waste of the land was a sin against both God and nature, and they felt the Indians didn't deserve to have it. Nonetheless, the land *did* belong to the Indians, and for a time the whites were restrained from taking it because they could find no solid moral justification for doing so. Then, in 1862, the Indians themselves (although not the Tetons) provided the "justification," and the good times of the Lakotah came to an end. The event that provided it was the Santee uprising known as the Minnesota Massacre. It so shocked the white world that the Tetons suffered from it both directly and indirectly for the next thirty years, in spite of the fact that they had absolutely nothing to do with it.

The Santee were Sioux also, but of a different branch. They called themselves *Dakotah*, and were the eastern cousins of the Teton Lakotah. At the time the Tetons moved out onto the western plains, the Santees remained behind in Minnesota where the advancing line of white settlement had overrun them. By 1862, they were already well settled on reservations (many in brick houses) and were adopting the white-man ways and were becoming farmers. To all outward appearances they had been "pacified" and were well on their way to becoming "civilized." Beneath the surface, however, they were angry. Their crops had been poor, their annuities had failed to arrive on time, they were heavily in debt to the traders, and many of them were hungry.

On August 17, 1862, when the Santee chief, Little Crow, made his regular attendance at the Episcopal church services and paused afterward to pass a few friendly words with the rector, things seemed peaceful enough. The peace was deceptive, however, for at the following dawn Santee warriors roared out of the reservation to begin what was one of the most savage bloodbaths in the history of the Indian wars. Their leader was the good Episcopalian, Little Crow.

Ironically, the Minnesota Massacre was not triggered by the Indians' discontent, but by an incident that was even more absurd than the one that had destroyed Grattan. It demonstrated that the Indians' ability to expand triviality into tragedy was fully as great as that of the whites, and it began with four young men arguing over a nest of eggs. One of the youths wanted to steal the eggs, which belonged to a settler named Jones. When one of his companions cautioned him, saying that Jones might make trouble if his eggs were stolen, the first youth accused the other of cowardice. The second young man responded hotly that he was not a coward and that he would shoot Jones to prove it. By the time their deadly "I dare you" game was ended, not only had Jones been killed, but also his wife, child, and two neighbors. As soon as the alarmed Santee tribal leaders heard of these killings, they called a council. There they jumped to the conclusion that the whites would impose severe punishment upon all the Santees for the boys' act, and thus, the Santees should strike before being struck.

As the chiefs designed it, the attack was to be directed only against the soldiers, the forts, and the agency. Unfortunately, as the Indians' resentments boiled to the surface, and the "pacified" Santee farmers of Sunday reverted to the painted Santee warriors of Monday, they reverted completely to the Sioux way of war. This meant warriors operating in small, independent bands, and it meant the merciless killing of the enemy wherever found—women, children, noncombatants, and the helpless included. That is the way the Sioux had always fought, and that was the way they would fight now. War parties swept the countryside, burning farms and killing their occupants. By the time army troops finally restored order, nearly five hundred settlers had been killed, and at least as many more were homeless.

As a result of the Santee uprising, the public mind was indelibly stamped with an image of the Sioux as treacherous savages who could never be trusted no matter how friendly they might appear, and also as bloody brutes who deserved to be granted no rights, nor given any favorable considerations. It was an image that was to influence white dealings with the Sioux for generations to come, and it would be applied not only to the Santees, who had committed the massacre, but also to the Tetons, who had not—simply because both the Dakotah and the Lakotah were "Sioux."

CHAPTER
5

.٨.٧.٨.٧.٨٠

Collision

As soon as news of the Minnesota Massacre was flashed across the talking wires, frightened whites began clamoring for protection from the Sioux, and new soldiers began pouring into the forts along the Missouri and the North Platte. To the Lakotah this was a bad thing. They had always regarded the soldiers rimming their lands as a worrying threat, especially after Whitebeard Harney had shown how easily he could march through Indian country when he had taken his troops from Fort Laramie to Fort Pierre. Unless the soldiers were planning either to make war or to take Indian land, the Lakotah could see no reason for them to be in the forts along the rivers. One of the reasons, in fact, that the years immediately preceding the Santee uprising had been such good years for the Lakotah was that the soldiers had been so few. Another good thing about that time was that since the soldiers had been too few to protect the Crows, the Sioux had been able to fight these ancient enemies again and to seize a piece of land from them as large as the white men's state of Connecticut.

However, with the soldiers pouring in again, it seemed to the Lakotah that they were being enclosed in a noose of blue-coats—a noose that was loose enough for the present, but one that the White Father in Washington could draw tight and choking whenever he took the notion. And even worse was the *kind* of soldiers that were coming now. They were volunteers who, having been aroused by the Santee uprising, had come west with an angry eagerness to "put those Sioux savages in their place." So they were not only impossible to get along with, they were also

36

actually dangerous. They made much fierce talk of fighting, and sometimes took shots at the Indians just for the fun of it. One day at Camp Cottonwood on the Platte a group of cannon soldiers even practiced their shooting by dropping shells among some Indians who were on an island out in the river.

Furthermore, it was not only the soldiers who were acting in this new hard way, but the white civilians also. There were few among them now that an Indian could call *kola* (friend), and most seemed to look at each Indian as if he, personally, had killed all those people in Minnesota.

In view of these new hard feelings and of the whites and Indians looking at each other in anger and fear more than ever before, it was plain to see that the good times had ended. As it turned out, they would have ended in any case, for other trouble clouds had been gathering, also, and the problems stemming from the Minnesota Massacre were but the first gust of a storm of affliction that now broke around the Lakotah.

Out on the south-central plains the white hide hunters, with their great booming rifles, were daily slaughtering thousands of the buffalo that were the Indians' staff of life. This was not being done on Lakotah land, but even so, the mass killing was shrinking the buffalo herds and breaking up their migration patterns so much that when they did make their annual meanderings through the Lakotah country, they were few and hard to find. So it was becoming harder and harder to fill the parfleches, and sometimes there was even hunger in the camps.

In 1862, the same year as the Santee uprising, gold was discovered in Montana. By the following summer caravans of white men crazy for the yellow metal invaded the lands of the Hunkpapa on their way to the mines. The wild Hunkpapa fought them, killing many and burning their wagons, but still they kept pressing in. Finally, in the spring of 1864, some of the big men of the Hunkpapa—Four Horns, Black Moon, Sitting Bull, and others—sent word to the whites that trespassing on the land of the Hunkpapa meant death. No matter how the whites came, the Hunkpapa told them, even with soldiers or by the Missouri River steamboat, they would be attacked and killed. The whites replied by sending an army against the Hunkpapa, and in July the two met in a big battle at Killdeer Mountain. Although the whites claimed they had defeated the Sioux, they still could not travel through Indian lands and live, so all the battle accomplished was to confirm that there was, indeed, all-out war in the Hunkpapa country of the north.

Also, in that turbulent summer of 1864, danger was building in the south. Along the North Platte the whites and Indians had become increasingly separated by the growing anger that now lay between them—dark and perilous as a heap of gunpowder.

Still farther south, a hot war was raging between Indians and the Colorado militia as the Cheyennes, assisted by some of their Sioux friends, attempted to shut down roads that had been cut through the Cheyenne hunting grounds to the new city of Denver. The fighting continued throughout the summer despite the efforts of a Cheyenne peace chief, Black Kettle, to negotiate an end to it. When fall came and Black Kettle had still failed to negotiate a peace, he moved his camp to Sand Creek, not far from Fort Lyon. There, he thought, his people would be out of the war's way. And to be sure the white people understood that Black Kettle's people were friends, both the American flag and the white flag flew daily from the top of his tipi. Tragically, and in spite of his precautions, the war found Black Kettle; it arrived in the form of Colonel John Chivington and his volunteer Colorado Cavalry. Colonel John Chivington was many things. He was a Methodist preacher and thus, presumably, a man of God. He was also a hot-eyed Indian hater. And finally, hoping to win high political office, he was out to make a reputation. In Colorado during that bloody year, the way to make a reputation was by killing Indians, and on a cold day at the end of November Chivington found Black Kettle's people at Sand Creek.

From both the Indians' present location and the peace conferences of the past summer, Chivington could not have failed to know that Black Kettle was friendly. Nor could he have failed to see the flags above the chief's tent. Regardless, this half-mad officer who had once startled a dinner party by announcing that he "longed to wade in gore" set out to do just that as he ordered his troops to attack to kill. What followed may well be the most cold-blooded slaughter of Indians by white troops in the entire history of the Indian wars. When it ended, one hundred twenty-three Indians had been killed, and of every eight of them slain, seven were women and children. The carnage was such that even some of Chivington's own men were sickened by it and wrote protesting letters to Washington—letters that led to an investigation and, ultimately, to Chivington's disgrace.

The Indian response, however, was much more immediate. Sand Creek was the spark that touched off the gunpowder of accumulated hostility on the Platte, and even though it was winter and a bad time for the Indians to make war, the Platte River country exploded. A thousand warriors—Cheyenne, Sioux, and some Arapahoe—attacked Fort Rankin on the South Platte killing fourteen soldiers. Then they sacked the trading post and stage company warehouses at nearby Julesburg. Following that, they raged up and down the South Platte valley, killing settlers, burning, and taking cattle. Then they struck Julesburg again, this time burning it down. And so it went, with the raiding continuing throughout the winter.

As spring came on, an unbelievably stupid act by an army officer fanned the war fires even higher. Two Face, a friendly Oglala chief, had bought a white captive—a Mrs. Eubanks—from some of the hostile Indians and had started with her to Fort Laramie to return her to her own people. On their way they were joined by Black Foot, another friendly chief. Once at the fort, Mrs. Eubanks sobbed out an hysterical (and highly overdramatized) story of her sufferings as a captive of the savages. Thereupon, the temporary post commandant—a man who was both an Indian hater and a drunk—promptly had Two Face and Black Foot arrested and hanged. Furthermore, they were not hanged quickly by a rope, but were suspended from chains placed around their necks—until they died of slow strangulation.

When the Indians learned of this additional atrocity, they were so incensed that during the summer of 1865 there was no place in the North Platte country where whites were safe, and for a time the Overland Trail was completely shut down. Finally, as the war grew hotter in both the Platte country of the south and the Hunkpapa country of the north, the government decided something had to be done. And so (as was becoming its habit in such cases) it called for another peace council.

The council met at Fort Sully on the Missouri River, just above the present Pierre, South Dakota. There a treaty was drawn up which the assembled "paper chiefs" meekly signed. According to its terms, the Indians were to receive the equivalent of thirty dollars per year per family for twenty years. In exchange, they acknowledged the government of the United States to be their master, and they promised to withdraw from any white-man roads that were either existing or *were to be established* across the Lakotah lands.

Flushed with easy victory, the government commissioners returned to Washington, where they announced that whereas the signing chiefs spoke for more than ten thousand Indians, the treaty had therefore been ratified by a majority of the Sioux and was valid. They were wrong on all counts.

In the first place, even if the chiefs had represented that many Indians, ten thousand did not constitute a majority of the so-called Sioux Nation. Second, these particular chiefs did not speak for ten thousand Indians; they spoke for almost none. Nearly all of them were merely "paper chiefs"—*appointed by the white men themselves*—and chosen from the "tame" Indians that the Lakotah scornfully called "hang-around-the-forts." In fact, about the only chief of any standing at all who signed the treaty of 1865 was a Minneconjou, Lone Horn—father of Big Foot. Furthermore, there was yet another reason why even if the paper chiefs *had* been real chiefs, and if they *had* represented a majority of the Lakotah, the commissioners would not have had a binding treaty. That reason was one the white men never did come to fully comprehend, and it was this: the Lakotah neither understood nor cared about this foolish thing the white men called "a majority." Just as no one chief could make a promise for another, neither could a "majority" of chiefs who signed a treaty bind those chiefs who did not sign; and those who did not sign saw no reason to honor the promises of those who did. Moreover, there were so many Lakotah bands, and therefore so many chiefs, that it is doubtful the white men could ever discover who they all were. And even if they could, it is certain they could never obtain unanimous agreement of all the chiefs on any given proposition. Thus, although the white men made treaty after treaty that they considered binding on all the Lakotah, they never made one that all the Lakotah themselves considered binding. Such a thing was impossible.

At any rate, under the Treaty of 1865, the whites thought they had an agreement (even if the Indians didn't) and under the "roads . . . to be established" provision they set out to take advantage of it by opening a new trail. It was to run from Fort Laramie northwest along the edge of Oglala country to Montana and was to be called the Bozeman Trail. Inasmuch as the road was not to really run *through* Sioux country, but only along the edge of it, the violence of the Oglala reaction to it was astonishing to the white authorities. This was because they didn't understand the Sioux view of the territory around them. So far as the Sioux were concerned, all the land rightfully belonged to them regardless of what other tribes might actually be occupying it. To the Oglalas the land beyond their western border was Oglala land, also, and the fact that they had not yet taken it away from the Shoshonis cast no cloud upon the validity of their title. Consequently, the Oglala saw the Bozeman Trail not as a road along their outer rim, but as a war lance thrust through the heart of their hunting grounds—and it was a lance they were determined to break and cast out.

The moving spirit of the Oglala resistance was a rising leader named Mahpiya Luta—Red Cloud. Born in the year of the Whistling Star and named for the red-burning meteor that gave the year its name, he was now forty-four years old and beyond the age when most men first begin to make strong leading. Nevertheless, Red Cloud was so forceful in rallying the Oglala warriors against the new road that in the spring of 1866, when the government announced that it was both open and safe, the truth was that no white man could travel it without being killed. When it became apparent that this was the case, the government sent an army to build forts along the trail and to protect its travelers. Although it was under almost constant attack from Red Cloud's warriors, the army did manage to build two forts; but as far as protecting travelers was concerned, the army could barely protect itself. Thus when the first wagons came up the trail bearing the brave markings "Virginia City or Bust!" they met the Sioux with no help from the army . . . and "busted." In August alone, the Sioux killed thirty-three whites on the trail, and by summer's end they had closed it completely. With that accomplished they paused long enough to make the fall hunt. But they only paused. In early winter they returned to try to do something about those hated forts.

The main part of the army, about three hundred men commanded by scholarly, mild-mannered Colonel Henry Carrington, was wintering at Fort Phil Kearney near the present Sheridan, Wyoming. And since the army was there, the Indians began gathering there, too. Not only were there Oglalas, but also—as a result of sending the war pipe around— some Minneconjou led by Hump and some Cheyenne led by Two Moon. By early December there were at least fifteen hundred warriors in camps scattered among the Big Horn foothills around the fort. And from there they tormented the surrounded garrison like wolves yapping and lunging at a surrounded buffalo bull. Despite the Indians' numbers and harassment, however, they probably wouldn't have been able to cause the army any serious difficulty had it not been for the great quantities of fuel the army needed in order to survive the cold of the mountain winter. The only way they could keep their stoves burning was to conduct a daily wood-cutting and hauling expedition. Wherefore, as regularly as the wood train ventured out, the Indians—recognizing it as the fort's vulnerable point—attacked. And just as regularly, when they attacked, a rescue force would charge out of the fort to drive them off. When this process had become established as a daily routine, the Indians used it to set a trap—one of the few such Sioux traps that actually worked the way it was planned. Usually their traps were spoiled by honor-hungry young men who gave them away by charging too soon. This time, however, the chiefs were able to hold the men back until the right moment came to charge. The trap still would not have worked, though, had there not been another of those eager officers at Fort Kearney who was fool enough to step into it.

Captain William Fetterman had joined the regiment in November and had been trouble since the day he came. A much-decorated officer in the Civil War, he allowed no one to forget that he was a fierce fighting man. He had come west to fight Indians and he wanted to get on with it. To his fellow officers he was openly contemptuous of the mild Carrington, accusing him of timidity in allowing the Indians to besiege the fort and to bedevil the wood detail. Were he, himself, in command, Fetterman often boasted, he would teach the Sioux a lesson they'd never forget. In fact, he claimed, "with eighty good men" he could "slice through the whole Sioux Nation."

Finally, on December 21, Fetterman got his chance. It was a bitingly cold day with a raw wind and with storm clouds piling up over the mountains. At ten o'clock in the morning, when the weather showed no signs of moderating, the wood detail faced the bitter cold and went out in spite of it. At eleven they were under attack. Straightaway Carrington ordered a force to its rescue and this time Fetterman was to lead it. Being aware of Fetterman's aggressiveness, however, Carrington cautioned him sternly, telling the captain that with so many warriors waiting in the hills it would be folly to pursue the Indians very far. Then he ordered, emphatically, "Under no circumstances pursue the enemy beyond Lodge Trail Ridge!"

There were seventy-six men in Fetterman's command as he mounted up, when at the last moment he was joined by four volunteers—two soldiers and two civilians. Thus, by one of history's little ironies, as Fetterman galloped out of the fort, he was followed by exactly "eighty good men."

The captain's intention was to force the Indians that were attacking the wood train to stand and fight, but as he charged them they frustrated him by simply running away. However, they ran neither very fast nor very far. Once out of the way of the charge they stopped and faced back toward the troops, all the while taunting them and shouting insults and making obscene gestures. Again Fetterman charged, and again the Indians ran . . . and then stopped. And then again the process was repeated—with the Indians always falling back toward Lodge Trail Ridge. Finally, the enraged Fetterman set out after the Sioux in a full, steady pursuit while they led him up and over the forbidden ridge and down its far side.

Then they sprang the trap. From the plum brush in the gulches, hidden chiefs cried, "Hopo! Hopo!" and were answered by more than a thousand warriors making the "Hi-yi-yi!" yell and by the hooves of a thousand war ponies thundering on the hard-frozen ground. In no more than forty minutes every man of Fetterman's command was dead. In a few minutes more their bodies (like those of Grattan's men) were stripped, gashed, gouged, and had many of their bones broken so they would go to the afterlife as naked cripples. Instead of "slicing through the whole Sioux Nation," Fetterman had gone scarcely five miles.

The extermination of Fetterman's troops outraged the whites. Again the newspapers cried "Massacre!" And the commanding general of the United States Army, William T. Sherman, went so far as to say, "We must act with vindicative earnestness against the Sioux; even to the extermination of men, women, and children."

To a great many people Sherman's statement seemed shockingly bloodthirsty and unjustified at the time he made it. Viewed today, from the perspective of more than a century, it still seems that way; but fortunately, it was never carried out. On the other hand, the charge of massacre did seem justified, and the perspective of history does not change that. The Fetterman affair not only *was* a massacre, it was a cold-blooded one besides.

There are some, however, who will still argue that point. One modern writer, for instance, has sought to excuse the Indians for the Fetterman massacre by saying they were simply imitating Chivington's actions at Sand Creek. Actually, the Indians *can* be excused for their behavior, but not on such absurd grounds. The Indians were imitating no one. Instead, they were merely fighting according to the Sioux code of war and, according to that code, fighting honorably. It was a harsh code. In war the Sioux expected neither to give mercy nor to receive it. There was no dishonor in killing the enemy, regardless of how or of whether they were warriors, women, children, or aged. The only dishonor lay in showing cowardice before the enemy. This was how the Sioux were taught; this is how it had always been. Consequently, from their point of view, fighting in this manner was both moral and just.

On occasion the whites, also, attempted mass killing although—restrained by a more confining set of ethics—they attempted it a good deal less often than the Indians. When they did do so, however (as in the case of Chivington at Sand Creek), they were usually more successful than the Indians because they had better equipment. Moreover, in view of the fact that the whites *taught* a code of war that included mercy for those surrendering and defeated as well as just regard for women, children, and the helpless, when they acted otherwise (as they sometimes did) it was to their dishonor for the reason that they were then violating their own moral principles. Thus, had the situation at Fort Kearney been reversed and had a thousand white soldiers entrapped, annihilated, and subsequently mutilated eighty-one Indians, the incident would no doubt be regarded now as another of those "blackest pages in army history." By the code of the Sioux, however, it was an honorable victory—and that is how history generally presents it.

Be that as it may, the Fetterman massacre was the worst defeat the whites had ever suffered in Indian warfare up to that time. It severely shook their confidence in their ability to open the Bozeman Trail, and the horde of warriors that had gathered to oppose them shook it even more. Nevertheless, as winter gave way to spring, and spring to the summer of 1867, they kept trying to open the trail. But the forces of Red Cloud kept trying to prevent them, and it appeared the Indians were the stronger. Although unable to force the soldiers out of the forts, they were able to keep them penned up inside. And they were able to keep the Bozeman Trail unusable. Thus, for all practical purposes the Lakotah were winning what would come to be known as the Red Cloud War.

The government officials also saw that the Indians were winning, and they found it most disturbing. It appeared now that they had only two choices—both difficult. One was to fight an all-out war and throw so many troops into the West that the Sioux would be completely overwhelmed and subjugated. However, this would be almost unacceptably expensive for a nation still exhausted by civil war. Their other choice was to attempt that which past experience seemed to indicate was nearly impossible—to make a peace treaty so solid, so practical, and so fair to both sides that war with the Sioux would be ended forever. They chose to attempt the latter, and the eventual result of their efforts was the Treaty of 1868—the most famous of all the treaties with the Teton Sioux and the one over which lawyers are still haggling and under which claims are still being made more than a century later.

As an inducement to the Lakotah to accept the treaty, the government officials had agreed among themselves that they would offer to abandon the Bozeman Trail. This meant, of course, that Red Cloud had, in truth, won his war.

CHAPTER
6
/\/\/\/\/\/\
"God Damn a Potato!"

DURING THE WINTER of 1867–1868, the White Father's messengers—busy as nest-building swallows—traveled among the scattered camps of the Lakotah carrying presents for the headmen along with the words that the White Father was inviting them to another peacemaking. He was asking the Brulé to meet with his peace chiefs at Fort Laramie in the Moon of Grass Appearing (April) and the Minneconjou and Oglala to do the same in the Moon of Ponies Shedding (May). So that the northern tribes would not have to travel so far, he was asking the Hunkpapa, Blackfeet, Sans Arc, and Two Kettle to council at Fort Rice near Bismarck, North Dakota, in the next month—the Moon of Making Fat. These meetings were so important, the messengers said, that the white peacemakers did not wish to deal with the paper chiefs but with the true leaders of the people. Thus, many wagonloads of presents would be given to those who came and talked and—it was said—they could keep the presents even if they did not touch the pen to an agreement. To most of the headmen these were kind words. Ah-h-h. It was good to be recognized as a true leader, and the presents would make a fine beginning for the summer—especially the guns and ammunition for hunting (or fighting if need be). Besides, perhaps the fighting with the Oglala had made the white men willing to pay much for peace. So at the proper time, lodges were struck and packed with other possessions on the travois poles to be dragged behind the horses of the women, and from all directions lines of people began moving like slow-flying arrows toward the place of meeting.

When the Brulé (who were to be the first to council) arrived at Fort Laramie, they discovered that the White Father had sent some very strong men to talk for him—possibly, the Indians thought, with the idea of making them afraid. Whitebeard Harney was there and, also, for a time, General Sherman, who had made such hard words after the fight at Fort Phil Kearney. But now these men seemed friendly and reasonable and showed no hard feelings for the happenings of the past. Consequently, as the Indians thought about it, they put aside their hard feelings, too. It was true that Whitebeard Harney had done a bad thing to the Brulé on the Blue Water, but it was no more than the Brulé themselves did to enemies in a fight. Nor had General Sherman's words been any stronger than those a Lakotah chief would have spoken had many of his young men been caught and killed and mutilated.

Therefore, the first meeting opened in a mood expressed by a Brulé who said, "When two persons talk together and their hands reach each other, it is all right. The Great Spirit sent you here. He has taken pity on us and I hope you will do the same."

During the two weeks following the opening statements, there was much talking in small groups as the peace commissioners and their interpreters explained the Great Father's offer to the Lakotah. Essentially, his offer was this:

Land. All of the present state of South Dakota west of the Missouri River would belong to the Lakotah absolutely, and would be known as the Great Sioux Reservation. No whites would ever be permitted to settle upon the reservation, and none but government employees on necessary Indian business would even be permitted to enter it.

In addition the Sioux were to have as a hunting ground an "unceded territory" consisting of all of the land "north of the North Platte River and east of the summits of the Big Horn Mountains." No white men could settle in this territory either, nor even cross it without prior Indian permission.

Annuities and Rations. For thirty years following the treaty each Indian would receive an annual issue of clothing.

Also, for thirty years each of the Indians who continued to "roam and hunt" would receive an annual cash payment of ten dollars, and "each person who engages in farming" would receive twenty dollars. Each Indian who was "settled permanently upon said reservation" was to receive a ration of one pound of meat and one pound of flour per day for four years "provided the Indians cannot furnish their own subsistence at an earlier date."

Education. A schoolhouse and teacher would be provided for each thirty children.

Inducements to Farming. Each Indian would have the right to "homestead" 160 acres of land, or to select and cultivate as his own up to 320 acres of reservation land. Indians who took up land and attempted to farm it would be given farm implements, seeds, "one good American cow," and "one good, well-broken pair of American oxen."

Other Assistance. The government would provide and operate for the Sioux a sawmill, a grist mill, and a shingle mill. It would also provide them with a physician, a carpenter, an engineer, and a farmer to instruct them in agriculture.

In exchange for all these things, the White Father was only asking the Indians to:

Remain within their prescribed boundaries.

Refrain from attacking or harassing whites or other Indians friendly to whites.

Compel all their children between the ages of six and sixteen to attend school.

These were the things the White Father was offering. Perhaps it was because the various "friends of the Indians" groups were now gaining a strong voice in Washington that the government's proposals for the Treaty of 1868 were good ones and were fair.

For one thing, the Great Sioux Reservation and the "unceded territory" together constituted almost exactly the same lands as the Lakotah were presently occupying. Thus, about the only land right the Indians were giving up was the "right" to seize any more. Moreover, in establishing definite boundaries, as well as stern rules for their observance, the government was both recognizing and attempting to deal with the problem that had destroyed far more Indian treaties than any other—the unlawful encroachment by whites. For contrary to both the Indians' belief then and what has become a popular myth since, most Indian treaties were not first violated *by* the government, but *in spite of it.* In nearly every case the first violaters were land-hungry whites independently pushing into Indian territory until they caused either an actual war or such a threat of one that the government would find itself compelled by voter pressure to force the Indians back. In the past the government had found this an almost impossible problem to solve, but according to the Treaty of 1868, it would try again.

The treaty also recognized what very few Indians were yet able (let alone willing) to perceive—that because of the diminishing game, their old nomadic way of life was doomed; thus, new sources of food would have to be found and a new way of living adopted.

It has often been said that each Indian treaty was but another in a series of robberies of the Indians by the white men. In many cases this has certainly been true. In the case of the Treaty of 1868, however, all evidence is to the contrary. There can be no question that it was a sincere attempt by the government not only to preserve a country for the Sioux, but also to help them, through education and encouragement in farming, make the adjustments which government officials of the time believed essential for survival of the Sioux in a world where change had become both constant and irresistible.

During their two weeks of learning about the treaty, the Brulé also began to think maybe it was a good agreement—although it was hard to be sure. There were so many words, so many things that were confusing. As they smoked around the lodge fires in the evening cool and spoke of what they had heard during the day, it always seemed that one of them had understood a thing one way and someone else another, until it was hard to tell what was meant. And yet . . . it sounded as if they would receive much and give up little. To force the little ones to go to school was not a good thing. But farming was worse. Ah! That was bad, indeed. Such a thing was woman's work and not for warriors. But it was also said they didn't have to farm if they didn't want to. And with having all the land, surely there would still be enough game. Most important, the white men said that if the treaty was made they would abandon their new forts and close the Bozeman Trail. In addition, both Spotted Tail and Red Leaf (the chiefs who had lived with the whites for a while after the mail coach raid) were speaking strongly for the treaty. Maybe it really was a good peace.

As a result of this kind of thinking, it took only two days of formal council for the Brulé to accept the treaty. The council opened on April 28, and on April 29 the chiefs touched the pen. Then—not knowing how much that day had changed their lives—they took their presents and went home.

When the Oglala and the Minneconjou came to the council at Fort
Laramie, things went much the same as they had with the Brulé. After
the talking and explaining, most of the assembled chiefs willingly
touched the pen. Among them was a young Minneconjou chief called
Spotted Elk, who later became known as Big Foot.

The whites, however, were troubled by the fact that two very
important men had not come even to listen, let alone to sign. One was
Hump of the Minneconjou and the other was Red Cloud of the Oglala.
The commissioners were not too concerned about Hump, but they were
very upset over the absence of Red Cloud. Since he had been the big
leader in the trouble on the Bozeman, they were sure that his was the
strong voice among the Oglalas. Actually, they were wrong. For one
thing, Red Cloud was not a hereditary chief as was, say, Man Afraid.
Also, many of the Oglala regarded Red Cloud as an ambitious upstart
who often set the people against each other so as to help himself.
Furthermore, he had had much to do with the big feud between the
bands of Smoke and Bull Bear back in the year of Snowshoes Worn
(1841), and there were some who said it was Red Cloud himself who had
killed Bull Bear. In any event, that fight had split the Oglala into factions
that still existed. Not knowing that, nor that Man Afraid (who had
signed the treaty) was actually the strongest of the Oglala chiefs, the
peace commissioners were convinced that their efforts would all be for
nothing without the agreement of Red Cloud. Before they pursued it
further, however, they must meet with the northern Lakotah at Fort
Sully.

There, in the first week of July, most of the chiefs of the smaller bands
signed the treaty without hesitation. However, of the most important
tribe—the Hunkpapa—the only truly strong leader who had signed was
Man-Who-Goes-in-the-Middle, the chief who later became famous
under the name of Gall. The others, such as Four Horns, Black Moon,
and Sitting Bull, not only stayed away, but sent word they would never
agree to this new white-man paper. Furthermore, they never did sign it.
They, as well as Hump and a few other "hostiles," thus became known as
"nontreaty chiefs." Insofar as these nontreaty chiefs were concerned, the
Treaty of 1868 never existed.

With the Fort Sully council behind them, the commissioners turned
back to the matter of Red Cloud. In an exchange of messages they
discovered the problem to be the Bozeman Trail forts. The whites had
promised to abandon them, but the soldiers were still there. Quite

properly Red Cloud expected the whites to keep their promise before he signed the paper. Thus, in late summer the forts were vacated—with the exultant Indians riding in so closely behind the departing army that they had all the buildings burned before the troops were even out of sight.

However, now that Red Cloud had discovered his power with the whites, he set out to demonstrate it. With the forts gone, his promise to sign the treaty became "maybe." Throughout September and then October he kept the commissioners waiting. Finally, on November 4 he rode into Fort Laramie. There he hesitated for two days more, all the while telling the commissioners what he thought of such foolish ideas as expecting warriors to farm. But on November 6 he went to the council tent, washed his hands with the dust of the floor, and touched the pen.

With Red Cloud's signature the Treaty of 1868 became a fact, and with it a romantic rumor circulated that has persisted ever since. The treaty, it is often said, includes the promise that its conditions shall endure "so long as the grass shall grow and the rivers flow." The actual provision for its endurance, however, is considerably different in both style and meaning. It says:

> No treaty for cession of any portion or part of the reservation herein described which may be held in common shall be of any force or validity as against said Indians, unless executed and signed by at least three-fourths of all the adult male Indians, occupying or interested in the same. . . .

As it turned out, things would have been much simpler had the romantic rumor been a fact; the interpretation of the actual provision was to cause a great deal of bitterness and misunderstanding for years to come.

Nevertheless, with the treaty now in effect, government officials thought they had the "Sioux Problem" solved forever. Despite the fact that the restlessly nomadic Lakotah were penned inside a corral, it was a wide corral and more than ample. Containing about ninety thousand square miles, including the unceded territory, it was occupied by no more than twenty-five thousand Indians. And the beloved Black Hills that were the hub of the Lakotah's universe were firmly inside the Great Sioux Reservation itself. Moreover, along with all that land, the Lakotah would also have rations for survival during the time they were discovering the joys and rewards of agriculture—rewards which the government planners considered so enticing that they predicted it would require no more than four years for the heretofore free-roaming Sioux to become settled and self-sufficient farmers. Unfortunately, the mere writing of a treaty cannot impart wisdom to its administrators or patience to its beneficiaries—nor can it rewrite human nature. And it was human nature—on both sides—that caused the treaty to be doomed from the moment it was executed.

As a matter of practical administration, the whites had expected the Indians to establish permanent camps near the agencies through which treaty benefits were to be provided. Many bands did establish such camps—and in so doing planted the seeds of increasing animosity among the Indians themselves. The so-called wild Indians scorned these agency Indians, calling them "coffee coolers" and "loafers." Sitting Bull expressed their feelings in a message in which he said, "You are fools to make yourselves slaves to a piece of fat bacon, some hardtack, and a little coffee and sugar." These words (and others like them) were stinging to the pride. Also stinging to the pride was the way in which the rations were distributed. The people found themselves waiting in long lines, and because rations were given only to "the heads of families," it was the men who found themselves standing in the lines and thus "doing women's work." On top of that, they were not called up in order of importance, as was proper, but were called alphabetically so that the chiefs were made to appear the same as anyone else. Finally, the white men were inclined to give these things in a way that said they were charity instead of honest payment for an agreement. But the rations were only one thing. Another was the matter of the new schools; their children were being told that the ways of their ancestors had been the ways of heathens and savages and that they must disregard and forget the teachings of their parents. Worst of all, however, was the deadly idleness of the agency camps. Their old activities were gone, and the Indians were not yet equipped to find constructive new ones to replace them. As a result, there began to be much gambling—with even the women playing the plum stone game to win each other's blankets and rations. There was drinking, too, whenever whiskey could be obtained to relieve the slow-dragging time. The inevitable consequence of the Indians' damaged pride, resentment, gambling, alcohol, and idleness was that the agencies constantly seethed with fermenting trouble. As one official said of them, "They abuse the agents, threaten their lives, kill their cattle, do anything they can to oppose the civilizing movement, but eat all the provisions they can get."

As the early 1870s passed and the ferment in the agencies continued, treaty violations also occurred—the first, probably, by the Indians themselves. They had promised not to attack Indians friendly to the whites, but the war with the Crows continued and was, if anything, more intense than before. Admittedly much of it was conducted by nontreaty bands of Hunkpapas, but many of the treaty Indians fought the Crows, as well. Also in the early 1870s, more trouble developed in the north. Survey crews appeared along the Yellowstone River to lay out a line for the new Northern Pacific Railroad. As far north as the crews were, and as vaguely as the boundary of the unceded territory was defined, they were not in violation of the treaty by the white interpretation. But by the Indian interpretation they *were* in violation and, furthermore, nontreaty Hunkpapa bands, not recognizing the treaty, were claiming the Yellowstone. So again, there was fighting between the soldiers and the Indians in the north.

By the summer of 1873, although the treaty had been in effect for nearly five years, the Lakotah country was as stormy as ever, not only in the north but in the south, also. That summer a strong band of Sioux warriors—ranging south of the Platte and, therefore, outside the treaty territory—came upon a band of Pawnees making the summer hunt. The result was a massacre in which more than fifty Pawnees died—many of them women and children—and all of the Pawnees' meat and hides were taken and their camp destroyed. Additionally, at about the same time, a war party led by Red Cloud's son had turned its attention to the whites and was raiding along the Platte and the Sweetwater.

Thus, after five years, there continued to be such turmoil that it appeared the Treaty of 1868 had accomplished absolutely nothing. As things were, it had not. Yet, had there been no additional problems, peace likely would have been its eventual result. After all, the Indians were suffering from the most extreme possible case of what would be referred to in the following century as cultural shock. Their way of life, unchanged for thousands of years, was being swept away by a new culture like a sandbank is swept away by a flash-flooding river. And although their loss of the old life was inevitable, it was the only life they either knew or cared about, so their transition could hardly be expected to be other than turbulent.

However, there were additional problems, and they were building up fast. The line of white settlement had advanced until it was pressing against the Sioux boundaries like rising waters against a dam, and the whites were looking hungrily at the empty land on the other side. They wanted it; they wanted it now; they were convinced that rightfully they should have it—and their justifications were many. Recalling the Minnesota Massacre, they thought it wrong for "those savages" to be rewarded with ownership of so vast a territory. They considered a farm of anywhere from 160 to 320 acres as "aplenty" for any family, yet the Great Sioux Reservation alone contained nine hundred acres for *each Indian.* Adding in the unceded territory jumped the figure to about two thousand acres—eight thousand acres for a family of four—which they saw as a preposterous amount of land . . . especially for people who didn't even use it anyhow. Beyond that, there were the treaty supplies given to the Indians who attempted to farm, as some of them were now doing. Seeing those Indians receiving farm machinery and seeds and oxen—things the white farmers had to provide for themselves—they were provoked mightily by what they considered to be inexcusable charity on the part of a soft-headed government. Finally, because the settlers generally labored hard and nevertheless were sometimes hungry, when they saw the idleness in the agency camps and the rations distributed to those who did not work, they did not see a painful readjusting process of displaced and bewildered people. They saw an outrageous pampering of "a bunch of shiftless Indians" who would not work their land and support themselves.

Thus, as the rising settlement tide pressed against the Sioux border dam, it could be only a matter of time until the dam was breached. When the breach was made in 1874, however, it was not done by the white settlers, but by a column of a thousand troops of the Seventh Cavalry under the direction of the government and led by Lieutenant Colonel George Armstrong Custer. The objective of the expedition was made clear enough—reconnaissance of the Black Hills—but its purpose never was. One of the government explanations was that since the Black Hills constituted the only remaining American territory to be totally unknown to the white man, it should be explored and charted. Still, this was hardly justification for violating the treaty clause that forbade white men to enter the Great Sioux Reservation. After all, if white men were never to enter the Black Hills, why did they need to know what was in them? General Phil Sheridan gave another reason. He said Custer's mission was to investigate the feasibility of a fort near the Black Hills for control of those Indians who were continuing to raid settlements to the south of the reservation. The true reason, however, may have been an unspoken one.

Not only had it long been rumored that there was gold in the Black Hills, but Custer's column also included two experienced gold miners who (it was later explained) "just happened" to go along.

Unfortunately for the Indians' cause, Custer's men found their sacred Paha Sapa (Black Hills) to be an oasis in the plains—a little Switzerland of rugged pine mountains separated by flower-carpeted valleys and clear, cold streams. Even more unfortunately, on July 30 they found the rumored gold. Custer's report of the find was guarded: ". . . until further examination is made regarding the richness of the gold, no opinion should be formed." But when the news reached the outside world, the newspapers were not so guarded. The Yankton (Dakota Territory) *Press and Dakotian* exulted:

PREPARE FOR LIVELY TIMES!

Gold Expected to Fall 10 per Cent!
Spades and Picks Rising.—The
National Debt to be Paid
When Custer Returns!

The *Bismarck Tribune* announced, "This immense section bids fair to become the El Dorado of America!" In Chicago, the *Inter-Ocean* devoted an entire page to the new strike and declared, "From the grass roots down it is 'pay dirt!' "

Now, with a gold rush added to the pressure from the land seekers, the destruction of the Great Sioux Reservation was inevitable. Even so, its destruction was not immediate. For a time the army did its best to carry out its orders to prevent whites from entering the reservation. And for a time it was successful enough to incur the intense resentment of almost every Westerner and to trigger such irate outbursts as the following editorial in the Yankton *Press and Dakotian* of September 3, 1874:

This abominable compact [the Treaty of '68] with the marauding bands that regularly make war on the whites in the summer and live on government bounty all winter, is now pleaded as a barrier to the improvement and development of one of the richest and most fertile sections in America. What shall be done with these Indian dogs in our manger? They will not dig the gold or let others do it. . . . They are too lazy and too much like mere animals to cultivate the fertile soil, mine the coal . . . bore the petroleum wells, or wash the gold. Having all these things in their hands, they prefer to live as paupers, thieves, and beggars; fighting, torturing, hunting, gorging, yelling, and dancing all night to the

beating of old tin kettles . . . if they have to be supported at all, they might
far better occupy small reservations . . . than to have the exclusive control
of a tract of country as large as the whole State of Pennsylvania or New
York, which they can neither improve nor utilize.

Despite the mounting public indignation, however, the army continued to do its job well enough that by the following spring of 1875, only
a few hundred of the thousands of would-be miners had actually slipped
through the military net and made it to the Black Hills. Obviously,
though, these were a few hundred too many to suit the Lakotah, and they
set about defending their beloved Paha Sapa with bloody vigor. Thus, as
increasing numbers of fortune hunters were deprived of their scalps, the
wrath of the American public grew until the government again found
itself in an intolerable bind. On the one hand, voter pressure would no
longer allow it to refuse protection to the trespassing citizens. On the
other hand, it could not afford the costly war that would result from
giving them protection. Past attempts to escape similar dilemmas
through treaties had shown very poor results. Accordingly, government
officials decided, they would escape this dilemma by a different door.
They would *buy* the Black Hills.

The commission, therefore, set to council with the Sioux and make the
purchase. The Lakotah response was immediate and strong. Hiya!
Tohanniyelo! No! Never! The land was their church and the Paha Sapa
was its altar, and the mountain thunderings were the voice of Wakan
Tanka speaking to his children. One does not sell such a thing. But,
finally, some of the chiefs said maybe for six hundred million white-man
dollars they might sell after all. Thinking they were making some
progress, the commissioners countered with an offer of six million. At
that, angry mounted warriors—war-whooping and waving rifles—
charged the council tent. The startled commissioners retreated, all the
way back to Washington, in fact, and the negotiation was finished.

The government, however, was not finished. Stung by their failure and
incensed by what one called the "high and mighty attitude" of the Sioux,
government officials decided that the backbone of the Indian resistance
lay in the so-called wild bands and in the nontreaty bands of Sioux in the
unceded territory. Consequently, it was decreed that all Sioux in that
territory must return to their agencies on the reservation proper and that
any who had not done so by January 31, 1876, would suffer military
consequences.

The legality of their action was questionable. On the one hand, the treaty did not give the Indians ownership of the unceded territory as it did the reservation itself, it granted them only the right to occupy it. On the other hand, the treaty made no provision for termination of that right. So, as usual, the government saw things one way and the Indians another . . . but the Indian reaction was violent.

The January 31 deadline came and passed and not one band of the affected Indians had come in. Such being the case, in the spring the government sent an army to the Powder River and the Yellowstone River country to round them up. At the same time, Sitting Bull sent messages to all the bands of all the tribes of the Lakotah inviting them to "come out for one more big fight with the soldiers." A great many came—gathering on Rosebud Creek in southern Montana until their camp was the greatest assembly of Lakotah since the Great Council of 1857.

On June 16 the Indians discovered an army led by General George "Gray Fox" Crook advancing up the Rosebud from the south. At dawn on the seventeenth, a thousand warriors led by Crazy Horse attacked it. The ensuing battle, fought amid showers of chokecherry and wild plum blossoms dislodged by the charging horses, lasted six hours. As in the case of most battles between the soldiers and the Indians, however, there was a great deal of shooting but very few casualties. According to army records Crook's twelve hundred men fired over twenty-five thousand rounds of ammunition that day, and the army losses were only ten killed and twenty-one wounded; the Indians' losses were about the same. Even so, the warriors of Crazy Horse had forced the Gray Fox to turn his army around and retreat to the Big Horn Mountains.

That night, as the Lakotah danced the victory, they felt very strong. For the first time they had fought in the white-man way—charging right into the enemy and fighting for a victory more than for counting coup and winning personal honors. And, more important, for the first time in their history warriors from all the seven council fires of the Lakotah had fought together, and they had fought as a *nation*.

Next day they moved over the divide to the banks of the Little Big Horn. They were found there on June 25 by a force of six hundred troopers of the Seventh Cavalry led by Pehin Hanska, Lieutenant Colonel George "Long Hair" Custer. Again the Indians fought in the new way, and by nightfall they had killed two hundred sixty soldiers, including Pehin Hanska himself, and had won the greatest victory in their history.

But the very greatness of their victory also made it their worst defeat. It aroused the whites to the point that they would never rest until the Sioux were completely subjugated. The Indians must have realized that themselves, for immediately after the battle they scattered. Most bands went directly to the reservation. The remaining few were easily gathered up by the army and taken there . . . all, that is, but one. Sitting Bull took his people and fled to the country of the little old lady in the white bonnet (Queen Victoria), which the Indians called Grandmother's Land and the white men called Canada.

Shocked by the Custer disaster, the whites were no longer in any mood to dilly-dally in the purchase of the Black Hills, and the matter was brought before Congress. There, on August 15, the Honorable Jefferson Kidder, congressional delegate from Dakota Territory, declared to the House:

> The Indians . . . have never attempted to utilize the country known as the Black Hills . . . to them it had no attractions until the white men came and gave them an easy chance to add to their decorations bleeding scalps. . . . And yet Sir . . . these Indians we have always carefully protected and made them honored guests, while at their waists hung the scalps of our bold pioneers.
>
> . . . The Black Hills have become occupied by a large population of the bold and hardy yeomanry of our country . . . pursuing the even tenor of their ways. . . . But the Indians . . . are continually murdering innocent men, women, and children . . . and committing such nameless crimes as the contemplation of which makes humanity's warm lifeblood congeal at its source.
>
> We are told to wait until a different policy or a new treaty may enable these Indians to vacate this valuable country; but Young America never waits. . . . Remove this dusky cloud from a portion of the reservation . . . (and) it will stop the shedding of innocent blood. Men and women will earn their daily bread in quiet, and lay down to sleep without fear of being awakened by the yell of the bloodthirsty savage or the glare of the midnight conflagration. . . .

The members of Congress, rarely able to look with more than one eye at any proposition, because the other eye must always be fixed on the ballot box, found this idea appealing. After all, the government was under no legal obligation to feed the Sioux. Under the Treaty of 1868, it *had* been, but for only four years, during which time the Sioux had been expected to learn to support themselves. That obligation ended at the beginning of 1872. When it did, the Sioux were, if anything, even less capable of self-support than before, and it was obvious that without continued rations they would quickly starve. As a moral duty, therefore, and at the cost of millions of dollars, Congress voluntarily continued making the annual rations appropriations. This action was exasperating to most voters, for they saw it becoming a program of perpetual support whereby their tax dollars would be endlessly and outrageously squandered on the feeding of "a bunch of lazy savages." Now, however, the use of the ration program as a crowbar for prying concessions from the Indians gave the members of congress an opportunity to justify their previous "waste."

On the day that Kidder made his speech, the annual appropriations bill was passed, with a rider attached specifying that the money would be appropriated *only* if the Lakotah agreed both to vacate the unceded territory and to give up the Black Hills. Without delay another purchase commission was sent to negotiate with the Sioux, and it held a strong hand. The choice was "sell or starve." The Lakotah sold. On October 27, 1876, they surrendered from the western edge of the Great Sioux Reservation a strip of land fifty-two miles wide and two hundred miles long which contained the Paha Sapa.

In its haste to secure the Black Hills, the Congress overlooked a vital point. The Treaty of 1868 clearly provided that no Indian cession of reservation land would be valid unless consented to by "three-fourths of all the adult Indian males occupying or interested in the same. . . ." The commissioners had neither obtained such consent nor even tried to. All they had received was the agreement of the chiefs under a certification clause that read, "We, the undersigned chiefs and headmen of the Sioux Indians . . . do hereby consent and agree to all stipulations therein contained. . . ." Regardless, on February 28, 1877, Congress ratified the agreement. Because the Indians were in no position to protest—and the whites were not disposed to—the fact that the agreement was clearly illegal made no difference to any of those who passed it. It would, however, rise to plague their great-grandchildren.

The ten years following the sale of the Black Hills was a deadly decade of stagnation on the Great Sioux Reservation. The Lakotah were adapting, but only to survival under reservation conditions and not to any constructive new way of life. They drew their rations and their annuities, and they idled and existed. Their children were learning to read and write after a fashion, but they could find no profitable use for it afterward. They were also being taught that Indians were inferior people and that the only worthwhile people were whites, which they could never be. Thus, gradually, among both old and young, morale decayed and hope died.

As for the farming program, it was a failure for several reasons. One was that the men still retained enough of the old warrior ways and spirit to see farming as a demeaning thing beneath the dignity of a man. Red Cloud told his agent, "Father, the Great Spirit did not make us to work. He made us to hunt and fish. He gave us the plains and the hills and covered them with the buffalo. He filled the streams and rivers with the fish. The white man can work if he wants to, but the Great Spirit did not make *us* to work. The white man owes us a living for the lands he has taken." Sitting Bull was more brief: "I don't want anything to do with a people who make an Indian warrior to carry water on his shoulders or haul manure." But the attitude of the Plains Indian toward agriculture was most pungently expressed by the Shoshoni chief, Washakie. When the white men told a council of his people that they should farm, Washakie drew himself up to his full height, faced the white commissioners, and said with deep feeling, "God damn a potato!"

Despite that attitude, a few Indians did make an attempt at farming. But since they didn't know how and since much of the soil was poor and the weather dry, the crops failed. After a few such failures, all but the most persistent gave up.

The whites, however, had by no means given up on the idea of Indian farming. In fact, they had just started. The greatest pressure was coming from various "friends of the Indians" groups. By the late 1880s there were many of these with large memberships and a growing influence in Washington. They were sincerely dedicated to what they considered the Indians' welfare, but, unfortunately, their group contained too many members who knew nothing of either farming or Sioux Indians. They were of the opinion that 160 acres of Dakota land was more than ample to provide for a family. They further believed that agriculture was such a "civilizing" occupation that once the Indians commenced to hoe and plant, they would automatically also begin to wear overalls and gingham aprons and attend box socials on Saturday nights and prayer meetings on Sundays; then the "Indian Problem" would disappear for lack of Indians—they would all have become dark white men. The fact that they were mistaken in both their opinions in no way diminished the enthusiasm of their efforts to force the Indians to farm.

Another group pressing for Indian agriculture consisted of those who were tired of "wasting tax dollars" to support Indians and simply wanted them to become self-sufficient. And a third and politically the most powerful of these pressure groups was the "land boomers," the people who wanted more land. They thought the Indians still had too much land, and they reasoned that if each Indian family was given a farm, the remainder of the reservation would become "surplus" and could be justifiably taken by the whites.

Once the would-be benefactors, the land boomers, and the taxpayers in general all decided that their widely differing goals could be reached by the same means—forcing the Indians to farm—action was inevitable and resulted in the Dawes Act of 1887. It provided for the breaking up of the Great Sioux Reservation into six smaller reservations. Each family head would be allotted 160 acres which he would be expected to farm. Then the reservation "surplus" would be sold at fifty cents per acre and the money put in trust at five percent interest, with the income therefrom to be used for the benefit of the Indians "in advancing them toward civilization." Senator Dawes—one of the sincere but uninformed would-be Indian benefactors—thought the Lakotah would welcome the allot-ment act. He could not have been more mistaken.

In the summer of 1888 a government commission took the act to the reservation for the Indians' approval—this time being under instruction to secure the signatures of "three-fourths of the adult male Indians" as prescribed under the Treaty of 1868. But, in the meantime, word had gone ahead of the commission's coming, and the chiefs had sent runners to all the camps saying that the Wasicun (white men) were coming to steal half the reservation and to force the Indians to farm the balance. The commission failed miserably.

Still, the whites did not give up. They rewrote the act to provide 320-acre allotments per family head, $50 to be paid to each family when it began farming, and $1.25 per acre for the nine million acres that would be declared surplus. In the summer of 1889, a new commission went to the reservation to present the amended agreement. It was headed by General "Gray Fox" Crook who—although he had fought the Indians— was their dedicated friend and supporter of their rights. Also, despite the fact they had fought *him,* the Indians knew General Crook to be a friend,

and they respected his word. He was determined to sell the Dawes
agreement to the Indians, for he realized (even if they did not) that if the
Indians did not give up part of their land, the whites would never rest
until they had taken it all, and the Indians would be left with nothing.
Furthermore, as low as it may seem now, $1.25 an acre for the surplus
land was not a bad price at that time (in fact, it was more than some of
that same land sold for fifty years later), and Crook was convinced that if
the Indians didn't accept it, they would be forced to accept less later. So
all that summer there were councils—with the commissioners giving
feasts and making long speeches, and with the Indians responding with
even longer ones.

All during this time Indian resentment was high and Indian suspicion
even higher. At Pine Ridge the commission was met by a band of
painted warriors, and at Cheyenne River, when a line of Indians had
formed to sign the agreement, Chief Hump sent warriors leaping through
the windows of the meeting hall swinging war clubs to disperse them. As
the bitterness grew and fights broke out between those Indians who were
for the agreement and those who were against it, the commissioners left a
divided people behind them when they left each agency. Even so, their
list of signatures grew until finally the commission announced that it had
enough. Whether it actually did or not is still a matter of debate, but at
the time some people accused the commission of using juggled figures,
and others charged that they had even helped babies to touch the pen
and then counted them. But whether or not the charges were true, the
main challenge to the commission's claim of having obtained sufficient
signatures lay in the question of who should be considered "an adult
male."

Be that as it may, General Crook could not have obtained the
signatures he did had he not faithfully promised the Indians that their
approval of the bill would in no way reduce their rations. He was sincere
in his promise and remained embittered to his death when, shortly
afterward, Congress broke it. Just two weeks after the departure of the
commission, Congress (in an economy move) reduced the annual Sioux
appropriation bill; that, in turn, reduced the Lakotah's daily meat ration
by about forty percent.

There was hunger in every family that winter. And along with the
hunger came an epidemic of influenza, and many died. The influenza
was followed by whooping cough, to which the Indians had not the same
resistance as the whites, and more died. With the hunger and the sickness

and with the land diminished and the knowledge that the old life was gone came hopelessness. No more was there anything the people could do to help themselves. What was needed now was a messiah.

CHAPTER
7

./\./\./\./\./\.

Messiah

THERE HAD BEEN Indian messiahs in the past—many of them. Almost every time the pressure of the whites upon the Indians had become too painful to be endured, an Indian prophet had arisen to comfort the people with a promise to lead them out of their afflictions and into a happy new world. Thus, Tenskwautawa had come to the Shawnee, Smoholla had come to the Wanapum, and Nakaidoklini to the Apache. Their teachings had been diverse and had contained some unusual concepts. Smoholla, for instance, had preached that "God made the Indians first. Then He made a Frenchman, and then He made a priest. A long time after that came the Boston Men [Americans], and then the King George Men [English]. Later came the black men, and last God made a Chinaman with a tail. He is of no account and has to work all the time like a woman. All these are new people. Only the Indians are of the old stock." In general, however, the message of all the Indian messiahs had been the same—that a new world was soon to come which would be only for the Indians and would have no white people in it.

It is doubtful until the winter of 1889–1890 that most of the Lakotah had ever heard the stories of those past prophets or of the troubles that had precipitated their appearance. But when the Lakotah's own pain became too great to endure, a rumor of another such messiah began to circulate among them, too. In the evenings as they sat smoking by the iron stoves in their cabins, they listened to Oglala visitors from Pine Ridge telling strange stories of an Indian holy man who lived far to the west. It seemed he was saying that since the white men had spoiled the

Indian's old world, Wakan Tanka (God) was sending them a new one in which there would be plenty of buffalo and no white men at all. Such a thing was hard to believe and doubtless the words were not true. Nonetheless, the visitors said, a delegation of Lakotah was even now in Nevada to learn more of this man who—some said—was actually the Son of God.

As a matter of fact, the rumor circulating among the disheartened Lakotah that winter was true. In the sagebrush country of Nevada's Mason Valley, not far from Lake Tahoe, there *was* an Indian holy man preaching of a beautiful new world that was soon to come. And although this prophet's new world sometimes had whites in it as well as Indians, sometimes it did not. But it was always a place where all the dead Indians would be alive again and where there would be plenty of game, and where they would live the old life again and be forever happy.

This holy man was a Fish-eater—a Paiute—whom the whites knew as Jack Wilson and whose Indian name was Wovoka. At least it had been until he started his ministry; then he had changed it to his grandfather's name, which was Big Rumbling Belly. Mercifully, however, it is as Wovoka that history knows him. He was a gentle man teaching a gentle faith of peace which, nevertheless, would eventually bring bloodshed upon the Lakotah.

For a Paiute, Wovoka was a big man, stockily built and nearly six feet tall. His hair was bobbed closely below his ears, and his face was round and his features heavy. He tended to wear white-man clothing and preferred a flat-brimmed white felt hat. He didn't look much like an Indian prophet, nor, despite his keen interest in religion, had he intended to become one. Neither had his father, Tavibo, intended to become a prophet, but after receiving what the white men would describe as "a call" he became one anyway. With Wovoka it happened the same and after receiving *his* call, he carried on the work of his father.

The ministry of Wovoka's father had begun on a day when (as a young man) he had been up in the mountains and had heard the voice of the Great Holy speaking to him. The voice told Tavibo that the old earth was tired out and that God was going to renew it—but only for the Indians. All the white men's buildings and tools and things would be allowed to remain for the Indians' use, but the whites themselves would be wiped away. At that time all the Indians who had ever died would come back to life and all of them would be young again and would enjoy the new earth forever. But this wonderful thing could not happen,

Tavibo was told, unless the Indians not only believed it, but also prepared themselves for it by regularly performing a sacred dance called the Dance of Souls Departed, or the Ghost Dance. God then taught Tavibo the sacred dancing ceremony and instructed him to carry the message of the new world to the people and to teach them this dance they must do to make it come to pass. Faithfully, Tavibo gave the Great Holy's words to his people and led them in the dance, and (for a while) they both believed and danced. But as time passed and the new world proved unsatisfactorily slow in coming, the new faith faded away.

When Tavibo died, Wovoka, who was then about fourteen, was adopted by the family of a white rancher, David Wilson. The Wilsons gave the young Paiute the name of Jack Wilson and treated him as one of their own, and the Wilson boys came to consider him a brother. The Wilsons were a religious family, and it was at their nightly Bible readings that Wovoka became interested in Christianity. Once his religious curiosity was aroused, Wovoka went on to learn more from the Mormon missionaries who were working among the Paiutes. Then he spent two years working in the hops fields on the West Coast where he studied the beliefs of the Shakers. Regardless of his keen interest in the things of the spirit, however, when he returned to the Mason Valley, Wovoka still showed no missionary tendencies of his own. He married, settled down to a steady job—mainly working for his adopted father—and established a reputation among the local whites as a hard worker and a solid citizen.

One day when Wovoka was about thirty years old, he was cutting wood in the mountains when (like his father) he heard the voice of God. On his return from the mountains he told his friend Josephus, who was captain of the Indian police, what had happened. Later Josephus repeated it as follows:

> Wovoka said that he heard a great noise which appeared to be above him on the mountain. He laid down his ax and started to go in the direction of the noise, when he fell down dead, and that God came and took him up to heaven and showed him everything there; that it was the most beautiful country you could imagine; that he saw both Indians and whites, who were all young; that God told him that when people died here on this earth, if they were good, they come to heaven, and he made them young again and they never grew to be old afterwards; that the people up there were dancing, gambling, playing ball, and having all kinds of sports; that the country was nice and level and green all the time; that there were no rocks or mountains there, but all kinds of game and fish; that God

brought him back and laid him down where he had taken him from. He woke up and went to camp and went to bed.

God came to him again that night and told him to tell all the people that they must not fight, that there must be peace all over the world; that people must not steal from one another, but be good to each other, for they were all brothers; and when he had finished this work God would come after him again.

Wovoka heard no more from God for three years. During that time he continued working for the white men as before. At the same time he was preaching to the Indians, as he had been told to do, and performing an occasional miracle as well. It was one of these miracles (unorthodox as it may have been) that firmly established him as a holy man of the Paiutes. Because not everyone believed the story of his visit to heaven, Wovoka announced that on a certain day in July, in order to prove that he really *was* God's messenger, he would make ice to appear in the Walker River. As the day approached, the Wilson boys became increasingly concerned that their adopted brother would fail and thereby lose much face. Secretly they decided to give him some insurance. So while the curious and doubting Paiutes were waiting on the riverbank to see the miracle, the Wilson brothers were hauling a wagonload of ice from their father's ice house and dumping it into the river upstream. When the floating chunks drifted past the astonished Indians, all their doubts vanished and Wovoka's reputation was made.

It could be argued, of course, that this was not a real miracle. But Wovoka had *said* he would make ice appear, and although it appeared by means unknown to him, it *did* appear. So if it is true that God works in mysterious ways, who can say for sure that Wovoka's miracle was not a true one?

Even after the miracle, however, Wovoka's preaching and reputation were confined to his own people, until God came for him the second time. It was on New Year's day in 1889. The Nevada whites said there had been an eclipse of the sun that day. The Paiutes said it was the Day the Sun Died. When the sun died, Wovoka—who was in bed with a high fever—"died" also. He was taken to heaven again, and this time he received a new and more detailed set of instructions. Some of the new message was similar to the one received by Wovoka's father, but it was a little stronger. Now the old world was not merely to be renewed, it was to be destroyed and replaced by a fresh one. It was still to be a place where all the dead would live again and everyone would be young and happy forever, but this time nothing was said about removing the whites. However, since nothing was said about keeping them either, Wovoka never was quite sure which way it was going to be. One thing he was sure of, however, was that the new world could not come to pass unless the Indians both believed in and faithfully performed the sacred dance.

Wovoka was further informed that he was no longer merely a preacher; he had been promoted. God told him that whereas He intended for President Harrison to continue to run the East, that He (God) Himself would look after heaven, and He wanted Wovoka to take charge of the West. In this position Wovoka would have the power to control the rain and snow. More important, he would be given not only the power to destroy the old world and create the new one, but also the responsibility to decide when it should be done. The only restriction God put on this power was that first Wovoka was to summon Indians from all the tribes to come to hear his message. Next he was to instruct them that they were not to fight with the white man or with each other, that they were not to lie around in idleness, but to work, and that for five days every three months—after first purifying themselves—they must dance the Ghost Dance, which he would teach them. Then, when Wovoka was satisfied that all the Indians had received his teachings and had properly prepared themselves, he was to destroy their old, sad world and create for them a new, happy one.

As before, when Wovoka returned to earth and told his story, he could not spread the new faith as he had been instructed to because the people doubted. Especially they could not believe he had been given power over the rain and snow. Then he worked another miracle. At least the Indians said it was a miracle. The whites said it was luck. Both, nevertheless, agreed on what happened. In an interview with A. I. Chapman, who later investigated the Ghost Dance for the army, Josephus described how it came about. He said, "At this time I did not believe in the new Messiah and I thought I would try his power over the elements, as the country was very much dry; and unless they got rain they would have no kind of crops, and it looked like there was going to be a great suffering amongst the people." Josephus then went on to say that he rode to the Messiah's house, where he arrived late in the evening and told the man he called Jack Wilson how important it was for the people to have rain. According to Josephus, Jack Wilson spoke not one word, but sat with his head bowed for a while and then went off to bed. Early the next morning he came in to where Josephus was sleeping and said, "You can go home now, and on the morning of the third day you and all the people will have plenty of water." Shortly after Josephus returned home, the rain began. On the morning of the third day he arose to find the Walker River out of its banks and all the lowlands flooded. "Now," Josephus told Chapman, "I am a strong believer in the unnatural powers of the new Christ." Chapman went on to report that white employees of the agency corroborated Josephus's statement and that "All the white people I talked with around the agency and in the Mason and Smith valleys admitted that the rain did come, and they cannot convince the Indians that Jack Wilson had nothing to do with it."

The new Messiah was offended by this lack of recognition on the part of the whites, not so much because they were vocally ungrateful for the miracle of the rain, but because they were so *materially* ungrateful. After he had demonstrated his power over the elements, Wovoka went to Mr. J. O. Gregory, one of his white friends at the agency, and asked him to help prepare a letter to President Harrison. In the letter Wovoka proposed that in exchange for a small salary from the President he would agree to keep the Nevada people informed of all the latest news from heaven and he would also provide rain whenever requested. The letter was written, but Mr. Gregory, thinking it ridiculous, never mailed it. Not knowing that, the Paiute prophet was very disappointed when the President—whom God had made Wovoka's counterpart in the East— never saw fit to reply. Provoked by such shortsightedness on the part of the whites, Wovoka later complained to investigator Chapman:

> This country was all dry early last spring; there was nothing growing, and it looked like it was going to be a very hard time for both the Indians and the whites, and they came and asked me for a rain to make their crops grow. I caused a small cloud to appear in the heavens, which gave rain to all, and they were satisfied. I think all white men should pay me for this kind of a thing; some two dollars, others maybe five, ten, twenty-five or fifty or however much it does not hurt them to pay. Also, the white people of this country do not treat me and my people right. They do not give us anything to eat unless we pay for it. If the whites would treat me right I would have it rain in the valley, and snow on the mountains in winter, so the farmers could have good crops.

If the whites, however, were willing neither to believe that Wovoka had performed the miracle of the rain, nor to receive his "latest news of heaven," the Indians were ready to do both—enthusiastically. Thus the prophet's reputation and his comforting words soon began to radiate out to the tribes beyond the Paiutes—farther and farther like the warmth of a growing fire—from Paiute to Bannock, to Shoshoni, to Crow, to Cheyenne, to Sioux.

When the stories of the Messiah came to the Lakotah, they arrived a bit at a time, in confused little pieces brought by different messengers. One such fragment was described by Elaine Goodale, a young white woman who had just been appointed Superintendent of Indian Education in South Dakota and who spoke the Lakotah tongue:

> I [accompanied] a party of my wilder [Indian] neighbors on an old-time antelope hunt. . . . Our second night's camp in the wilderness found five families sleeping soundly after a hard day's travel. In my diary this item appears: *July 23, 1889.* So tired I fall asleep before supper. Later in the night a cry is raised, "A traveller comes!" Chasing Crane, on his way home from Rosebud, is welcomed with supper and a smoke. He tells a strange story of the second appearing of Christ! God, he says, has appeared to the Crows! In the midst of a council he came from nowhere and announced himself as the Saviour who came upon earth once and was killed by white men. . . . He was beautiful to look upon and bore paint as a sign of power. Men and women listen to this curious tale with apparent credence. A vapor bath is arranged and I fall asleep to the monotonous rise and fall of the accompanying songs. No intuition warned me of the bitter grief this self-proclaimed Messiah was soon to bring upon the Sioux.

At this same time the Sioux were also receiving letters from friends at western agencies telling of the Messiah and saying that he was asking all the tribes to send messengers to carry his words back to their people. It seemed that somehow most of the news and letters were coming to Pine Ridge, which was now the agency of the Oglalas and of such chiefs as Red Cloud, Little Wound, and American Horse. Man Afraid's son, Young Man Afraid, was also there. As the summer wore on, the chiefs heard more of this thing and sorted out the pieces of news until they began to believe that there really was a Messiah among the Fish-eaters of the West who was performing miracles and teaching of a new world that was coming for the Indians. It was not easy for the chiefs to believe that there was such an Indian working miracles, or that this new world was coming for just the Indians. Yet, this story was very much like the one told by the white holy men in the churches of Red Cloud, who was now a Catholic, and of Little Wound, who was now an Episcopalian. In the white men's story, however, the Son of God had come to a distressed little nation of *white* men as a white man. Could it not also be true that the Great Holy might send the Wanikiye (Saviour) to the distressed *Indians* as an Indian?

Although the chiefs doubted more than they believed, there was one thing that they *did* know for sure. During the weeks since Gray Fox Crook and his commission had been at the agency, the people had been badly divided, and there was much bitterness between those who had signed the agreement to sell the land and those who had not. The chiefs hoped that perhaps this new Messiah might have words that could bring them together again. Thus, in the fall of 1889, the chiefs finally did as the white men would do in similar circumstances—they appointed a committee to look into the matter of the Fish-eater Messiah. Broken Arm, Flat Iron, Good Thunder, and Yellow Breast were appointed from the Oglalas at Pine Ridge. The Minneconjous at Cheyenne Agency appointed Kicking Bear, and the Brulés at Rosebud selected Short Bull and one other.

The committee traveled west on the iron horse, stopping off and visiting with other tribes along the way. Each time they resumed their journey they were joined by other delegates who were also going to see the new Indian Messiah. When they finally reached the home of Wovoka in the Nevada wilderness, they were but a small part of a throng of Indians from many tribes . . . all of whom had come to hear the good words of this holy man. The Lakotah delegation was gone all that winter and did not return until the Moon of Grass Appearing (April, 1890). They returned as they had gone—in a leisurely way and with stoppings off for visiting. Good Thunder and two others came back by way of Oregon because they had heard that there was supposed to be a Messiah there also, and they wanted to hear his words. (It turned out, however, that they didn't find him.) Kicking Bear, on *his* way home, stopped off in Wyoming for a time to learn more of the Ghost Dance from the Blue Clouds (Arapahoes), who were already performing it.

When all the delegates finally returned to Pine Ridge, the chiefs called a council to hear their report. Unfortunately, the agent at Pine Ridge, H. D. Gallagher, had also heard of the committee's return and of the council called to hear its words. Gallagher didn't know just what was going on, but as restless and excited as the Indians were over it, he suspected it was troublemaking. Consequently, he ordered the Indian police to arrest Good Thunder and two other delegates and lock them up. Then, when two days of questioning the prisoners revealed nothing at all, Gallagher released them again on the condition that no councils would be held for discussion of their trip. Meanwhile the Minneconjou, Kicking Bear, had been telling the chiefs of the wonderful things he had seen at the Ghost Dances of the Blue Clouds. He said that after the people had danced a little while they would fall down and die for a time, and then an eagle would come and carry them up to the beautiful land of which the Messiah had spoken. Kicking Bear further related that while they were in this beautiful land, these people would meet their dead relatives—fathers, mothers, brothers, sisters, and even their own children—and visit with them for a little time. Moreover, there was plenty of food in that land and no white people at all, and everybody who had died was young and happy and wanted their relatives on earth to do the sacred dance so that they could come there also. These were such good words that, promise or no promise, the committee's report had to be heard in a council. Accordingly, one was called to meet on White Clay Creek, well away from the listening ears of the agent.

At the council the delegates produced a letter from the Messiah which he had sent home with the delegates from all the tribes who had come to hear him. His letter, rearranged and clarified from the original Carlisle English, said:

> When you return home you must make the dance, and all of you do it the same way. Dance five days and one night. Then everybody should take a bath in the river and go home.
>
> I, Jackson Wilson, like you all. You have brought me a good many gifts, and my heart is full of gladness.
>
> After you get home I will send you a good cloud [spirit] that will make you feel good. Also I give you some holy paint.
>
> I want you folks from all the tribes to come to see me again in three months.
>
> There will be a good bit of snow this year. Sometimes this fall there will be such a rain as I have never given you before.
>
> The Grandfather [God] says that when your friends die you should never no cry.
>
> Be a good behave always. It will give a satisfaction in your life.
>
> Do not tell no white man about this, but Jueses is now on the earth like a cloud. Everybody who was dead is alive again. I don't know when they will come here—this fall or in the spring. Then everybody will never be sick anymore and all will return to being young again.
>
> Work for the white man, and do not make any trouble with them until you leave them.
>
> When I shake the earth do not be afraid. It will not harm anybody.

I want you to make the dance every six weeks. First, put out food for everybody. Eat, and then wash good clean yourselves before dancing.

That is all I have to tell. I am with you and you will receive good words from me sometimes.

Do not tell lie.

After they read the letter, the delegates described their own visit to the land of the Fish-eaters and the Messiah. They told it thus:

The people there told us that the Messiah would appear at a place in the woods that had been prepared for him. When we went to that place there was a smoke descending down from heaven to the place where he was to come. When the smoke had disappeared there was, in its place, a man of about forty, and he was the son of God. The man spoke to us and said, "My Grandchildren! I am glad you have come from so far away to see your relatives. They are all your people who have died from your country."

Then he told us to come with him, and he took us to where we could see a land which he had created across the ocean, and on which all the nations of the Indians were coming home. Then, as the Messiah showed us that land which he had created and which reached across the ocean, it disappeared, and he said it was not yet time for that to take place.

Then the Messiah gave to Good Thunder some paints—Indian paint and a white paint—and a bunch of green grass. Then he spoke again and said,

"My Grandchildren, when you get home, go to farming and send your children to school.

"On the way home, if you kill any buffalo cut off the head, and the tail, and the four feet, and leave them, and that buffalo will come to live again.

"When the soldiers of the white people chief want to arrest me, I shall stretch out my arms, which will knock them into nothingness or, if not that, the earth will open and swallow them in.

"My Father commanded me to visit the Indians on a purpose. I had come to the white people first, but they not good. They killed me. You can see the marks of wounds on my feet, my hands, and on my back.

"My Father has given you life—your old life—and you have come to see your dead friends. However, I will not take you home to these things just yet.

"When you get home I want you to tell your people to follow my examples. You and all your people must use the paints and grass I give you. Any Indian who does not obey me, or who tries to be on the whites' side, will be covered up by the new soil I am sending to cover the old earth.

"In the spring, when the green grass comes, your people who have died will all come back, and you shall see your friends again if you have answered my call."

Then, from the many tipis that were there, the people sent for us to visit them, and they were all people who died many years ago. Chasing Hawk, who died not long ago was there, and we went to his tipi. He was living there with his wife, who was killed in a war long ago. He was living in a good buffalo skin tipi—a very large one—and he wanted all his friends to come to that place to live. Also a son of Good Thunder who died in war long ago was there, and took us to his tipi, and his father got to see him.

On our returning journey we come to a herd of buffaloes. We killed one and took everything except the four feet, the head, and the tail. Then, when we had come a little way past it, that buffalo come to life again and walked off. This was one of the Messiah's words come to truth.

There was another of his words that come to truth also. The Messiah had told us, "When you feel tired of the long ways, if you call upon me I will short your journey." Once, when we were tired, we did this. When the night had come upon us and we had stopped at a place, we called upon the Messiah to help us because we were tired of long journey. Then we went to sleep. When we awoke the next morning we found ourselves at a great distance from where we had stopped.

However, while that was how the Lakotah delegation understood and passed on the Messiah's message to their people, it was not quite the same way it was understood and passed on by the delegates of the thirty-odd other tribes that had heard and accepted it. Moreover, as the Sioux began to practice it, it underwent more change. This is understandable since listeners have ever been inclined to interpret the words of messiahs according to what they are hoping to hear and to shape them in memory to conform with what they would like to believe. It was no different with the Sioux. They so promptly forgot Wovoka's instructions to farm, to work willingly for the whites, and to send their children to school that it was as if they had never heard them.

Furthermore, the Sioux read more hostility to the whites into the prophet's words than did the other tribes. When the Sioux thought they had heard Wovoka speaking of knocking the soldiers "into nothingness," other tribes understood him to say that he would send soldiers against any tribe that "misbehaved." And whereas the Sioux believed he had come to earth for the Indians alone and would destroy any Indian who "tried to be on the whites' side," others understood he had come for *all* of God's children and that "all whites and Indians are brothers . . . they are going to be all one people." However, all of the tribes that adopted the Ghost Dance religion were agreed that their domination by the whites was soon to end and that a beautiful new world was coming in which everyone would live forever, and that they must perform the dance in order to bring these things about. And all the tribes except the Sioux understood that they were to keep peace with the whites until the new world came. The Sioux were never quite sure about that—no doubt because they were the last of the Ghost Dancing tribes to have been subdued by the whites, and their warrior memories were still fresh. Although many of the more farsighted Sioux were now teaching that with the old way gone forever the Lakotah had no choice anymore but to walk in a new road, some of the older men would still rather die fighting than take up farming or be forced to live like a Wasicun. Also, there were young men among the Sioux who were old enough to have learned the warrior's ways, but were still too young to have had a chance to count coup on an enemy or to win battle feathers. So it is probably because the Lakotah's need for war had not yet ended that they were never quite convinced that the Messiah really wanted them to wait for the new world in peace.

Thus it remained for Kicking Bear, the most militant of the Lakotah delegates, to give the Ghost Dance faith of the Sioux the one warlike touch—the bulletproof ghost shirt—that set it apart from the faith as it was adopted by all the other tribes. This happened at the council after the committee had told its story, when Kicking Bear repeated the things he had learned at the Ghost Dances of the Blue Clouds. Again he told how the dancers would fall down dead for a little time during which they went to heaven to visit the *wanagi* (the ghosts of those who had died before). He said, "When the dancers come back from visiting the ghosts they brought . . . water, and fire, and wind with which to kill all the whites or Indians who help the chief of the whites." Then he said,

> All the men and women made holy shirts and dresses to wear in the dance. They paint the white muslin of the holy shirts and dresses with blue across the back, and along side of this is a line of yellow paint . . . a picture of an eagle is made on the back of all the shirts and dresses. On the shoulders and sleeves they tie eagle feathers. *They said that bullets will not go through these shirts and dresses, so they have all these dresses for war.* [emphasis added]

Actually, the Ghost Dance faith of the Blue Clouds did not include bulletproof shirts, nor did the faith of any of the other tribes; but because Kicking Bear—a strong warrior who had fought in the battles of the Rosebud and Little Big Horn and Slim Buttes—had told it otherwise, the Sioux adopted the shirt . . . with tragic results.

CHAPTER
8

·/\/·\/·\/·\/·\·

Ghost Dance
(The Spreading of the Gospel)

BY THE TIME of the Ghost Dance craze, fourteen years had passed
since the sale of the Black Hills, and western South Dakota had changed
greatly both on and off the reservations. In that 1876 sale, the Indians
had given up the western fifty miles of South Dakota together with a
small triangle of land that lay between the converging Belle Fourche and
Cheyenne rivers and projected from the east-central border of that
western strip to the point where those rivers joined. By 1890, all of that
purchase territory had been filled in by white settlement. Now it was
almost entirely occupied by fenced ranches and farms and frequent small
communities with stores, churches, and post offices. In the Black Hills
there were small cities now—trading centers with brick buildings and
banks, hotels and grain elevators, and shady residential streets lined with
solid and sometimes stately homes. At Deadwood and Lead the
Homestake gold mine was in the process of becoming the largest in the
United States. And although Deadwood was still served by stagecoach
(its final run, ironically, was made on the day of the battle at Wounded
Knee), Rapid City had a railroad and also a college. When Delegate
Kidder had made his fiery speech to the Congress in 1876, and had
referred to "the hardy yeomanry" of the Black Hills "pursuing the even
tenor of their ways," much of that "hardy yeomanry" had actually been
made up of questionable types of citizens such as Calamity Jane, Wild
Bill Hickok, Wyatt Earp, and Poker Alice. By 1890, however, the
brawling frontier days were gone. The gamblers, gunslingers, and

whooping cowboys had long since been replaced by sober farmers, and the Indians were tucked away out of sight and half forgotten on their reservations. As far as the local whites were concerned, their part of the country was no longer any wilder, say, than Pennsylvania.

Where the reservations were concerned, the most visible change was that the Great Sioux Reservation was no more. That of it which still remained after the Land Agreement of 1889, had been broken into six reservations, four of which figure in the story of the final struggle of the Lakotah. They were:

Standing Rock. Bounded on the east by the Missouri River and lying across the South Dakota-North Dakota border, it was the home of the seventeen hundred or so Hunkpapa. Also at Standing Rock were about an equal number of Yanktonais who had been moved there from east of the Missouri and who were not Lakotah at all, but were of the Nakotah, which is the third of the three language groups of the Sioux.

Cheyenne River. Bounded by Standing Rock on the north, the Missouri on the east and the Cheyenne River on the south, its population of about three thousand Indians was mostly Minneconjou, but there was also a sprinkling of Blackfeet, Two Kettle, and Sans Arc.

Rosebud. This was the home of about five thousand Brulé. It lay between the White River on the north and the Nebraska border on the south and extended from the Missouri River westward for about a hundred miles to Pine Ridge Reservation.

Pine Ridge. Formerly known as Red Cloud agency, Pine Ridge was occupied in 1890 by a few more than five thousand Oglala. Joining the Rosebud on the east and lying between the same north and south boundaries, it extended on westward for about another hundred miles.

Although perhaps not changed as much as the reservation itself, life on the reservation had changed, also, the most apparent change being in the Indian settlements. While they were still referred to as "camps," this was merely a matter of old habits dying slowly, for no longer did the Lakotah live in tipis. Now the camps were actually communities of log cabins scattered along creeks where the various chiefs at one time had settled their bands. In most of these communities there was a store, a school, a church, and often a post office. Also, all the communities were generally well connected by networks of wagon roads. Thus, to the casual observer it might have seemed that the Lakotah were readily and rapidly adapting to the white man's ways.

Actually, however, their lives, like their clothing, were all mixed up—part white, part Indian, and not satisfactorily either one. Completely overwhelmed by a new culture and dominated by its representatives, they were being expected to leap from the stone age to the near-twentieth century in one generation. It was too much to ask. Nevertheless, the white determination to make the Indians over in their own image was stronger now than ever before. They were no longer asking the Indians to make that giant leap, they were demanding it—and demanding that it be done immediately. To that end they had done such things as banning some of the old religious ceremonies (including the Sun Dance), forcefully and arbitrarily cutting off the braids of all boys attending school, and punishing any child who spoke Sioux while on school grounds. At some agencies it was even rumored that the Indians' receiving of their rations was, in some cases, dependent on their church attendance. Although there seems to be no solid proof of this, it does sound reasonable as it is entirely consistent with the whites' drive for the forced civilization of the Indians.

Moreover, the whites were better at taking the old things of the Lakotah away than they were at putting something else in their place. Consequently, the Sioux were living in limbo, unable to live entirely in the old way, yet incapable of living entirely in the new one. So at the same time that they attended church and became Christians, they quietly retained their old religion and ceremonies. At school their children were taught the white way of living, but at home they were taught the Indian way. And while they lived in their dank, sod-roofed, white-man cabins in the winter, they often moved out into canvas tipis in the summer and lived as their ancestors had.

Every two weeks the Indians loaded their tipis, blankets, and cooking things onto their wagons and journeyed to the agencies, where they first set up camp and then stood in line to receive their rations. Afterward there would be feasting and parties in the agency camps, for that was the old way of doing when there was food and the people were camped together. This practice nearly drove some of the Indian agents to despair. Being able to give the Indians few enough rations at best, they found it next to impossible to teach them to make the rations last until the next issue. As a result, most of the people ate well only at ration time and then starved until the next issue.

Almost as discouraging as the Indians' suffering itself was the fact that it was not caused by the bad intentions of the whites nearly so much as by their good intentions being wrong. The designers of the various Indian programs were keenly aware of the fact that the treaties and land agreements were neither intended nor written to provide Indian benefits (including rations) indefinitely, but for only a limited time—at the end of which the Indians were expected to go it alone. They also felt (correctly so) that when that time came, if the Indians had not yet learned how to function successfully in the modern world, they could not survive. Therefore, when it became apparent that the Indians had never been much inclined to plan ahead and had little interest in learning to do that sort of thing, the government officials decided (probably correctly) that if the Indians were to continue to exist in the future they must be forced to learn. But from that point forward the government planners and administrators went sadly astray. So convinced were they of the infinite superiority of the white culture in all its aspects that it seems never to have occurred to them that the Indians might make the necessary adjustment more successfully if they were allowed to remain *Indian*. Instead they proceeded on the assumption that the only way the Indians could ever become adapted to the modern world was by first being totally crushed as Indians and then totally remolded as dark-skinned whites. Tragically, the government's programs for the Sioux were designed to do just that.

It was with this same sort of reasoning that Congress justified its ill-timed (and also ill-advised) reduction of the appropriations for Indian rations, even though under the Agreement of 1876, Congress *did* have the right to do so. From the very beginning of the ration-issuing program, it became obvious that the Lakotah—being human—could see little reason to learn to feed themselves by their own efforts as long as they were being adequately fed by doing nothing. Thus, it was argued, if the Indians were allowed to be somewhat hungry now, they would be forced to take up farming and would thereby become prepared to avoid being totally starved later. But in this approach there was at least one fatal flaw. Congress could never seem to understand that because of the climate and quality of much of the reservation land, what they were demanding of the unskilled Sioux would be, in a good many cases, an impossibility for the most experienced of white farmers.

So, regardless of the intent of the various government Indian programs and actions, all they had actually accomplished this far was to reduce a

proud and self-sufficient people into a broken and dependent people
whose days of pride were still so recent that their association with the
whites was a bitter cup which they would accept only if they could find
no other. It was into this atmosphere that the Lakotah delegates' story of
a new world coming was carried from the council on White Clay Creek.

As soon as the council on White Clay was ended, those who had been
there brought the words they had heard back to the scattered settlements
of their people. Then, from the camps of Red Cloud and No Water on
the western edge of Pine Ridge reservation to that of Little Wound's
people on the eastern edge, and then east again across Rosebud
reservation, people began talking about this new religion. The words
they heard of it were good words; there was hope in them and the people
were in need of hope. Yet, despite the need for hope, there was also
doubt and hesitation. No matter how good the words might sound, they
were still only hearsay, and the people had already heard too many good
words and promises spoken about other things which had then fallen to
the ground and been forgotten. Besides, even if the words were true, of
what use were they without someone to teach the sacred dance and, also,
to lead it? Thus, it was clear with the Ghost Dance faith, as it was with
any other, that the good words could come to nothing if there were not
any apostles to keep the words alive and to give them strength. As it
happened, two such apostles *did* emerge from those who had gone to visit
the Messiah—tireless apostles without whom the Ghost Dance faith
would never have taken hold among the Sioux. One was Short Bull and
the other was Kicking Bear. They were brothers-in-law and were about
as unlike as two men could be.

Short Bull was a slightly built man of about forty-five and had the sort
of lean, sharp face and hooded eyes that make one think of an
introverted intellectual. Far from being introverted, however, he was
actually a smiling, outgoing man and a gracious host. And unlike the
stock image of an Indian medicine man (which he was), he often enjoyed
wearing—and looked rather dapper in—a white-man business suit with a
heavy gold watch chain across his vest. Short Bull was a medicine man of
Chief Lip's people, whose cabins were scattered along Pass Creek a little
way south of where it runs into White River. Things were a little mixed
up as to which tribe Lip's people belonged. They were of a band called
the Wazazas, which means a fringe, or something dangling, and in their
case that was about right. Since the time of the trouble with Whitebeard
Harney on the Blue Water, they had been sort of Oglala, but at the same

time, sort of Brulé, too. Presently they were considered more Brulé than Oglala, so it was among the Brulé that Short Bull would preach the new faith and lead the dancing.

Kicking Bear was a tall, tough-looking, heavy-boned and heavy-featured man who looked every inch the forty-one-year-old warrior that he was. He was not, however, lacking in intellect or imagination. Thomas Riggs, a well-respected missionary to the Indians, said of him, "I knew Kicking Bear of Cherry Creek on the Cheyenne River tolerably well. He would have been abundantly able to manufacture and publish the message [of the Ghost Dance] out of his imagination without assistance." In bygone days Kicking Bear had been a good friend of Crazy Horse and had fought beside him in the battles of the Rosebud and the Little Big Horn. And like that famous war leader, Kicking Bear had no affection at all for the white man or for any of the white man's works. As the Reverend Riggs also observed, "Every word of [the Ghost Dance message] was in accord with his past and his hopes of the future." Kicking Bear had been raised an Oglala, but since it was the old custom for a husband to join his wife's people, he became a Minneconjou when he married Big Foot's niece, Woodpecker Woman. Unlike Short Bull, who seems to have confined his preaching mainly to his own tribe of Brulé, Kicking Bear carried the message of the Ghost Dance not only to the Minneconjou, but to any of the Lakotah who were willing to listen to him.

During the spring and early summer of 1889, busy as the pocket gophers that run about carrying earth in their cheeks, Short Bull and Kicking Bear carried the words of the new faith to their people. Strangely, they seem to have met with only small success at first. Perhaps this was because for the moment the suffering of the Lakotah had eased. It was true that their rations were still short, but the sicknesses had ended, and it was the season when they could move out of their dank, dirt-floored cabins and pitch their tipis on the spring-fresh land. Moreover, the land was unusually fresh that spring. Regular rains had come to break the long drought, so that now the wind smelled clean and the hills were soft-carpeted with new grass and the valleys were bright with wildflowers, and the farmers' crops were coming up thick and strong. Truly the land was smiling, and so close to their land were the Lakotahs, that when it smiled they smiled also, and were hard to agitate. Even so, the apostles were creating some excitement—although it was kept as secret from the whites as a hidden fire, with only an occasional

faint and uncertain whiff of smoke to hint at its existence. One such whiff
was detected by Charles Hyde of Pierre, South Dakota, on May 29 when
he received a letter from a young Indian friend which prompted him, in
turn, to write this letter to the Secretary of the Interior:

Secretary Noble
Washington D. C.

Dear Sir:

The information has come to me confidentially, through a source I have
confidence in, that the Sioux Indians or a portion of them are secretly
planning and arranging for an outbreak in the near future, probably, tho',
several weeks or months off. . . .

> Yours Resp.
> *Chas. L. Hyde*

Secretary Noble immediately passed Hyde's letter to Acting Commissioner of Indian Affairs Robert Belt, who promptly wrote to the agents of
the various reservations asking if they had detected any trouble brewing.
Their answers were received in mid-June:

McChesney—Cheyenne River
    So far as the Indians at Cheyenne River Agency are concerned, I speak
with some confidence and I do not hesitate to say that no fears need be
entertained of any outbreak on their part.

Gallagher—Pine Ridge
    There is no ground for apprehension. I have the assurance of the
[Indian] police from all parts of the Pine Ridge reserve that the Indians are
peaceably disposed.

Wright—Rosebud
    The idea of an outbreak is scoffed at by the large majority of well
disposed Indians at this agency.

McLaughlin—Standing Rock
    Insofar as the Indians of this agency are concerned, there is nothing
either in their words or actions that would justify such a rumor.

These were the last such reports the agents would send. In July both
the land and the Indians smiled no longer. The rains had stopped and
the hot winds came—carrying gritty dust from powder-dry fields; the sun
was a blazing iron ball that burned the corn shoots back into the earth
that bore them; and in July, the Indian appropriation funds had run so

low that rations had to be reduced again, so that there was hunger in every household. In fact, many of the Brulé were journeying from the Rosebud clear down to Valentine and Fort Niobrara in Nebraska just to beg for food or even garbage to feed themselves and their children. Now, with the hunger and the drought, the spirits of the Lakotah were again on the ground, and their empty stomachs opened their ears to the words of the Ghost Dance apostles. This time, as they heard the message of a new green world containing many buffalo and no white men, the words warmed their hearts as a buffalo robe warms one who is freezing . . . and the dancing started.

No white man seems to have ever known for sure just when the first Sioux Ghost Dance was held, or where, but by late July increasing numbers of Indians on Pine Ridge and Rosebud reservations were abandoning their homes and farms to gather in camps of canvas tipis along the creeks to dance for the coming of the Wanikiye and the end of the white man.

The Ghost Dance, as taught by its apostles in these camps, was not a simple thing. If it were to remain *wakan* (a thing of holy power), it had to be done in the proper way, and that required much preparation and much attention to form. First, the dance tree—usually a slim, fresh-cut cottonwood log—was set up in the center of the dance ground, and since it was a holy tree, the setting up had to be done in a ceremonial way. The tree was then decorated with colored streamers, eagle feathers, and other such things; sometimes, even, an American flag was flown from its top. All of this except the flag was done very much the same as for the Sun Dance—which was the holiest dance of all, but which the whites had now forbidden. In that dance the tree was the Holy Center and the people who circled around it were the nation's Sacred Hoop; in the Ghost Dance it seems to have been about the same.

For twenty-four hours before starting a dance, the leaders fasted. Then, early on the morning of the dance day, all the men went to the small sweat lodges to purify themselves. They did this by sitting in the steam from water poured over hot stones by the medicine men until all their inside evil was sweated out onto their skin where it could be bathed away in the creek. After bathing and drying themselves with sweet-grass, they lined up before the lodges of the holy men for painting. As each one's turn came, he laid his hands on the holy man's head and said, "My father, I have come to be painted so that I may see my friends [the dead ones]. Have pity on me and paint me." Since the dancers remained fully clothed in the Ghost Dance, only their faces were painted. This was done in a variety of colors, but red was used more than any other because it was the color that belonged to Anpetu Wi (the sun) and was, therefore, the holiest color of all.

In their hair the dancers twined eagle feathers—even the women did, who had never worn feathers in dances before. It was necessary for everyone to wear these feathers in the Ghost Dance, for it was by the feathers that the faithful were going to be lifted to safety when the new soil came rolling over the earth to bury the unbelievers and the white people.

On the sacred shirts and dresses which were always worn in the dance, and which were believed to be bulletproof, there were both drawings and feathers of Wanbli Gleska (the spotted eagle), for he was the holiest of all birds and was the guardian of the nation's Sacred Hoop. Flying so high that he could see all things (and could even fly up to heaven), Wanbli Gleska was the special messenger of the Great Holy, and his feathers were the rays of the sun. Furthermore, it was Wanbli Gleska, with his powerful wings, who carried the spirits of those dancers who had "died" for a little while up to heaven to visit the ghosts. Often the picture of Kangi (the crow) was also drawn on the shirts; he, too, was a special messenger, and was the one who told the hunters where the buffalo were grazing.

When all these preparations were completed, usually around noon, the people who were to do the dance seated themselves in a great circle around the dance tree. Unlike the other Sioux dances, this was a dance for all of the people, so the circle included little children and often even old people with canes. Also unlike most of the other dances was the fact that no drums or other musical instruments were allowed, nor was a fire ever built within the circle.

When the leader signaled that the ceremony was to begin, the visiting of the crowd fell hushed, and a young woman in a white buckskin dress walked to the holy tree and shot four arrows, one to each of the four directions. Remaining at the tree, she then extended a ceremonial pipe toward the west—the direction from which the Messiah was expected to come. She continued to hold the pipe thus until the dance was ended.

After the arrows were fired, the people (still seated) chanted a praying song and then, in a form of communion, each ate a bite of holy food from a bowl passed around the circle. Then the leader extended his arms to heaven and made an opening prayer such as this:

O Great Holy: We are ready to begin the dance as you have commanded us. Our hearts are now good. We would do all that you ask, and in return we beg that you give us back our old hunting grounds and our game.

O Great Holy: Carry such of our dancers as truly believe to the Land of the Wanagi [departed spirits] and let them see their dead relatives. Show them the good things you have prepared for us, and then return them safely to earth again.

O Great Holy, hear us, we pray.

Following the prayer, the people arose and stood motionless with their arms extended toward the west as they sang the opening song. The words of the Ghost Dance songs were not always the same, but their pattern was. In the opening song the worshippers first offered themselves, then they asked for the good things to come. One such opening song went:

> *Father, I come*
> *Mother, I come*
> *Brother, I come*
> *Father, give us back our arrows.*

Next the actual dancing began. Joining hands by interlacing their fingers, the worshippers began a slow side-step shuffle to the left while singing of the promise of a new world:

> *You shall see your Grandfather—E'yayo*
> *You shall see your Grandfather—E'yayo*
> *The Father says so*
> *The Father says so*

Then came songs about God's reply:

> *My son, let me grasp your hand*
> *My son, let me grasp your hand*
> *Says the Father*
> *Says the Father*
> *You shall live*
> *You shall live*
> *Says the Father*

By this time the first of the many dancers who would fall unconscious and have visions were already on the ground. The other dancers stepped over them as they continued circling and singing of the happy new life coming:

> *Why, they say there is to be a buffalo hunt over here*
> *Why, they say there is to be a buffalo hunt over here*
> *Make arrows! Make arrows!*
> *Says the Father, says the Father.*

Finally, the voices swelled up in a joyful chorus as they sang of the prophecy as it would be fulfilled:

> *The whole world is coming*
> *A nation is coming, a nation is coming*
> *The Eagle has brought the message to the tribe*
> *The Father says so, the Father says so.*
>
> *Over the whole earth they are coming*
> *The buffalo are coming, the buffalo are coming*
> *The Crow has brought the message to the tribe*
> *The Father says so, the Father says so.*

The dance continued for hours, with many other songs and with occasional pauses for resting and smoking and sometimes even meals. It was during these pauses that the dancers who had already "died" and visited the ghosts told of their "trips" to heaven. The Oglala chief, Little Wound, described his trip this way:

> When I fell in the trance a great and grand eagle came and carried me over a great hill, where there was a village such as we used to have before the whites came into this country. The tipis were all of buffalo skin, and we used the bow and arrow, and there was nothing in that beautiful land that the white men had made. Neither would Wakan Tanka let any whites live there. The land was wide and green and stretched in every direction and made my eyes glad.
>
> I was taken into the presence of the great Messiah, and He said these words to me, "My child, I am glad to see you. Do you want to see your children and relations who are dead?"
>
> I said, "Yes, I would like to see my relations who have been dead a long time." Then the Messiah called my friends to come up to where I was. They appeared, riding the finest horses I ever saw, they wore clothes of bright colors that were very fine, and they seemed very happy. As they came near I recognized the playmates of my childhood and I ran forward to embrace them while the tears of joy ran down my cheeks.
>
> Then we all went together to another village, where there were very large

lodges of buffalo skin, and there held a long talk with Wakan Tanka. Then He had some women prepare us a meal of many herbs, meats, wild fruits and *wasna* [pounded dried beef and chokecherries]. After we had eaten, the Great Holy made a prayer for our people upon the earth, and then we smoked together using a fine pipe ornamented with beautiful feathers and porcupine quills. Then we left the village and looked into a great valley where there were thousands of buffalo and deer and elk all feeding.

After seeing the valley we returned to the village while the Great Holy kept on talking to us. He told me the earth was now *bad* and *worn out* and that we needed a new place to live where the rascally whites could not bother us. He also told me to go back to my people, the Lakotah, and say to them that if they would keep on making the dance and pay no attention to the whites that He would shortly come to help them. If the holy men would make for the dancers medicine shirts and pray over them, no harm could come to the wearer; that the bullets of any whites that wanted to stop the Messiah Dance would fall to the ground without hurting anybody, and the person who fired the shots would drop dead. The Great Holy said He had made a hole in the ground and filled it with hot water to put all the white men and the nonbelievers in. As soon as He had finished saying these things He told me to come back to earth.

When those Sioux who had not yet joined the Ghost Dance faith heard words such as these, the new Messiah religion spread across the Pine Ridge and Rosebud reservations like fire sweeping through dry grass. After all, who would not want to visit heaven and see their dead relatives who were alive and happy there, and to talk with the Great Holy and eat his food?

Not only did those who had danced and had visions tell the good news to their neighbors, but many of them also sent word to their friends and relatives far away. One of the dancers at Pine Ridge wrote to his brother in Oklahoma (free rendering from Carlisle English):

Dear Brother,

Yes, it is so about Jesus, and all the Indians are talking about it. He has come with long hair to save the Indians. It is the first time he has come to save just the Indians. It was too far to go to him where he was before, up in the sky. Now it is not half so far to where he is. So, you may come to him, and all the Indians may.

Jesus gave me some berries. Some black and some red. I ate two.

How are you all getting along up in Darlington. Please send me some money and tell Red Neck's wife to send money too.

I am your brother,
Crooked Nose

Once the dancing was well established, dozens of stories were told of marvelous visions and of trips to heaven to visit with dead relatives who were living there and were young and happy. Considering all these stories and the Indians' despair and need for hope, as well as the evangelistic fervor of the believers, it seems strange that the Ghost Dance was not adopted by all the Sioux. A great many of them, however, never accepted it at all. Its greatest appeal was to those so-called nonprogressive bands who clung doggedly to the memories of the life that was gone. And since of all the Lakotah tribes in 1890, the largest number of the nonprogressives were found among the Oglala and Brulé, that was probably why the greatest part, by far, of the Ghost Dancing took place on the Pine Ridge and Rosebud reservations. Still, it has been estimated that even on those reservations, well over twenty-five percent of the Indians never had anything to do with the Ghost Dance. Nonetheless, the nonbelievers were so completely eclipsed by the fanatic zeal of those who did believe, that by mid-August the casual observer might well have concluded that there were no nonbelievers.

Now that the fires of religious fervor among the Oglala and Brulé were well stoked, in August (or possibly a little earlier) Kicking Bear set out to carry his new theology home to his own people on Cheyenne River reservation. However, either because the Minneconjou were "tamer" than their southern relatives, or because a prophet truly *is* "not without honor save in his own country," or because of some other reason, the majority of the Cheyenne River Indians ignored his message. There were two notable exceptions—the people of Hump and Big Foot, the most nonprogressive of all the Minneconjou bands, adopted it immediately and passionately.

Hump was the warrior chief who had led the charge against Fetterman at Fort Phil Kearney and, also, who had refused to sign the Treaty of 1868, and who in just the past summer had sent war-club-swinging warriors to break up a line of people waiting to sign the Land Agreement. Since then (with the inconsistency that made perfect sense to the Sioux but totally baffled the whites), Hump had taken a government job as District Farmer for the Cherry Creek District. Once exposed to the Ghost Dance, however, he again became the old Hump and resigned his job to devote himself to the full-time leadership of Messiah ceremonies at his settlement at the mouth of Cherry Creek on the Cheyenne River.

The cabins of Big Foot's people were scattered about the mouth of Deep Creek, also on the Cheyenne River, near the extreme western edge of the reservation. In his camp there was inconsistency also. Big Foot—as his father, Lone Horn, had also been—was a diplomat, a peacemaker, and a friend of the whites. Nevertheless, even before the Ghost Dance excitement began, his band had become so unruly that since the past April the army had felt it advisable to maintain a camp of two hundred soldiers at the mouth of the Belle Fourche River, a few miles to Big Foot's west, in order to make sure his people didn't molest the settlers west of the reservation.

If the army's reason for establishing its watchdog outpost (called Camp Cheyenne) was sound, and there actually *was* an ominous attitude among Big Foot's people, it was due at least partly to the work of the medicine man, Yellow Bird. Yellow Bird was not only one of the most anti-white and one of the most dedicated-to-the-old-ways of all the Lakotah, but he was also a skilled agitator. So when the Messiah faith came along, Yellow Bird was provided with a religion that exactly suited both his feelings and his talents. Consequently, he kept Big Foot's people so worked up over it that they danced, as an observer from Camp Cheyenne put it, "both day and night, so long as they are able to move and to keep awake."

As the hot summer wore on, more and more Indians left their homes and farms to go live in the dance camps. Meanwhile, the agents at Pine Ridge and Rosebud and then at Cheyenne River pondered the problem and finally concluded they had no choice but to try to put an end to the dancing. There were some who criticized them for their decision at the time, and there have been many who have roundly condemned them for it since. The critics at that time, for instance, argued that the agents actually had no problem. They maintained that if the agents would permit the dancing to continue without interference, the Indians would eventually realize the new world was not coming after all and the craze would die of its own failure. The more recent critics have continued to support that argument, but the basis of their most bitter denunciation of the agents has been the argument that the Ghost Dance was purely a religious rite and that the agents had no business interfering with religion.

Unlike their critics, however, the agents and their superiors did not have the advantage of historical hindsight. Furthermore, since they were the ones who actually had to cope with the situation, they were in no position to engage in detached ethical philosophizing. They were directly responsible for the welfare of the Sioux Indians on their reservations, and the Ghost Dance was giving them two very real problems. The main one was the Indians' food supply. Their rations had already been reduced to the point that even with such of the Indians' farm and garden crops as had survived the drought, plus the fairly substantial number of meat animals the Indians were raising, they faced a winter of semi-starvation. But if the Indians continued to remain in the dance camps, and their crops and livestock continued to be unharvested and untended, the winter's hunger could become catastrophic.

Their second problem was that law and order on Pine Ridge and Rosebud reservations and to some extent at Cheyenne River was beginning to be undermined by the few (so far) Indians who were inclined to take advantage of the supposed invulnerability in their ghost shirts and do what they pleased, when they pleased, and to whomever they pleased without fear of consequences. Until now there were only a few Indians with that attitude, but even a few were trouble enough on the reservation; and if they should wander off it, they could easily get both themselves and other people killed.

In addition to these very real problems, the agents also had other concerns which were real to *them,* but which no one can say even today were justified or not. The agents understood that the Ghost Dance religion had sprung up as just that—a religion. Their concern, however, was that it would become twisted into something more. They recognized in the dance a sort of mass hysteria that could easily produce highly emotional mobs which a skilled leader could influence to his own purpose, even if that purpose were war. Furthermore, since the true believers were firmly convinced that the new world was to be created in the following spring (at which time all the dead Indians would be resurrected to live in it), the agents worried that a true believer would not fear dying in war. In fact, he might see it as a desirable thing if it would allow him to sleep peacefully through what would be a hungry winter and then awaken in the new Indian paradise. Finally, there was the matter of the ghost shirts. The agents wondered why the Indians were being told they were bulletproof unless someone were planning for the Indians to face bullets.

So it was that the concrete problems of the food shortage and the maintenance of reservation order, together with the possibility of the Ghost Dance's becoming the foundation for a bloody uprising, caused the agents to decide to stop it. Although it seems clear now that a better decision would have been to allow the dancing to continue and let the craze die of itself, the agents were by no means unjustified or unreasonable at the time in deciding to put an end to it.

The first time an agent tried to break up a Ghost Dance was in August when H. D. Gallagher of Pine Ridge attempted to disperse a crowd of believers who had gathered at Torn Belly's camp about twenty miles northwest of Pine Ridge agency. The Torn Belly settlement lay along White Clay Creek near where it joins White River in the southwestern corner of the Makoce Sica (the Bad Lands). This was and still is a lonely and starkly beautiful place where the grassy bottoms of the tree-lined creek curve among wildly eroded and delicately colored buttes and mesas. It is a place where man seems far away, but God seems close—which may very well be the reason why more than six-hundred Indians had come to pitch their lodges on the heat-browned flats around the cabins of Torn Belly's people to dance to the coming of the new world. Hearing of the gathering at Torn Belly's, Gallagher became concerned that such a large number of Indians was assembled there, and on Friday, August 22, he sent a squad of Indian police to break it up and send the people home. The police returned the following day and reported that not only had they been unable to disperse the camp, but that the defiant Indians there had sent word to the agent that they were going to dance again on Sunday. Hearing that, Gallagher decided to handle the matter himself.

Accompanied by visiting Special Indian Agent E. B. Reynolds, by the mixed-blood interpreter Philip Wells, and a troop of twenty mounted Indian police, Gallagher set off early the next morning up White Clay Creek road for Torn Belly's camp. After some four hours of riding, Gallagher's little brigade arrived at the Indian settlement to find it eerily quiet. There were some hundred and fifty lodges pitched among the cabins, and there was a tall dance tree standing in the center of a well-worn and dusty dance ground, but aside from the soft, dry rattling of the cottonwood leaves in the hot summer breeze, there was no sound; and except for the rippling of the American flag flying from the top of the dance tree, there was no movement—because despite the fact that smoke was still drifting from the cooking fires, there were no people.

As Gallagher's company rode closer, two warriors suddenly sprang from the cottonwood grove by the creek, knelt, and leveled their Winchesters at the agent. Gallagher promptly halted his troop. Then— ever the imposing Civil War colonel that he had been—Gallagher rode directly toward the two riflemen, speaking in a stern voice and asking,

"What do you mean, when I come here as your agent, to draw your guns on me?"

Philip Wells was one of the best and most diplomatic and level-headed of all the Pine Ridge interpreters. When he heard this dangerous kind of talking, he spurred his horse forward and pushed in front of the advancing agent. By this time several more rifle-carrying Indians had come out of the trees. Wells knew one of them particularly well and spoke to him in a friendly tone of voice and in a manner that made it sound as if he were translating Gallagher's words and that the agent had really made a very polite invitation to the Indian to put down his gun for a talk. At this the Indian did put his gun on the ground. Then, looking all the while at the armed policemen, he asked, "If you have come to talk to me as my Father [agent] why have you brought so many guns?"

Before the agent could answer, more armed Ghost Dancers appeared. One of them shouted in an angry challenge to the lieutenant of Indian police, "Where is Thunder Bear? Why does he not stand in sight?"

"Here I am!" called back the lieutenant. "If you cannot see me I will come closer to you!" And with that he began riding forward. As he did so the other police unholstered their revolvers. From the trees where the Indians were concealed, they could hear the metallic *chick-chack* of cartridges being chambered in repeating Winchesters, and it became abundantly clear, as Agent Reynolds later observed, that "the Indians were ready to seal their religious convictions at the mouths of smoking rifles."

Then, into that tense moment of "things-about-to-happen," Young Man Afraid—tall, straight, and projecting an inner power like his father—rode between the two opposing groups, stopped, and held up his hand. Such was the strength of his action that the tension was broken to the point that in a few minutes Gallagher, Torn Belly, and the other leaders were engaged in friendly conversation. Regardless of the friendliness, however, it was plain to the agent that he and his twenty police were in no way going to be able to stop the dance. That being the case, Gallagher (to his credit) accepted Torn Belly's invitation to remain as a guest and watch the dancing. Reynolds stayed, also, and when it was over, both men came away considerably shaken by the frantic intensity of what they had seen. Reynolds, in fact, was moved to report to Washington that ". . . steps should be taken to stop it. . . . This can be done only by the military unless the cold weather accomplishes it."

In Reynolds's message he mentioned what soon emerged in the minds of all the Indian Affairs officials as the only two possible solutions to the Ghost Dancing problem—"the military" and "the cold weather." But while military assistance could be obtained upon request, cold weather could not, and it was the latter that the people in Indian Affairs much preferred. Their reason was that the government agencies of 1890 were no less jealous of their own fiefdoms than they are today, and things had not yet reached a point where either the Commissioner of Indian Affairs or his superior, the Secretary of the Interior, could accept or even tolerate the thought of War Department intervention in their particular provinces. Thus, the official policy became that of encouraging the agents to hold the line and maintain control to the best of their ability until winter set in, and to hope that when it did, it would be so severe that the Ghost Dances would be impossible.

While they waited for winter, the disorder continued to grow— although not everyone seemed aware of it. Early in September the Reverend Thomas Smith Cook, rector of the Holy Cross Episcopal Mission at Pine Ridge and himself a full-blooded Sioux, wrote to Bishop Hare:

> . . . because of the large and ever increasing number of souls already caught within the meshes of the gospel net . . . no previous year has been so full of the visible results of the husbandman's work. For all these tokens of His favor and goodness, and for the unmistakable signs of constant growth in grace and righteousness of living on the part of the Christianized Indians, it is but honest and proper to sing, *"Deo gratias! Laus Deo!"*

At the same time that the Sioux Reverend Cook was singing *Deo Gratias*, the Sioux on White Clay and Wounded Knee and Porcupine and a dozen other creeks were singing *"Father, give us back our arrows"*! Nevertheless, as time went by that fall, many of the missionaries did come to believe and often to acknowledge openly that they and the Ghost Dancers were, indeed, praying to the same Great Holy and recognizing the same Christ—although they differed with each other considerably on the details.

In September, Agent J. George Wright of Rosebud reservation announced to his Indians that there would be no more rations issued until they had all stopped dancing and had returned to their homes. This strategy worked for a short time, and the dancing did stop and the people did return home. But a little later in the month Wright was called to Washington to defend himself against charges of misappropriation of Indian funds (of which he was found innocent), and during his absence Special Agent E. B. Reynolds took temporary charge of the agency. Reynolds did not know the people of the Rosebud, and they did not know him. He immediately lost control. When he did, the Ghost Dancing Brulés—which were most of them—went wild. They began dancing constantly and everywhere. They started killing breeding stock for feasts, and they were selling their personal property (and agency property, also, when they could get hold of it) for money to buy guns and ammunition.

Rosebud was not the only reservation on which the turmoil was compounded by the replacement of an agent. South Dakota had been admitted to the Union only a few months before, and now its new congressmen were taking advantage of their right to repay political debts by making such patronage appointments as were allowed to them under the spoils system. This included the right to appoint the Indian agents in their districts. Thus, on September first, the able McChesney of Cheyenne River was replaced by Perain P. Palmer, and Gallagher at Pine Ridge was put on notice that he would be replaced shortly.

When trouble had exploded on the Rosebud after Reynolds had taken over, Kicking Bear had been there to help it along. Then when it appeared to him that Rosebud was in a satisfactory state of anarchy, he returned home to see what additional opportunities for disorder might exist at Cheyenne River reservation under its new agent, Palmer. On his arrival he found that the majority of the Minneconjou were no more inclined to take up the Messiah faith than before, and that the disturbance on Cheyenne River reservation still remained pretty much confined to the valley of Cheyenne River, itself. However, Kicking Bear was now well established as the high priest of the Ghost Dance among the Lakotah, and when he returned to his home on Cherry Creek, it became the Vatican and the Mecca of the new faith. He received a steady stream of disciples from Pine Ridge and Rosebud, as well as from the dance camps on the Cheyenne River, but as yet he had few visitors from Standing Rock. Even now the Ghost Dance had still not reached the Hunkpapa.

In September it was the religious frenzy of Big Foot's people (on the western edge of the Cheyenne River reservation) that caused the Ghost Dance craze to alarm the white settlers for the first time. Actually, considering the increasing disorder on both the Pine Ridge and Rosebud reservations and also along the southern edge of Cheyenne River reservation, it seems strange that there had been no earlier fright among the nearby whites. But there must not have been, for the local press made absolutely no mention of such a thing during the summer and fall of 1890, and Indian disturbances were not something the area newspapers were likely to ignore. However, in late September the tumult in Big Foot's camp caught the attention of settlers immediately to the west of the reservation sufficiently to prompt the following petition to the Commissioner of Indian Affairs:

> Sept., 26, 1890
> Mead County
> State of South Dakota SD

We the under-signed settlers of eastern Mead County South Dakota, and United States of America,

Do hereby ask in humble prayer for military protection during the trouble on the opening Reservation against the Sioux Indians.

Indians residing in viliges along the Cheyenne River, from the forks down to Cherry Creek.

> Chiefes Spoted Elk, or Big Foot
> Brave Eagle and Red Skirt, and
> their bands.

We ask in most humble prayer, and further demand that we have protection of our lives and our childrens and our homes and our property.

> [signed] [blanks are illegible signatures]

Elbert Jones   ———
Peter Quinn   ———
J. W. Wicks
J. B. Slicks   *A. J. Culbertson*
———   *J. W. Duvall*
John Reynolds   *P. T. Lemly*
                          Peter Dunn
                          John Dunn

I, Thomas Crowell, living at the forks of the Shian river, being personal by none [unrelated] to the above named sitsens, I do sertify that they are frmers [and] not ranchers in this versinety, [and that] they are squaters [and] not freeholders [of] Land not open for setelment. [punctuation added]

But however strange it may seem that the reservation disturbances had not caused white settlers to request protection before now, it is far stranger that the first to do so were these particular ones. As indicated in their petition, they lived around "the forks of the Cheyenne River," which was actually the junction of the Belle Fourche with the Cheyenne. It was at that junction that the army had established Camp Cheyenne, which was occupied by three troops of cavalry and two of infantry for an overall total of about two hundred men. Thus, these settlers were petitioning for protection which they already had, and which they had had for the past six months! Moreover, during the past months of Camp Cheyenne's existence these particular farmers had been doing a brisk business there selling butter, eggs, meat, milk, and hay. They just *might* have decided that the addition of more soldiers would expand their market, but no one knows for sure.

With the coming of October and with tension along the Cheyenne River still building, Agent Palmer sent the following message to the Commissioner:

> . . . a number of Indians living along the Cheyenne River and known as Big Foot's band are becoming very much excited about the coming of a Messiah. . . . These Indians are becoming very hostile to the [Indian] police. Some of the police have resigned. Information has been received here [that] . . . nearly all of these Indians are in possession of Winchester rifles and the police say they are afraid of them. . . . The Christian Indians are all quiet and well behaved.

> *Perain P. Palmer*
> U. S. Indian Agent

Also in early October, and more important, six young Standing Rock Indians called on Kicking Bear at his Cherry Creek headquarters. They carried a message from Sitting Bull. Sitting Bull, they said, wanted Kicking Bear to bring the Ghost Dance to the Hunkpapa.

CHAPTER
9
∧∴∧∧∴∧∧

Panic in the North

DESPITE THE MOUNTING fever of the Ghost Dance on the more southern reservations, throughout the summer of 1890, Standing Rock had remained quiet. The people there knew about the Messiah, of course. The nomadic Lakotah were great visitors and were always traveling back and forth to see their friends and relatives, and they had carried the stories of the new dance to them. But the Hunkpapa and the Yanktonais had sent no delegates to see Wovoka, nor had they been visited by any of his dedicated Lakotah disciples so they were not very excited about the Ghost Dance faith.

Nonetheless, there was a conflict at Standing Rock. It was not one of excitement and turmoil, however, but was a quiet war between two strong-minded men. Both were dedicated to the improvement of the lives of the Indians, but they differed completely on the definition of "improvement." To James "Whitehair" McLaughlin, agent at Standing Rock, improvement meant propelling the Indians into the future as rapidly as possible. To Chief Sitting Bull, it meant returning them to the past—also as rapidly as possible. As constant adversaries, neither McLaughlin nor Sitting Bull had ever had anything good to say about each other, yet reading between the lines seems to reveal that deep down they shared the sort of grudging and unadmitted friendship that sometimes exists between strong enemies.

James McLaughlin was forty-eight years old in 1890, and was a handsome, trimly built man with firm features, prematurely white curly hair, and a white handlebar moustache. Born a Canadian, he had entered the American Indian Service in 1871, married a gracious half-blood Santee named Marie, and become one of the first (and the few) Indian agents to become fluent in the tongue of the Sioux. He was also a stubborn, autocratic, hot-tempered, competent, unbluffable, totally honest man who was devoting his life to what he considered to be the best interests of the Sioux. He was determined to prepare them for survival in the new world that had overtaken them, whether they liked it or not. He had progressed to the extent that there was now more farming, or at least more *successful* farming, on Standing Rock than on the reservations to the south. There were also more Indians working at paying jobs, so there seemed to be somewhat less hunger and suffering among his Indians than among the others. Because of his effectiveness, when politicians passed the patronage jobs around to their friends, they never quite dared to replace agent McLaughlin.

Tatanka Iyotaka, Sitting Bull, lived in the settlement of his band of Hunkpapa on the north bank of Grand River about forty miles southwest of Standing Rock agency. He had a little farm there on which were three cabins—one for general living, one for his wives, Seen-by-Her-Nation and Four-Times, and one for his grown daughter, Standing Holy. In addition to the cabins were a stable with a corral and a small henhouse. The farm was near where Sitting Bull had been born, although no one was quite sure when that had been. His mother, Her Holy Door, said it was in the Winter the War Bonnet Was Torn, which the Wasicun—who number such things—called 1838. Others said it was in the Winter When Yellow Eyes Played in the Snow (1831). Whichever, in 1890, he was somewhere between fifty-one and fifty-nine years old, and everyone called him an old man. However, they called him this mostly as a mark of respect to one who was an "old man chief" rather than because he looked or acted old, which he did not. He was, to all appearances, a man in his prime.

Although Sitting Bull and the whites rarely agreed on anything, there was one point on which they were in perfect accord. For many years now both he and the whites had believed Sitting Bull to be the most important and powerful Sioux alive. And in bygone days he had, for a fact, been a power among his people, though not nearly so great a one as either he or the whites believed. During the white-man years since 1876, however, his once wide power had been shrinking and drawing in on itself like a rain pool drying in the summer sun, until in 1890, his importance among the

Indians was confined mainly to the three hundred or so Hunkpapas of his band on Grand River.

If Sitting Bull realized (as he probably did) that his influence had shrunk, he never let on; he clung instead to the memory of the day when he had been made supreme chief of all the seven tribes of the Lakotah. That had happened at a council back in the Year of the Sleety Season (1867). Some of the leaders that year had felt that in order to fight the white people effectively, the Lakotah needed to have one head chief, and through the manipulations of his powerful uncle, Four Horns, they had chosen Tatanka Iyotaka. He found it good to recall how Four Horns, Loud Voice Hawk, Red Horn, and Running Antelope had carried him on a spread buffalo robe to the council lodge, and to remember the feeling of power rising inside himself like a silent singing when they had announced that he was now a great chief above all other chiefs. The fact of the matter was that the council had been very much only a Hunkpapa affair—with some support from the minor northern tribes. The Oglala, Brulé, and Minneconjou had never recognized his appointment, and because of the independence of the chiefs, some of Sitting Bull's own tribe had not either. But regardless of how much or little the appointment had meant at the time, its only importance now was in Sitting Bull's memory, and possibly in the memory of some of his old cronies of the Midnight Stronghearts warrior society. Running Antelope, who had helped to carry Sitting Bull on the robe that day and whose camp now was just a few miles on down the river, had become a good Congregationalist and had gone over to walking the road of the whites. Gall, a traditional chief and famous warrior of much influence, who had lost two wives and three children to the attack of Custer's men at the Little Big Horn and who had then led the countercharge that wiped Custer out, had become an Episcopalian, going over to the white ways, also. Sitting Bull found this most disgusting. Even Gray Eagle, the brother of Sitting Bull's wives, who used to stand tall with pride in the importance of his famous brother-in-law, had gone over to the whites and had even gone so far as to try to get Sitting Bull to farm.

Yet, in spite of all these things and of how the old Indian life seemed to be crumbling around him, Tatanka Iyotaka stood fast against the white-man ways. A few years back, when he had seen some of the people giving in to the whites, he had snorted scornfully, "Indians! There are no Indians left but me!" He still felt the same. The one concession he had ever made to the white ways was the time it had appeared that his family might go hungry and he had tried a little gardening. He had hated every minute of it. Fortunately, at about that time, the rich white woman the Indians called Woman-Walking-Ahead (and the whites called Catherine Weldon) had come along. She had given him many presents of money so that he not only didn't have to farm any more, but he could even afford to have feasts and hold councils to decide how to keep Whitehair McLaughlin from making white people out of the Indians.

Among the whites, Sitting Bull's reputation was mostly a matter of publicity. It had begun back in 1876, when the white newspapers had jumped to the conclusion that it was he who had been the supreme leader of the Indians that had destroyed Long Hair Custer at the Little Big Horn. Actually, according to most of the evidence, Sitting Bull had never taken part in that fight at all, but had remained in his lodge making medicine while Gall, Crazy Horse, and the others had done the fighting. Since the newspapers had told it otherwise, however, the whites had believed it. Then in 1885, Sitting Bull had spent a few months traveling the East with Buffalo Bill's Wild West Show, where he was paid fifty dollars a week for being introduced as the killer of Custer and for being roundly booed and hissed by the crowd. By the end of that tour Sitting Bull was firmly established in the public mind as towering in a sort of dangerous greatness above all other Sioux—an impression that still held in 1890. Thus, because the whites *thought* Sitting Bull had a great deal of influence among the Indians, and also because he had a strong personality, he *did* have influence among the whites.

Like McLaughlin, Sitting Bull was hot-tempered and bull-headed, although he was also known to be thoughtful, kind, and (except when provoked) extremely gracious. He was a big, stockily built, and ruggedly handsome man who exuded a charisma which often charmed men and which women found irresistible.

McLaughlin, however, was never charmed by Tatanka Iyotaka. On the contrary, he found him a source of constant irritation. Like the old days, when Sitting Bull had refused to even talk about any treaty—let alone sign one—just this past summer he had done his level best to thwart the Land Agreement that McLaughlin had been pushing. Now the old fool was sitting down there in his Grand River cabin dreaming of the buffalo days, and of fighting the Crows, and talking against the farming program, and the Indian police, and the other Indians who held white-man jobs, and cooking up Lord only knows what kind of trouble.

Not only that, but he was developing a small corps of followers who were also opposing every progressive idea McLaughlin advanced. Thus, more and more the agent thought that, for the welfare of the reservation as a whole, Sitting Bull should be removed from it. On June 18 he made such a suggestion to the commissioner. His suggestion was not strongly put, however, and when the commissioner did not accept it, McLaughlin said no more about it for the rest of the summer. That did not mean he had given up on the idea of removing the irritating old goat; it simply meant that as long as things remained peaceful, he could find no convincing excuse to do so.

McLaughlin also had another irritant to put up with that summer—a large, good-looking, overdressed and overjeweled, graying widow in her mid-forties named Catherine Weldon. The Indians called her Woman-Walking-Ahead. She was a woman of substantial means who back in Brooklyn, New York, had been a teacher of modern languages and also a painter of sorts. In the late 1880s, she had become involved with a group called the National Indian Defense Association and, as their representative, had come west in 1889 to encourage the Indians to fight the Land Agreement. Almost immediately upon her arrival she had crossed swords with McLaughlin. She wanted to take Sitting Bull with her from Standing Rock to Cheyenne River reservation to speak against the Land Agreement. McLaughlin, who was promoting the agreement, refused to give the chief permission to leave Standing Rock. He also told Mrs. Weldon, plainly and clearly, what he thought of meddlers from the East. Unfortunately, there happened to be a news reporter hanging around the agency office while this discussion was going on. As a result, a wildly sensational story appeared in the *Bismarck Tribune* of July 2, 1889.

SHE LOVES SITTING BULL
A New Jersey Widow falls victim to
Sitting Bull's Charms.

A sensation is reported from the Standing Rock Agency, the chief participants being Mrs. C. Wilder, of Newark, New Jersey, and Sitting Bull, the notorious old chief. Sitting Bull has many admirers and among them is numbered Mrs. Wilder. . . .

No sooner had the agent refused [permission for Sitting Bull to leave the reservation] than Mrs. Wilder flew into a rage . . . those who came from Standing Rock state that she used the most scathing and abusive language. . . . Mrs. Wilder is a widow and is visiting the reservation. She is a great admirer of Sitting Bull, and it is gossip among the people in the vicinity of the Agency that she is actually in love with the cunning old warrior . . .

Provoked by both her encounter with McLaughlin and the news story (which she also blamed on McLaughlin), Mrs. Weldon wrote a letter to Red Cloud in which she said:

> . . . I asked him [McLaughlin] if he was afraid of a woman & a woman's influence & threatened to report him at Washington. High words passed between us both & I rose indignantly & left the office . . .
>
> In order to lessen my influence as a member of the N.I.D.A. he makes me ridiculous by having the story printed, in which it is stated that I should have said that I came all the way from N. York to marry Sitting Bull. Red Cloud, is there no protection for defenceless women? . . .
>
> The Agent fears my presence & did all he can to destroy me.

Her unfortunate experiences notwithstanding, Catherine Weldon developed so deep an affection for the Lakotah that during the following winter she made a momentous decision. She would devote the rest of her life to the "Saving of the Sioux" in general and to the "Saving of Sitting Bull" in particular. In April of 1890, McLaughlin, who had thought himself rid of this flighty woman who always traveled in the midst of an emotional whirlwind, was dismayed to receive a letter from Mrs. Weldon in which she said, "It has been my intention for years to spend the remainder of my life in Dakota among or near my Indian friends." She then went on to request permission to build a home on the reservation. If that were not permitted, she made clear, she would settle at the edge of the reservation and operate from there. Just what she intended to do to aid the Indians was not made clear except,

> I have set certain days apart for Ind. women and girls to come to me for instruction in useful domestic accomplishments,

And in regard to Sitting Bull,

> I have no intention to become either Sitting Bull's wife or squaw . . . [but] nothing can ever shake my faith in his good qualities and what I can do to make him famous I will certainly do and I will succeed. . . .

Predictably, McLaughlin refused to give her permission to settle on the reservation, and just as predictably, Mrs. Weldon established residence on the very edge of it, at Cannon Ball. When she arrived, accompanied by her fourteen-year-old son, Christie, she brought with her fine furniture, silver, books, paintings, and carpets. Then, having established herself in opulent elegance (for Dakota), she set about Helping the Indians. Just what help she gave them has never been clear, but (much to McLaughlin's irritation) she kept Sitting Bull well supplied with money, which the agent thought only contributed to the old chief's general worthlessness and capacity for troublemaking.

In July Mrs. Weldon again wrote to McLaughlin, this time asking for a teaching job on the reservation. Again he refused; wherefore, sometime after the middle of August and without agency permission, Catherine Weldon went to Grand River to live in Sitting Bull's camp. She remained there, acting as the chief's secretary, painting his portrait, and financing his activities until the Ghost Dance made such hard words between them that she was driven away.

Although he had not admitted it to Mrs. Weldon, all through the summer Sitting Bull had had the Ghost Dance on his mind, and as his curiosity grew, he had repeatedly asked permission of Whitehair to visit Cheyenne River reservation. Just as repeatedly, Whitehair had denied it. Finally, Sitting Bull sent six of his young men to Cherry Creek to ask Mato Anahtaka (Kicking Bear) to come to Grand River to tell his people of this Messiah and the sacred dance.

Responding to Sitting Bull's invitation, Kicking Bear and a party of his disciples came on October 9 to bring the new gospel to the Hunkpapa in the Grand River bottoms. It was a poor day for gathering people to hear a preaching. There had been cold, drizzling rain the day before, and everything was still chilly and wet under low, gray clouds. And besides that, Bishop Hare was holding an annual convocation for Episcopalians only twenty miles away at Oak Creek, and some of the people had gone over there. Nevertheless, it was a good-sized crowd that gathered on the cold wet grass around Sitting Bull's place to hear the new prophet, Mato Anahtaka, speak these words:

> My brothers, I bring to you the promise of a day in which there will be no white man to lay his hand on the bridle of the Indian's horse; when the red men of the prairie will rule the world. . . .
> I bring you word from your fathers the ghosts, that are now marching to join you. They are led by the Messiah who came once to live on earth with the white men, but who was cast out and killed by them. . . . I traveled far and am sent back with a message to tell you to make ready for the coming of the Messiah and return of the ghosts in the spring.

In my tipi on the Cheyenne river reservation I arose after the corn-planting sixteen moons ago, and prepared for my journey. . . . I traveled far on the cars of the white men, until I came to the place where the railroad stopped. There I met two men, Indians, whom I had never met before, but who greeted me as a brother and gave me meat and bread. They had three horses, and we rode for four days. . . .

Two suns we had traveled, and had passed the last signs of the white man—for no white man ever had the courage to travel so far—when we saw a fierce-looking black man, dressed in skins. . . . He had medicine with which to do what he wished. He would wave his hands and make great heaps of money. Another motion, and we saw many spring wagons, already painted and ready to hitch horses to. Yet another motion and there sprang up before us great herds of buffalo.

The black man told us he was the friend of the Indian, that we should remain with him and go no farther, and that we might take what we wanted of the money and spring wagons and buffalo. But our hearts turned away from that black man, my brothers, and we left him and traveled for two days more.

On the evening of the fourth day, weak and faint from our journey and looking for a camping place, we were met by a man dressed like an Indian, but whose hair was long and glistening like the yellow money of the white man. His face was beautiful to see, and when he spoke I forgot my hunger and the toil I had endured.

And he said, "Hau, my children. You have done well to make this long journey to come to me. Leave your horses and follow." And our hearts sang in our breasts and we were glad. He led the way up a great ladder of small clouds, and we followed him up through an opening in the sky.

My brothers, the tongue of Kicking Bear is straight and he cannot tell all that he saw for he is not an orator, but the forerunner and herald of the ghosts.

He whom we followed took us to the Great Holy and his wife and although we lay prostrate on the ground I saw they were dressed as Indians.

Then through an opening in the sky we were shown all the countries of the earth, and the camping grounds of our fathers since the beginning. All were there—the tipis, the ghosts of our fathers, and great herds of buffalo, and a country that smiled because it was rich and the white man was not there.

Then he whom we followed showed us his hands and feet, and there were wounds in them which had been made by the whites when he went to them and they crucified him. And he told us he was going to come again on earth, but this time he would remain and live with the Indians, who were his chosen people.

Then we were seated on rich skins of animals unknown to me, before the open door of the tipi of the Great Holy, and told how to say the prayers and make the dances I am now come to show my brothers.

And the Great Holy spoke to us, saying: "Take this message to my red children and tell it to them as I say it. I have neglected the Indians for many moons, but I will make them my people now if they obey me in this message.

"The earth is getting old and I will make it new for my chosen people, the Indians. . . . I will cover the earth with new soil to a depth of five times the height of a man, and under this new soil will be buried the whites, and all the holes and rotten places will be filled up. The new land will be covered with sweet-grass and running water and trees, and herds of buffalo and ponies will stray over it so that my red children may eat and drink and rejoice. The sea to the west I will fill up so that no ships may pass over it, and the other seas I will make impassable.

"While I am making the new earth the Indians who have heard this message and dance and pray and believe will be taken up in the air and suspended while the wave of new earth is passing, and will then be set down among the ghosts of their ancestors, relatives and friends. But those of my children who doubt will be left in undesirable places. They will be lost to wander around until they believe and learn the songs and the dance of the ghosts.

"And while my children are dancing and making ready to join the ghosts, they shall have no fear of the white man for *I will take from the whites the secret of making gunpowder, and the powder they now have on hand will not burn when it is directed against the red people, my children, who know the songs and dances of the ghosts. But that powder which my children have will burn and kill when it is directed against the whites by those who believe.* [emphasis added]

 . . . "Go then, my children, and tell these things to all the people, and make all ready for the coming of the ghosts."

We were given food that was rich and sweet to the taste. And as we sat there eating there came up through the clouds a man, tall as a tree and thin like a snake, with great teeth sticking out of his mouth and his body covered with short hair, and we knew it was the Evil Spirit. And he said to the Great Holy, "I want half the people of the earth." And the Great Holy answered saying, "No. I cannot give you any. I love them all too much." The Evil Spirit asked again and was refused. He asked a third time, and the Great Spirit then told him he could have the whites to do with as he liked, but he would not let him have any Indians as they were his chosen people for all time to come.

Then we were shown the dances that I am bringing you, my brothers, and were led down the ladder of clouds by him who had taken us up. We rode back to the railroad, the Messiah flying along in the air with us and teaching us the songs for the new dances.

At the railroad he left us, telling us to tell all the people of the red nations what we had seen. And he promised that he would return to the clouds no more, but would remain at the end of the earth and lead the ghosts of our fathers to meet us when the winter is past.

On the day he made that speech, the tongue of Mato Anahtaka the prophet was even stronger than the arrows of Mato Anahtaka the warrior had been. When he finished, a murmuring of marvel rippled through the crowd as the people at once believed. Warmed by the thought of removing the white man's hand from the bridle of the Indian's horse, they forgot the cold and began preparing to make the sacred dance.

Such an agent was Whitehair that a sparrow seldom fell on Standing Rock but what he heard it strike the ground. Thus, when the dancing started, he knew it immediately. On October 12 he sent his police chief, Crazy Walking, with thirteen men to break it up. When they returned on the fourteenth, they not only had not broken it up, but they acted as men who had been dazed by some strong power. Straightaway, Whitehair called in tough Police Lieutenant Chatka and sent him with eleven other police to try again.

On the morning of the fifteenth, Chatka and his men were riding down the grassy benches above Grand River when they saw below them a circle of dancing Indians at Sitting Bull's. Without hesitating they rode into the circle, removed Kicking Bear and his companions, escorted them directly south to the border of the Cheyenne River reservation, and there Chatka ordered them to go on home. The warrior prophet and his friends meekly obeyed.

At the time the police were removing Kicking Bear and his group, neither Sitting Bull nor the dancers had made any move to interfere. But that night, before a gathering of Ghost Dancers, Sitting Bull held up a peace pipe which he had kept since the day he brought his people home from Grandmother's Land. Then with his strong hands he snapped it in two as he shouted that he was now ready to fight and die for his new religion.

The story of Sitting Bull's words and the breaking of the pipe reached Whitehair the next day. He also heard that Sitting Bull's people were dancing harder than ever and that the chief himself was leading them. That, McLaughlin decided, was enough. Sitting Bull must be removed from the reservation. Accordingly, he wrote to the commissioner:

Standing Rock Agency, October 17, 1890

Hon. T. J. Morgan
Commissioner of Indian Affairs
Sir:
    . . . I have the honor to state that there is now considerable excitement and some disaffection among certain Indians of this agency.

I trust I may not be considered an alarmist . . . and do not wish to be understood as considering the present state of excitement so alarming as to apprehend any immediate uprising or serious outcome, but I do feel it my duty to report the present "craze" and nature of the excitement existing among the Sitting Bull faction of Indians over the expected Indian millennium, the annihilation of the white man and supremacy of the Indian, which is looked for in the near future and promised by the Indian medicine men as not later than next spring, when the new grass begins to appear, and is known amongst the Sioux as the return of the ghosts.

. . . Sitting Bull is high priest and leading apostle of this latest Indian absurdity; in a word he is the chief mischief-maker at this agency, and if he were not here this craze, so general among the Sioux, would never have gotten a foothold at this agency. Sitting Bull is a man of low cunning, devoid of a single manly principle in his nature or an honorable trait of character, but on the contrary is capable of instigating and inciting others (those who believe in his powers) to do any amount of mischief. . . . He had announced that those who signed the agreement ratifying the act of March 2, 1889, opening the Sioux reservation will be compelled to accept a small corner to be set apart and subdivided into small tracts for them to settle upon, where they will be obliged to remain and support themselves, but those who refused to ratify the act . . . and refuse to accept allotments, will have all the unoccupied portion of the reservation to hold in common and continue to enjoy their old Indian ways and . . . freedom and therefor will have to be rationed by the government for all time to come, and it is not to be wondered at that, among an uneducated and ignorant people, he finds supporters and followers. He is an Indian unworthy of notice except as a disaffected intriguer who grasps every opportunity to maintain his power and popularity. He is opposed to everything of an elevating nature and is the most vain, pompous, and untruthful Indian that I ever knew. His word is not believed by the more intelligent Indians of this agency, but . . . is . . . the idol of the disaffected and worthless element of the Sioux. . . . He is such an abject coward that he will not commit any overt act . . . himself, but does the intriguing and directs the mischief to be done by his less cunning followers. . . .

Sitting Bull is a polygamist, libertine, habitual liar, active obstructionist, and a great obstacle in the civilization of these people, and he is so devoid of any of the nobler traits of character, and so devoted to the old Indian ways and superstitions that it is very doubtful if any change for the better will ever come over him at his present age of fifty-six years. He has been a disturbing element here ever since his return from confinement as a military prisoner in the spring of 1883, but has been growing steadily worse this past year, which is partly to be accounted for by the presence of a lady from Brooklyn, N. Y., who came here in June of 1889, announcing herself as a member of Dr. Bland's society, the Indian Defense Association, and opposed to the Indians ratifying the act of March 2, 1889, and demanding of me permission to pass through the Sioux Reservation to Cheyenne River

Agency, and to take Sitting Bull with her. The Sioux Commission being
then engaged negotiating with the Indians of the southern Sioux agencies,
I, as a matter of course, refused to permit her either to pass through the
reservation or allow Sitting Bull to accompany her, and compelled her to
cross the Missouri River at this point and travel over the public roads
outside of the Indian reservation, in consequence of which she was very
hostile to me and wrote several letters to different parties in condemnation
of my course of action. While here she bestowed numerous presents upon
Sitting Bull, considerable being money, which had a demoralizing effect
upon him, inflating him with his importance. After her departure she kept
up a correspondence with Sitting Bull until early last spring, when she
again returned and located on the north bank of the Cannon Ball River,
just outside of this reservation and about 25 miles north of the agency.
Sitting Bull has been a frequent visitor at her home, and has grown more
insolent and worthless with every visit he has made there. Her lavish
expenditure of money and other gifts upon him, enabling him to give
frequent feasts and hold councils, thereby perpetuating the old-time
customs amongst the Indians and engrafting, with their superstitious
nature, this additional absurdity of the New Messiah and the return of the
ghosts, and in this coming, Sitting Bull, whose former influence and power
being so undermined and tenure so uncertain, asserts himself as high priest
here, and like a drowning man grasping at a straw, is working upon the
credulity of the superstitious and ignorant Indians and reaping a rich
harvest of popularity. . . .

. . . I would respectfully recommend the removal from the reservation
and confinement in some military prison, some distance from the Sioux
country, of Sitting Bull and the parties named in my letter of June 18
[Sitting Bull, Circling Bear, Black Bird and Circling Hawk of Standing
Rock, Big Foot of Cheyenne River, and Crow Dog and Low Dog of the
Rosebud]. With these individuals removed the advancement of the Sioux
will be more rapid and the interests of the Government greatly subserved
thereby. . . .

One of the problems which McLaughlin had complained of in his
letter—that of Catherine Weldon—was about to be solved. She was
living in Sitting Bull's camp when the Ghost Dance arrived, and in the
dance she found her greatest opportunity yet to save the Sioux from
something. She attacked the dance with all the force of her crusading
nature and said to the people:

It is not true!

I love you more dearly than life, and to prove it I will meet Mato
Wanahtaka and tell him he is either insane or crazy or that he deceives
you!

Do not be blinded or cheated. Mato Wanahtaka has no more power than any of you!

I who love you dearly, who have made greater sacrifices for you than any of you think of, tell you this because I do not want any Dakotas cheated by evil people who doubtless have their motive for leading you into trouble.

I have spoken to Sitting Bull . . . & warned him not to be deceived.

These were but a few of the things she said. There were many more, but the people's ears were closed. In calmer times they had more or less accepted Woman-Walking-Ahead as a friend and had most willingly accepted whatever she might do for them. But things were different now. Now she was just another meddling white, and she could no more change their direction than a dove could change the direction of a hawk. Most of her arguing, of course, was directed to Sitting Bull himself. But now that he was involved in leading the new dance and, as a medicine man, also painting the dancers, he had little time or inclination to listen to the strident clamor of this woman as she condemned it. From Mrs. Weldon's later letters and from some of her notes found in Sitting Bull's cabin after his death, it appears that harsh words passed between them. On one sheet of her notes, for instance, are such fragmentary observations as:

S. Bull's heart, secret, not open like to a friend, but secret, like to an enemy . . .

Memorandum of what to say to S. B.

Yanayan—to cheat.
Owa Kanka—also to cheat.

Eyi Jate—forked tongue.
Leji Nonpa—double meaning.

I think myself as great as Sitting Bull & my *Hankake** have been much greater.

Finally, on October 22, Catherine Weldon sadly left Sitting Bull's camp for the last time and returned to Cannon Ball. From there she wrote to McLaughlin:

*Author's note: *Hankake* means "sisters-in-law," but Mrs. Weldon's meaning is not clear. An affectionate term for Sitting Bull's wives perhaps?

Cannon Ball
Oct. 24 —90

Major McLaughlin
Dear Sir:

. . . All was quiet at the Grand River on the 22nd when I left there. . . . By attacking and defeating "Mato Wanahtka" I have turned my former Uncpapa friends into enemies, & Some feel very bitter towards me. Even Sitting Bull's faith in me is shaken & he imagines I seek his destruction in spite of all the proofs of friendship I have given him for many years. In fact His brain is so confused that he does not know friend from foe. . . . I believe the Mormons are at the bottom of it all & misuse the credulity of the Indians for their own purposes. I have every reason to believe the 5 tribes are ready to fight. . . . They believe that some terrible fate will overtake me for my sacriligious utterances against their Christ. Poor mis-guided beings, so earnestly desiring to seek God, groping blindly for the true light & not finding it. If I had known what obstinate minds I had to contend with, I would not have undertaken this mission to enlighten & instruct them. It was money, health & heart thrown away.

I am very Respectfully,
C. Weldon

On October 29 the commissioner replied to McLaughlin's letter of the sixteenth in which he had requested permission to remove Sitting Bull and others from the reservation. McLaughlin snorted in disgust when he discovered that instead of arresting and removing Sitting Bull, he was to *chide* him. Specifically, the message said:

. . . the honorable Secretary of the Interior . . . directs me to instruct you to inform Sitting Bull and the other Indians named by you as engaged in encouraging the ghost dance . . . that he is greatly displeased with their conduct, and that he will hold Sitting Bull to a strict personal responsibility for the misconduct, acts of violence, or any threats, actions, or movements to which any of the Sioux Indians may be guided, influenced, or encouraged by him or as a result of his bad advice and evil councils. . . .

Very Respectfully,
R. V. Belt
Acting Commissioner

Meanwhile, agent McLaughlin's letter of October 17 to the commissioner had somehow fallen into the hands of the press, and the press made the most of it. In fact, from this point on until the Battle of Wounded Knee there was a "war" with the Sioux, but it was entirely a "newspaper war." On October 28, the *Chicago Daily Tribune* fired the opening gun. It printed McLaughlin's letter almost verbatim, but headlined it:

TO WIPE OUT THE WHITES

What The Indians Expect Of The
Coming Messiah

FEARS OF AN OUTBREAK

Old Sitting Bull Stirring Up The Ex-
cited Redskins

A WOMAN'S EVIL INFLUENCE

Mrs. Weldon Partly Responsible For Sitting
Bull's Conduct

On the same day the *Chicago Daily Tribune* also carried the following story:

SOLDIERS ARE READY FOR HIM

The Army In The Northwest Prepared
To Quell Any Uprising

Standing Rock Agency, ND, Oct 27—Special—For the last four weeks Sitting Bull has been inviting the Sioux Indians in this vicinity to an uprising. He enlisted the sympathy of a large number of young bucks by telling them the story of his great bravery on the field of the Custer Massacre, and several hundred of them have agreed to go on the warpath at his bidding. . . .

Sitting Bull has just recovered from a long illness and is very ugly, but any move on the part of the aged chief and his 300 or 400 followers would be quickly checked. Companies G and H, 12th Infantry and Troops F and G of the 8th Cavalry are at Fort Yates could probably quell it instantly without other assistance. But if affairs should assume a serious phase through a general uprising of the Sioux along the Missouri the regulars at Fts. Totten and Sully could be brought into service in a few hours.

The *Tribune* story provided editor R. M. Tuttle of the *Mandan* (Morton County, North Dakota) *Pioneer* with additional ammunition for

a campaign—already in progress—to save Fort Abraham Lincoln. This
was a matter of both pride and profit to Mandan. Fort Lincoln, only a
few miles south of town, had once been one of the most famous of the
western forts. In fact, it was from Lincoln that Custer had marched with
General Terry's army to the Little Big Horn. Furthermore, Lincoln was
not only the source of much profitable business for Mandan, but
originally it was the reason for the town's very existence. Now Lincoln
was being phased out. Its only remaining garrison was an infantry
company of about fifty men, and even that was to be removed in a few
months. Thus editor Tuttle, disturbed that the *Tribune* had mentioned
Forts Totten, Sully, and Yates but had ignored Lincoln (and disregarding the fact that the well-garrisoned Fort Yates at Standing Rock agency
was only fifty miles to the south of Mandan), wrote the following:

> The . . . report of Major McLaughlin to the Indian department . . .
> should convince the authorities of the importance of retaining Fort A.
> Lincoln as a permanent post. When Lincoln is removed . . . the settlers
> that are located between the reservation and this city will have no
> protection whatever. . . . Sitting Bull is reported to be posing as a Saviour
> of the people, and the Indians are reported to be awaiting the deliverance
> of their tribes from the control of the white men. Next spring is the time
> fixed for the uprising, and it behooves the authorities to put Sitting Bull in
> chains or in some other way curb him. He should be today reposing
> peacefully in a grave, but under our policy of clemency to treasonable
> individuals and murderers, he is still at large causing trouble to the citizens
> of this republic.

On November 1 the *Philadelphia Telegraph* added its voice:

> If the Army had charge of the Indians, as common sense and common
> prudence demand, Sitting Bull would be shut up very shortly; but the
> Army has no authority until the murdering redskins have broken out,
> burned a dozen ranches, slaughtered a score of women and children. . . .
> The Army officers may be perfectly well informed of Sitting Bull's
> intrigues, but they can do nothing until he deliberately perfects his rascally
> plans and gets ready to start his young bucks on a raid. . . .

During the following two weeks, with absolutely nothing more to go
on than that one McLaughlin letter, the newspapers kept up a steady
drumfire of "scare" stories. Actually, during that time the only disturbance at all on Standing Rock reservation was the Ghost Dancing at
Sitting Bull's camp, and of the more than four thousand Indians on the

reservation, never more than about four hundred of them were involved in it. Moreover, so far the dancers had neither bothered anyone else nor shown any hostile intentions. Nevertheless, the settlers read the newspapers and then listened to the rumors which the news stories spawned, and those between Mandan and the reservation recalled the *Pioneer*'s saying that they were without protection and their tension grew. A large number of the farmers near Standing Rock were recent German immigrants who were strangers in a strange land besides, and they found the thought of an Indian uprising particularly frightening. There were also a good many people in the area who had had relatives in the Minnesota Massacre, and they, too, were especially (and understandably) frightened. Finally, on November 16, the settlers panicked. And when they did, the newspapers helped them along. Under dateline of November 16 the *Chicago Daily Tribune* reported:

> Settlers on the farms and ranches south of Mandan are fleeing their homes, believing that an Indian uprising is at hand. They urgently demand protection and many a farmhouse in North Dakota will soon be deserted unless the settlers receive some assurance that they will not be left to the mercy of the murderous redskins, who are now whetting their knives in anticipation of the moment when they may begin their bloody work. The Indians are trading their horses and all other property for guns and ammunition. . . . Joseph Buckley rode in today from the reservation and says . . . every Indian on the reservation will shortly go on the warpath and that they have got possession of Custer's rifles, which the U. S. Army has never found.

On November 17 a remarkably well-detailed rumor swept Mandan to the effect that at exactly half-past ten that morning a Sioux army had left the reservation with the specific intention of capturing Fort Lincoln and its guns and ammunition, and then proceeding on to Mandan to kill all its citizens and burn the town. Mandan went wild.

Morton County Sheriff, George Bingenheimer, wired the U. S. Marshal at Fargo, ". . . The Indians are crazy and likely to go on the warpath at any minute. Have telegraphed Governor Miller for arms. The government will not protect our unarmed settlers." Also, he wired McLaughlin at Standing Rock and asked for a report of the situation but received no immediate answer.

The special correspondent of the *Chicago Tribune* filed a story from Mandan saying, "It is reported that the Indian police have torn off their badges and revolted. . . . Roving bands that are travelling through the country say that the war of the Messiah will begin shortly, then every white man will be killed. . . ."

The men of Mandan loaded women and children onto railroad cars and sent them to Bismarck, ten miles east across the Missouri River for safety.

The depot agent at New Salem, twenty miles west of Mandan, spread the panic throughout the entire area by putting out a general telegraph call in which he announced that he had been ordered to close his office and flee for his life.

The Chicago *Daily Tribune* correspondent at Bismarck ominously reported, "All sorts of rumors are afloat. Telegrams to Standing Rock are unanswered. . . ."

That report was not true. The fact was that McLaughlin had been on a visit to Sitting Bull's camp and did not return to the agency until fairly late in the afternoon. It had been a remarkably friendly visit considering the circumstances, and when McLaughlin got back to the agency, he answered the anxious wires of Sheriff Bingenheimer and the others saying that he had just returned from Sitting Bull's camp where everything was calm and that there was absolutely no cause for alarm.

This was no comfort to the aroused men of Mandan, however, and that night they held a mass meeting to decide on a course of action. When the meeting was assembled, every man who owned a gun was carrying it—which resulted in the first and only white casualty of the entire Ghost Dance disturbance at Standing Rock. A railroad brakeman named Wilcox had come bearing a huge revolver. As he shouldered through the crowd it somehow fell to the floor where it discharged and fired a bullet entirely through the body of Fred Clark, paralyzing him at the time and killing him later. That seems to have been only a minor interruption of the principal business of the meeting, however, which was that of educating the President of the United States on the problems of Mandan. The result was what may have been the longest telegram in the history of the town and which said, in part:

> There are located on the Sioux reservation south of this county, a large number of Indians, of whom probably there are at least 2,000 warriors [the fact was that there were fewer than 2,000 males all told, including old men and infants]. . . . Settlers by the score come to town and tell of Indians armed to the teeth, who . . . act insultingly—draw mysterious circles around their heads, indicating there will be some scalping done—start fires

. . . which, if not extinguished would burn much property. . . . They are spending all their means to buy guns and ammunition. They are . . . beginning to domineer. They assume menacing attitudes, tap their guns ominously and show their scalping knives . . . it is utterly impossible for the ordinary white man to see why Indians should be permitted to roam all over . . . armed to the teeth. . . .

The most conservative men of this community will be powerless to suppress the determination of the majority of the settlers to kill off every Indian that presents his face . . . unless the government does something to protect us. There are scores of men in this immediate neighborhood who were sufferers by the Minnesota Massacre in 1862, and they don't propose to be annoyed and harassed any longer. Their property has been destroyed and their children and wives frightened by these worthless nomads who are permitted by a lax government to prowl over the country with arms that would not be allowed on the person of a white man. They will stand it no longer.

In the meantime, thanks to the wire sent by the New Salem depot agent, while the Mandan men were meeting and on through the night of the seventeenth, settlers to the west and south were in a ferment of fear. At Glen Ullin, forty miles west, the citizens organized a militia company complete with chaplain and surgeon, then worked all night digging trenches and throwing up breastworks.

At Hebron, ten miles west of Glen Ullin, young Paul Reveres galloped through the night warning the settlers (mostly German) with cries of "Die Indianer kommt! Die Indianer kommt!" The settlers loaded families into wagons and dashed for town. (One driver later confessed that in the wild dash over the rough night prairies he had gone some distance before discovering that his family had been bounced out of the wagon and left behind.) Meanwhile, in Hebron itself, the residents began construction of what was to become an elaborate defensive structure named "Fort Sauerkraut."

The next day, the commandant from Fort Lincoln observed the settlers coming into Mandan and commented afterward, "It was a sad sight to see women and children with all their worldly goods being hauled through the streets in wagons . . . several women were dangerously ill from excitement. . . ."

On November 18, General Ruger, who had just returned to St. Paul, Minnesota, from an inspection of the disturbances on the various reservations, told the press, "In regard to the probability of an attack upon the citizens of Mandan . . . Mandan is in no more danger than is

St. Paul." Over the following days, the panic gradually began to subside, but it resulted in McLaughlin's finally receiving permission to arrest Sitting Bull. Acting Commissioner Belt wired him on November 20:

> If condition now . . . requires that the leaders of excitement and fomenters of disturbances should be arrested . . . telegraph me names at once so that assistance of military . . . may be had to make arrests.

By this time, however, McLaughlin had changed his mind. He still thought the diehard "nonprogressives" of Standing Rock should be arrested and removed, but after his visit with Sitting Bull he had come to the conclusion that it would cause considerably less upheaval if they were arrested later. Accordingly, he wired the commissioner:

> Replying to telegram of yesterday, Sitting Bull, Circling Bear, Black Bird, Circling Hawk, Iron White Man, and Male Bear, being leaders of excitement and fomenters of disaffection, should be arrested before next spring, but everything quiet here at present . . . do not think it prudent to make arrests now. . . .

But the matter was no longer in McLaughlin's hands. While the panic had been building in the north, the southern reservations were heating up also, and in mid-November the Secretary of the Interior finally and reluctantly asked the army to take over his problems with the Sioux. Consequently, General Nelson Miles, commander-in-chief of the Department of the Missouri, was now in charge of restoring order to the reservations. General Miles had had long experience with Sitting Bull and knew him personally, but he, too, had an exaggerated idea of the chief's influence among the Indians. Miles once went so far as to say of him that "since the days of Pontiac, Tecumseh and Red Jacket no Indian has had the power of drawing to him so large a following of his race, and molding and wielding it against the authority of the United States. . . ." Besides that, the general was of the opinion that Sitting Bull was plotting to use the Messiah disturbance for the basis of a general armed uprising of all the Lakotah in the following spring. General Miles therefore decided that Sitting Bull should be arrested. He later explained, "I concluded that if the so-called Messiah was to appear in that country, Sitting Bull had better be out of it, and I considered it of first importance to secure his arrest and removal from that country."

Nevertheless, the general did respect the old chief, and, also he didn't want to stir up any more hornets than were necessary. He would have the arrest made as tactfully and gently as possible. Recalling that Sitting Bull had once been a member of Buffalo Bill Cody's Wild West Show, he sent for Cody.

Buffalo Bill assured the general that, yes, he and Sitting Bull were, indeed, old friends. By combining persuasion with presents, he was sure he could bring the chief in peacefully. Miles thereupon gave Buffalo Bill the following order:

CONFIDENTIAL
Headquarters, Division of the Missouri
Chicago, Ill., Nov. 24, 1890

Col. Cody,

You are hereby authorized to secure the person of Sitting Bull and deliver him to the nearest com'g officer of U.S. Troops, taking a receipt and reporting your action.

Nelson A. Miles
Major General
Comd. Division

Also, on the back of one of his personal visiting cards, Miles penciled:

Com'd officers will please give Col. Cody transportation for himself and party and any protection he may need for a small party.

Nelson A. Miles

Although Cody had been a frontier scout at one time, he was now entirely a showman, and publicity was his business. Even so, he managed temporarily to respect the confidentiality of his orders and to resist the urge to broadcast the news of his dramatic mission. This did not, however, prevent him from doing a little stage setting for his anticipated coup. Within hours after Miles chose him to bring Sitting Bull in, because he and the chief were friends, Cody issued a press statement on the Indian situation in which he declared, "Of all the bad Indians, Sitting Bull is the worst. . . . If there is no disturbance he will foment one. He is a dangerous Indian."

CHAPTER
10
ΛΛΛΛΛΛ

"Indians Are Dancing in the Snow..."

NOW THAT GENERAL MILES had set in motion what he hoped would be the solution to the Sitting Bull problem, he returned his attention to the reason the army had been called in—to suppress the disturbances raging at Pine Ridge and Rosebud where, so far, things weren't going nearly so well as he had planned.

The fact that they weren't did not mean that Miles was either inept or unprepared; he was neither of these. On the contrary, such was his ability that with less than a high school education he had risen from a clerk in a Boston crockery store at the beginning of the Civil War to a brevetted (temporary) major general by the war's end. Moreover, he had continued to advance until he was now a permanent major general and, as such, was one of the five highest ranking officers in the entire army.

Insofar as experience with the Sioux was concerned, Miles had been dealing with them off and on since 1876. They called him "Bear Coat," and although it is doubtful that they and Bear Coat ever had a great deal of affection for each other, they *had* developed a considerable amount of mutual respect. Also, Miles had prepared himself well for dealing with the current Sioux problem. A month or so earlier he had come to the conclusion that sooner or later the matter of the Ghost Dance disturbances would have to be turned over to the War Department where, since Miles was Commander of the Department of the Missouri, it would come to rest squarely in his ample lap. Accordingly, he had already sent General Ruger, his subordinate and Commander of the

Department of Dakota, to visit the reservations involved to find out just what *was* going on.

On November 14 when the army actually did take over, Ruger's investigation was not yet complete, but it had gone far enough for General Miles to have decided what he thought the real problems were and, also, to have devised a strategy for meeting them. First he concluded (correctly) that the real reason the Sioux were making mischief was not the Messiah excitement itself, but the simple fact that they were all but starving. Furthermore, he made it clear that he blamed their hunger on the failure of Congress to honor its treaty obligations.

Militarily, the Sioux had Miles worried. According to his information, they now had more and better weapons than ever before in their history. He knew that in the event of an actual and general uprising they could field at least four or five thousand warriors and perhaps more—in any event, more than the soldiers Miles had in the entire Department of the Missouri. Besides that, the land around the reservations was so well populated with cattle and horses now that a Sioux war force could seize enough to provide itself with food and remounts almost indefinitely. He observed that "they are in better condition for war than ever before," and added that in case a Sioux war did break out it would be "the bloodiest Indian war ever fought." That being the case, the general was convinced that either forcing or provoking the Sioux into war, *or* allowing them to organize and/or inflame themselves into provoking one would be a bloody folly that must be avoided at almost any cost.

Therefore, as soon as he inherited the Sioux problem, the general attacked first things first. He immediately began a campaign of trying to convince the War Department that it was cheaper to feed the Sioux than to fight them, and to get it to provide them with the necessary food from the army's own appropriation until (hopefully) Congress could be persuaded to fulfill its Indian obligations properly.

Accomplishing this would take time, however, and meanwhile there loomed (in the general's mind at least) the specter of "the bloodiest Indian war in history" unless he could somehow manage to control and extinguish the existing turbulence before it grew beyond peaceful solution. To accomplish this, Miles decided to arrest and remove the leaders he regarded as storm centers of the revolt—especially Sitting Bull and Hump. Also, as quickly as the necessary troops could be alerted and moved, he intended to encircle the reservations with sufficient soldiers to prevent the Indians from massing in large numbers or from raiding off-reservation settlements. And to minimize the danger of sparking a fight with this operation, he ordered his field commanders to "keep pressure on the Indians by your presence only. Do not come into active contact with them unless it is impossible to avoid doing so."

Where the general's plans suddenly went astray, however, was when—before he could either make the proposed arrests or encircle the reservation—conditions deteriorated at Pine Ridge and Rosebud to the point that he felt himself forced to send troops to occupy them and thus to risk touching off the war he was trying to prevent.

Earlier in the year, when September had faded into October, and the early days of October had then passed, it appeared that the Indian Office strategy of "hang on and hope for the best" was working effectively on the southern reservations. Things had quieted down considerably on the Rosebud since the September outburst, and probably no more than half the Brulés, at most, were involved in the Ghost Dancing. On Pine Ridge it was much the same. In both places, the Indians who were involved in the dancing were intensely involved, but for the others, life was going on pretty much as usual. (As we look back on it today with the advantage of the long view from the hill of history, it seems likely that with a combination of strong, knowledgeable agents and a great deal of patience, things would have gradually returned to normal.) Unfortunately, however, on October 9—the same day Kicking Bear had carried the Messiah gospel to Sitting Bull—agent Gallagher at Pine Ridge had been replaced by Dr. Daniel F. Royer. Now, except for McLaughlin at Standing Rock, there was no longer strong, knowledgeable leadership on any of the affected reservations.

Dr. Royer wasn't appointed because he knew anything about Indians. He didn't. Nor did he care to. He feared them, in fact, to the point that the Sioux promptly named him Lakotah Kopegla Koskala, which meant Young-Man-Afraid-of-Lakotah. Before receiving this political appointment Royer had been a physician-druggist at Alpena, South Dakota, and inasmuch as he had eagerly sought the $183-a-month agent job, it might conceivably be assumed that he hadn't been too successful at it. When he reported to Pine Ridge, Royer found orders already waiting from the commissioner instructing him to inform the Indians that "the Ghost Dance will not be allowed on any occasion." Royer told them. They, in turn, told Royer to mind his own business.

At the time Royer took over, things weren't nearly as bad at Pine

Ridge as they sounded. There *was* Ghost Dancing, to be sure, and a good deal of it. But so far the dancers had harmed neither persons nor property. Also, there were a good many strong chiefs at Pine Ridge—men such as American Horse, Young Man Afraid, Fast Thunder, Standing Soldier, and others—who were trying to help keep the reservation orderly. Even old Red Cloud, who was cannily steering a middle course so that no one knew exactly where he stood, was not, openly at least, abetting disorder. Royer, however, had been expecting a simple government sinecure in which, in addition to collecting his paychecks, he would have been expected merely to keep records and count supplies—neither of which ever had ideas of their own or talked back. It took him four days to discover that his actual job was to keep order among several thousand people who did both. At that time, on October 12, he wired the Indian Office requesting that soldiers be sent to back him up and protect him. The Indian Office, however, was still determined to prevent military interference in its affairs, so Acting Commissioner Belt gave Royer no comfort. He responded that Royer should be able to handle matters through persuasion.

So Royer suffered on through the month, his authority eroding day by day as more and more Indians bluffed him and faced him down, simply because he was so *bluffable.* Finally, according to a teacher in the Pine Ridge school, things reached the point that Royer occasionally locked himself in his house and refused to come out, allowing the running of the agency to fall upon his staff. By the end of October, his disintegrating authority was reflected in the report he sent to Acting Commissioner Belt:

> The believers defy the law, threaten the police, take their children out of school, and if the police are sent after the children, they simply stand ready to fight before they will give them up. When an Indian violates any law the first thing they do is join the ghost dance, and then they feel safe to defy the police, the law, and the agent . . . the only remedy for this matter is the use of the military . . . [these people] are tearing down more in a day than the Government can build up in a month.

At the same time Royer was having his troubles on Pine Ridge, Reynolds was facing a new crisis at Rosebud. The last few days of October, 1890, had been beautiful. There were gorgeous Indian summer days with rich blue autumn skies—days that were almost hot and nights that were mild. There was even a full moon. It was a time when everyone wanted to be out-of-doors, and for the Indians it was the ideal time for Ghost Dancing. Short Bull had taken advantage of it to assemble a large dance camp at Red Leaf's village on Black Pipe Creek on the Rosebud. There he had announced that the coming of the new world had been dramatically speeded up, and he instructed the Indians how to prepare to meet it saying:

> My friends and relations: I will soon start this thing in running order. I have told you this would come to pass in two seasons, but since the whites are interfering so much, I will advance the time from what my father above told me to do, so the time will be much shorter. Therefore you must not be afraid of anything. Some of my relations have no ears, so I will have them blown away.
>
> Now, there will be a tree sprout up, and there all the members of our religion and the tribe must gather together. That will be the place where we will see our dead relations. But before this time we must dance the balance of this moon, at the end of which time the earth will shiver very hard. Whenever this thing occurs, I will start the wind to blow. We are the ones who will then see our fathers, mothers, and everybody. We, the tribe of Indians, are the ones who are living a sacred life.
>
> . . . My father has shown me these things, therefore we must continue this dance.
>
> If the soldiers surround you four deep, three of you, on whom I have put holy shirts, will sing a song, which I have taught you, around them. Then some of them will drop dead. The rest will start to run but their horses will sink into the earth. The riders will jump from their horses but they will sink into the earth also. Then you can do as you desire with them. Now you must know this—that all the soldiers and that race will be dead. There will be only five thousand of them left living on the earth. My friends and relations, this is straight and true.
>
> Now we must gather at Pass Creek where the tree is sprouting. There we will go among our dead relations. You must not take any earthly things with you. Then the men must take off all their clothing and the women must do the same. No one shall be ashamed of their persons. My father above has told us to do this, and we must do as he says.
>
> You must not be afraid of anything. The guns are the only things we are afraid of, but they belong to our father in heaven. He will see that they do no harm.
>
> Whatever white men tell you, do not listen to them, my relations.
>
> This is all. I will now reach my hand up toward my father and close this that he has said to you through me.

In order to feed their gathering, the Indians killed two cows from the agency's breeding stock, whereupon Reynolds sent two officers and eight police to arrest the offenders. They returned to say that they had been surrounded by seventy-five or more Indians armed with Winchesters and, furthermore, that the Indians had sent word that they would rather die from fighting than from starvation and the new world was about to come anyhow, so they had no fear of dying. Hearing this, Reynolds added his voice to Royer's and wrote to the commissioner:

> . . . they are daily becoming more threatening and defiant. . . . This . . . may in a measure be attributed to the scant supply of rations, to which my attention has almost daily been called by the Indians. . . . They kill cows and oxen issued to them for breeding and working purposes and make no secret of doing so. . . .
>
> These Indians have within the past three weeks traded horses and everything else they could trade for guns and ammunition. . . . To me there appears but one remedy (and all here agree with me) . . . and that is a sufficient force of troops to prevent the outbreak which is imminent. . . .

On November 5 the weather turned bad and the harried agents got a short reprieve. On the sixth there was light snow, and on the eighth came the year's first blizzard. The tenth, however, dawned bright and clear with a warming sun, and like children kept in the house too long, the Indians on Pine Ridge and Rosebud swarmed to the dance camps.

At Pine Ridge Royer immediately wired the commissioner:

> . . . I deem it for the best interests of the service that I am permitted to come to Washington to explain [the situation] to you personally. Please grant authority as circumstances justify it.

Belt dryly responded that if times were as troublesome as Royer indicated, it would be best for the agent to remain at his post. Early the next morning Royer tried again:

> Very important I come to Washington at once. . . . Indians will remain quiet during my absence. You will agree with me when I see you personally that it is important for me to come. Please grant me authority to come at once.

The following day, Wednesday, November 12, was beef-issue day at Pine Ridge, and the agency area was swarming with Indians. In the combination dispensary and police headquarters Dr. Charles Eastman, a full-blood Sioux physician, was seeing patients from the outlying districts. In the same building the chiefs were holding a council, as they usually did when they were in town for an issue. Suddenly there was a great hubbub outside. Police Lieutenant Thunder Bear, seeing an Indian named Little who was wanted for cattle stealing, had attempted to arrest him. Almost immediately, according to Dr. Eastman, the police found themselves surrounded by as many as two hundred of Little's fellow Ghost Dancers. The Indians seized the police and freed Little, who drew a butcher knife and threatened Thunder Bear with it while his rescuers waved their guns and shouted that they were going to burn the agency and kill the whites. Next, American Horse—imposing even in his agency-issue white-man clothing—strode out of the chiefs' council, pushed his way to the entrapped police, and called out, "My Brothers! Think! What are you going to do? Kill these men of your own race? Kill helpless white men, women, and children? And then what? What will these brave words and deeds lead to in the end? Your country is surrounded by railroads; thousands of white soldiers will be here within three suns. . . . What will happen to your families? . . . This is a child's madness!"

For a moment the crowd fell still. Then Jack Red Cloud, son of the old chief, thrust a cocked pistol into American Horse's face and snarled, "It is you and your kind that have brought us to this condition!" At that American Horse did a brave thing. He looked at Jack Red Cloud as if he were something small; then he turned his back on him as a Great Dane might turn away from a yapping puppy and walked back into the council room. Impressed, the crowd fell silent and then dispersed, taking Little with them.

Royer instantly wired the story of the incident:

> . . . the agency is at the mercy of these crazy dancers. . . . I deem the situation at this agency very critical, and believe that an outbreak may occur at any time, and it does not seem to me to be safe to longer withhold troops. . . .

With that wire Royer got Washington's attention. On the following day Interior Secretary Noble gave in and recommended that the War Department be instructed to take whatever action it deemed necessary to prevent a Sioux outbreak. President Harrison promptly complied with Noble's request, and on November 14 the agents on the four affected reservations received this message:

The President has directed the Secretary of War to assume a military responsibility for the suppression of any threatened outbreak among the Indians. . . .

Now the army was finally into the act—running the show, in fact—and General Miles had the responsibility of restoring tranquility to Sioux country. He sat back and thought about Royer and his wires and also about Reynolds's reports from Rosebud. Both sounded bad. But then, what did these agents really know about outbreaks? By and large (in Miles's opinion) Indian agents were incompetent blockheads who held office because of whom they knew rather than what they knew. And he regarded even that opinion a bit too flattering for Royer, whom he had met while inspecting Pine Ridge agency three weeks previously. At that time the gibbering agent had practically hung onto Miles's coattails while pouring out his tale of tribulations at the hands of his Indians. The general had given Royer small comfort then, and since Royer's idea of moving large numbers of troops onto the reservations could be like setting a powder keg too close to the fire, he was little disposed to give the agent any more comfort now. On the other hand, the general did know from his own sources that things definitely *were* in a mess at Rosebud, and as he also had no confidence that Royer could handle the situation at Pine Ridge, matters just might possibly be reaching the point where sending troops could be the only answer. Hence, to be on the safe side, Miles wired Brigadier General John Brooke, Commander of the Department of the Platte, at his headquarters in Omaha and instructed him to have troops prepared for reservation duty—just in case.

That was on Friday, November 14, and it took Royer only another day or so to take care of Miles's "just in case." After the excitement over the attempted arrest of Little, Royer had retreated to the safety of Rushville, Nebraska, twenty-eight miles south, for a couple of days of nerve-calming. On Saturday the fifteenth, he returned to Pine Ridge, took one look around, and promptly sent yet another wire:

Indians are dancing in the snow and are wild and crazy. I have fully informed you that the employees and government property at this agency have no protection and are at the mercy of the Ghost Dancers. . . . We need protection and we need it now . . . nothing short of 1000 troops will stop this dancing.

With that telegram Royer did it. On Sunday General Ruger, who had been investigating the agencies, recommended dispatching troops to Pine Ridge and Rosebud. Following a conference on Monday with Secretary of War Proctor, Miles agreed and instructed General Brooke accordingly. Thus, all day Tuesday in the Omaha rail yards, quartermasters and supply officers checked their lists while swearing sergeants and sweating troopers loaded railcars with tents, provisions, wagons, horses, ammunition, clothing, and all the thousand other things required by an army in the field. Then, after dark that night—November 18—two troop trains chuffed their way out of Omaha and northwestward toward Indian country.

While all this was going on, Royer had still another fright. On the seventeenth an Indian had waved a butcher knife at him, whereupon Royer had loaded his family into his buggy, informed Issue Clerk R. O. Pugh that he was in temporary charge of the agency, whipped up the horses, and dashed for Rushville to await the arrival of the army. According to several sources (probably just gossip, but still revealing of his personality), when the Royers arrived in Rushville, the agent galloped his team down the main street shouting, "Protect yourselves! The Sioux are rising!"—or words to that effect. At the time Royer was fearfully loading his buggy with his family, Elaine Goodale, the young white Superintendent of Education, was calmly loading hers with camping equipment. At the time the Royers fled Pine Ridge for Rushville, Miss Goodale left Pine Ridge, unescorted, for an inspection trip to schools across the reservation. And as Royer waited in Rushville for rescue by the army, Miss Goodale, among other things, was visiting Ghost Dances and (she later reported) finding the reservation peaceful and the people friendly—until the moment they heard of the coming of the troops.

Aboard one of the troop trains chugging through the Nebraska darkness on the night of the eighteenth was C. H. Cressey, a reporter for the *Omaha Daily Bee*. Having gotten himself authorized as a "war correspondent" for the Sioux disturbances, Cressey was determined to see that there was actually a war for him to correspond about. During that first night he was already at work on it, conducting interviews and preparing a story that appeared in the *Bee* on the nineteenth:

ON TO THE FRONT

The Bee's War Correspondent Pushing Forward
to Pine Ridge Agency

. . . I had another talk with Maj. Burke and Nelson, the old scout . . . who, by the way, has spent sixty years among those northern Indians. . . . Without saying a word to influence their reply, I asked them how they felt by this time.

"I wish it was morning. I wish this night was past and I wish we were safely at Pine Ridge Agency," said the major with a troubled brow.

"And I too wish it as strongly as a man can wish," said the old graybearded scout. . . .

"Tell me," I said, "Do you really fear that bloodshed is ahead of us . . . ?"

"No one can tell," said the scout with trembling emphasis. "My fear lies in the apprehension that they will be given fire water by some white dog on our arrival, but I hope to God that it will be otherwise. No one can tell, though. No one can tell."

Nothing was plainer, as I watched the old man's face, than his heart quaked with fear of what the morrow would bring forth. . . .

On the afternoon of November 19 the troops arrived at Rushville, where they were to detrain and march to Pine Ridge. As Cressey's old scout had feared, there *was* firewater and there *was* bloodshed. The *Chadron* (Nebraska) *Advocate* (in its first official acknowledgment that there even was an Indian problem) put it this way:

The depot grounds at Rushville presented a busy appearance while the cars were being unloaded. And it was here that the first blood was shed in the campaign. Two 9th Cavalry negroes engaged in a drunken fight. One of them drew a revolver and struck the other a smashing blow in the ear. At this point Lieut. Wright rushed up, and in whipping out his sword in great haste, accidentally struck John Barry, the well known stock agent for the railroad, a sharp clip on the ear. Blood flowed freely. The ambulance corps, consisting of Dr. Waller and [*Advocate* reporter] John Maher came galloping to the rescue. A special dispatch of the battle was sent to the *Omaha World Herald*, while Barry retreated to the railroad right-of-way and proceeded to throw up entrenchements till darkness came and ended the sanguinary engagement.

As the troops prepared for the night march to Pine Ridge, a rumor swept through the news reporters who were with them that there had already been some sort of battle at Pine Ridge. The special correspondent for the *Chicago Daily Tribune* filed a story that was subsequently headlined:

REDSKINS BLOODY WORK

Stories Received of a Conflict at
Pine Ridge Agency

LOSS OF LIFE REPORTED

A Courier Declared the Killed and
Wounded Number 60

There was no truth to the report, of course. But—interestingly—while the correspondents for the "foreign" papers were busy playing it up, the reporter for the local *Chadron Advocate* concluded *his* coverage of the developing Indian "scare" by saying:

> There has been no great amount of fright on the part of the settlers between here and Pine Ridge. Farmers from Beaver and Dry Creek valleys report everybody jogging along as usual in their neighborhoods.

General Miles's strategy, as he had outlined it to General Brooke, was to take the Indians by surprise. Fighting was to be avoided at all costs, the purpose of the army being to quiet the turbulence on the reservations rather than to cause more. Hence, if the troops were to advance on Pine Ridge during the daytime, word would be spread in advance of them so that at best a great many Indians would flee in panic, and at worst a fight would break out. Therefore, the troops would march at night, planning to arrive at Pine Ridge about four o'clock in the morning. This would be some three hours before sunrise and would give the troops time to be properly organized and deployed while it was still too dark for the Indians to collect themselves for either flight or fighting. This strategy was to be applied at Rosebud as well. Thus, as Brooke marched from Rushville to Pine Ridge, Lieutenant Colonel A. T. Smith would be leading a similar force—a hundred and twenty miles to the east—from Valentine to Rosebud.

The soldiers in Brooke's force who were detraining at Rushville that afternoon, like so many of the troops that were sent to Sioux country during the Messiah disturbance, were in the main neither seasoned campaigners nor even very experienced army men. To be sure, there was a sprinkling of grizzled old veterans of ancient wars and Indian campaigns among them, but for the most part they were young and, never having been west before, knew nothing of Indians except what they had read in lurid dime novels and other melodramatic Indian fiction of the time. When it came to Indians, the sensationalism of the novelists then knew no bounds. One typical example from *Buffalo Bill's Raid of Death* (at a point where the hero is spying on the Sioux) reads:

> . . . they could hear the excited talk of the Sioux . . . recounting the acts of daring with which they would throw themselves on the hated whites.
> And the squaws, more fiendish, even, than the warriors, made themselves happy by talking of various plans of torture they would exercise on the white squaws and warriors and children who should be brought to the village.
> "Such people have no proper place on the face of the earth," was the thought of the scout, as he listened to them. . . . "They are really devils on earth, and I don't know that they deserve an atom of pity from the heart of any man. . . ."
> It was a conclusion that most soldiers and frontiersmen came to, who had much dealings with Indians.

With this sort of background for soldiers who were about to be thrown into close contact with a large number of Sioux, the unseasoned young troops were understandably nervous and excited. The people of Rushville were excited, too, with all the commotion in their ordinarily sleepy hamlet, and after an early supper most of them turned out to watch the confusion along the railroad tracks. Since the sun set well before five o'clock in November, night came on early. Thus, it was in gathering darkness that horses were being fed and watered and saddled or hitched to wagons, and the various units of infantry and cavalry were getting themselves and their equipment sorted out as they began gathering in their designated assembly areas. A haze of woodsmoke that rose and flattened in the evening calm lay over all as the fires of the field kitchens twinkled in the dusk and the troops were given supper.

Afterward, Brooke formed them up for travel. There were five companies of infantry totaling about two hundred men. In front of them, to lead the march into Pine Ridge, were three troops (about 170 men) of the impressive all-black Ninth Cavalry. The Sioux sometimes called these the Wasicun Sapa (the Black White Men), but more often they called them the Buffalo Soldiers. Some people said the Indians called them that because they thought the black men's hair was like that of the buffalo; others said it was because of their heavy buffalo-hide coats. But whichever, the Ninth would have little need for their coats tonight.

The day had been unseasonably warm, and the temperature at eight o'clock was still well above fifty degrees. Thus, it was a beautiful night for marching (if there ever *is* a beautiful night for it), and as they moved out of Rushville, there was a half-moon riding high in the clear night sky. Until it set at about midnight they had its light to help them along. After moonset the march did become more difficult—especially on the steep, winding trail down the Pine Ridge itself, just a few miles south of the agency. There swearing teamsters set wooden brake-blocks to rasping against iron tires as they tried to control their wagons on slopes they could not gauge, and occasionally a wagon overturned when the driver missed a bend he could not see. One wagon, in fact, fell on its driver and crushed his hip. Despite such hindrances, however, Brooke was not too far behind schedule when—with a newly confident Royer trotting beside him in a buggy—he led his detachment into the Pine Ridge agency.

When the Indians who were camped around the agency awoke on the morning of November 20, they were shocked, confused, and uncertain. They had heard stories that the soldiers were coming, but seeing them actually here . . . the Buffalo Soldiers and the walking soldiers, the Hotchkiss cannon and Gatling gun that were already in place for shooting, the tall white Sibley tents of the army being set up row upon row instead of in circles as a camp should be, the bugles sounding, and to the south a long line of white-topped supply wagons still coming (which meant the soldiers were planning to stay) . . . A-h-h-h! It was a thing that was both angering and frightening. This was not Wasicun land. It did not belong to the United States; it belonged to the Lakotah. All the treaty papers said so. These soldiers of the Wasicun had no business on it. Moreover, it was being said that they had come to stop the sacred Wanagi Wacipi (the Dance of the Ghosts) and they had no business doing that either. Some of the people, therefore, loaded their tipis on their wagons and fled in fright, part of them going where they could continue to dance. But most of them waited, bewildered and unsure, to see what their chiefs would have to say after talking with the soldier chief.

The moment Brooke arrived at Pine Ridge he had sent messengers riding to all the camps on the reservation with the message that he wanted the people to come immediately to the agency and camp there, and that those who did not come would receive no more rations. He also said that if the people did obey the order, the army would protect their rights to the fullest extent that it was able to, and that this included trying to get their rations increased. When the Lakotah heard the message, they would have found the last words hopeful had they not heard so many such words before that had come to nothing. The first part, however, the words about cutting off their rations, was frightening to people who were already hungry. And so, as hunger had opened many of their ears to the message of the Messiah, the prospect of even more hunger closed many of them again. Thus, by the end of the first day most of the Pine Ridge Oglala were ready to give up the dream of buffalo in the sky tomorrow in exchange for the actuality of something in the cooking pot today, and the people began coming in.

There were exceptions, of course. The bands of Big Road, No Water, Little Wound, and a few others not only stayed out, but began dancing for the coming of the new world with renewed intensity. One of them, Little Wound, sent a return message saying,

> . . . What have we done? We have done nothing. Our dance is a religious one, and we are going to dance until spring. If we find then that the new Christ does not appear we will stop dancing, but in the meantime, troops or no troops, we are going to start our dance at [Medicine Root] creek this morning. . . .
>
> I have also been told that you intend to stop our rations and annuities. Well, for my part I don't care. The little rations we get do not amount to anything. . . . We do not intend to stop the dancing.

Then Little Wound sent couriers galloping that night to all the Pine Ridge communities to say that those who wished to keep the sacred dance should gather on White Clay Creek near where Agent Gallagher had tried to stop the dance last August. As a result, there were some from every community who headed for White Clay instead of to the agency. All in all, however, the army's first day at Pine Ridge was peaceful, and the prospects for continued peace were encouraging.

On the other hand, when the Easterners read the news stories filed from Pine Ridge that day, they hardly got that same impression. Most of the correspondents at Pine Ridge were so convinced (or hopeful) that they were about to be involved in the wildest of Indian wars that they had arrived draped with bandoliers of ammunition and were so heavily armed that, as one of them wryly observed later, they were "round-shouldered because of the weapons and missiles they have had to carry around." Moreover, they seemed determined to pass on their own convictions to the reading public. Some of their first-day stories were headlined:

Chicago Daily Tribune

IN A STATE OF TERROR

Great Excitement at the Pine
Ridge Agency

Indians Dancing with Guns

. . . . . .
. . . . . .

Women and Children Still Fleeing to Points
Of Safety

Fighting Expected at Any Moment

New York Times

The Messiah Expected To Arrive At
The Pine Ridge Agency To-day,
When The Savages Will Fight

Omaha Daily Bee

WITH RIFLE ON BACK

The Red Skins Are Dancing The
Dreaded Ghost Dance

Had the correspondents been at Rosebud when the Indians awoke that day to find soldiers in their midst, they would have found the facts a good deal more in keeping with the stories they were writing. Many of the Indians at Rosebud did exactly as the ones at Pine Ridge had done—they started for the agency with the intention of camping peacefully there as they had been ordered to do. But through many of the Brulé bands, when they heard the order of the soldier chief, anger swept quick and hot as fire through a pine grove. Most of them had heard the good words of Short Bull at Black Pipe Creek when he had told them that the Wanikiye was coming after only one more moon. Part of that moon had already passed. Now the new world was so near they could almost hear the buffalo cropping at the green grass beside its clear streams. Should they stop dancing now and give up that heaven that was so close, just because of the order from a soldier chief, especially when Short Bull had told them that any soldier trying to stop them would sink into the earth? Hiya! No! They would not give it up! They would die first! The soldier chief had also sent word there would be no more rations for those who stayed out and danced, but that was all right. They would move away from the soldiers, and they would seize food wherever they found it. And so, before the sun had even touched the top of the sky, the bands of Eagle Pipe, Turning Bear, High Hawk, No Flesh, Lance, Crow Dog, Pine Bird, and Two Strike—well over a thousand people—began moving westward, ready to fight anyone or anything that tried to stop them.

On the second day of the army's occupation, November 21, the roads across the vast expanses of both reservations were alive with lines of people and wagons and horses. Except for those already camped at the agencies or those in the few scattered dance camps, all of the eleven thousand Indians of the two reservations were in motion—going somewhere. To General Brooke, in overall charge of both the Rosebud and the Pine Ridge operations, the giant question now was, *where* were they going? While trying to find out, the general continued his policy of restraint and was careful to make no threatening moves. He went so far, in fact, that, contrary to standard military practice in such situations, he didn't even send out any military scouting patrols for fear the Indians might misunderstand their intentions. Instead, he depended entirely on the reports of the Indian scouts and Indian police that he had out crisscrossing the reservations, talking to people and observing.

The general was well aware, that second day, that his troops at both agencies were substantially outnumbered by well-armed Indians of as yet unknown intentions, and it is reasonable to assume that as he waited for enough reports to come in to give some sort of picture of the situation he was having an anxious time of it. But General Brooke (portly, round-faced, moustachioed, and with white hair combed back in such a way that the top of his head looked flat) was an austere, withdrawn man. If he did feel any anxiety, it was securely hidden beneath an exterior of cold, detached calm.

By evening things began to sort themselves out. At Pine Ridge Indians had been flocking into the agency all day, and about the only Oglalas who were still out and not on their way in were the people of Big Road, No Water, and Little Wound, plus a fairly small gathering at the mouth of White Clay Creek. On the Rosebud, all but one of the hostile bands that had started west had now turned north toward Short Bull's dance camp at the mouth of Pass Creek where (he had said) the sacred tree was sprouting. That was the band of Nomp Karpa (Two Strike). Fierce old Two Strike, declaring that he, personally, was going to stab General Brooke to death, was reported to be heading directly toward Pine Ridge agency, eighty miles or so to the west.

Throughout the following days, Brooke continued his policy of patience and restraint, thereby incurring a considerable amount of criticism by the press for not aggressively pursuing the "redskins" and forcing them to heel by sheer armed might. Nevertheless, his tactics were showing good results. On November 23, Big Road and No Water and their people came in to camp peacefully at the agency. On the twenty-sixth, the diehard Little Wound did the same. By the morning of Thanksgiving day, the twenty-seventh, the only Pine Ridge people still out were the ones who had gathered at the mouth of White Clay Creek, and there weren't too many of those. On that day Brooke ordered Royer to make a full issue of beef in accordance with the terms of the Agreement of 1876—the first such issue at Pine Ridge in several years. Thus, on Thanksgiving day the people of Pine Ridge feasted.

At Rosebud, however, the Indians weren't giving up so easily. Two Strike's people, plundering the deserted Indian cabins and taking Indian livestock as they traveled, had reached Wounded Knee Creek, only fifteen miles east of Pine Ridge agency. Seemingly, Two Strike had given up his idea of killing Brooke, for he stopped on Wounded Knee and joined forces with a small band of Wazazas who were already there and then resumed the dancing.

Meanwhile, after the other Rosebud hostiles had joined the prophet, Short Bull, at the mouth of Pass Creek, he began leading the entire group southwestward along White River, taking cattle from the agency's White River herd as they went. On about the twenty-seventh, they came to the Oglalas gathered at the mouth of White Clay, and there the Brulés pitched their lodges and began to dance again for the coming of the new world and the end of the white man.

On the second night of the dancing, as Short Bull told it later, four stars came down from heaven and spoke to him. They told him to lead the people north into the Makoce Sica (the Bad Lands) to the place the Indians called the Stronghold. Christ was now ready to return to earth, the stars said, and as soon as the people were assembled and dancing in the Stronghold, He would come to them there. Now Short Bull was certain the new world was truly at hand, and he wanted to save all the Lakotah who still had ears for the glorious message of the Messiah. He therefore sent swift messengers to Two Strike at Wounded Knee, to Kicking Bear at Cheyenne River, and even to the far north to Sitting Bull at Grand River and asked all of them to come to the Stronghold to greet the Wanikiye when he arrived.

On the following day—Saturday, November 29—Short Bull and his throng of now nearly a thousand Indian pilgrims began moving northeastward down the White River preparatory to turning north into the Makoce Sica. At about the same time, the Two Strike people started north down Wounded Knee toward White River, again (and strangely for people about to enter the new world) thoroughly plundering the vacant Indian settlements along the way. On December 1, Two Strike and Short Bull met on the White River. Now, for the first time, all the remaining Ghost Dancers of both reservations were gathered together into one group.

From the points of view of Generals Miles and Brooke, their strategy of patience was proving to be successful. Now the hostiles were not only identified and collected together but were also isolated, and behind them the reservations were calm. Furthermore, Pine Ridge had received massive military reinforcements—including the famous Seventh Cavalry —and Rosebud had been reinforced, also. And finally, still other troops were now on their way to carry out Miles's plan of throwing a cordon around the disturbed areas. When that was done, the one remaining hot spot of turbulence and hostility would be sealed off, and (hopefully) the Indians surrounded there could then be persuaded to give up. If they did not, their excitement would probably soon die out anyhow. If neither occurred, as a last resort, they could be starved into submission. So, all in all, from the army's point of view, on December 1 things look encouraging.

At the same time, however, things also looked encouraging to the Indian pilgrims making their way into the Makoce Sica that day. To the white men it was now the month of December, but to the Lakotah, it was the beginning of the Moon of Popping Trees—a moon so named because of the way the jack pines made a sound like the crack of a rifle shooting when they became very cold. And ordinarily it was a moon of endings, with all of the growing things of the past year frozen and dead and with a long wait yet before the living things of the coming year could sprout and grow. But not this year. This year the Moon of Popping Trees was a moon of new beginnings, with the Indian Christ and the green spring grass of the new world so near now that the people would see them at the Stronghold.

There was a great throng of them going north, maybe as many as twelve hundred people, and the line of wagons and horses and food cattle plundered from the agency herd stretched along the trail for miles. And because they were so many, the people felt very strong now, not only for keeping the soldiers away, but also for making such strong praying that the Wanikiye would be sure to hear and to come to them. Moreover, Kicking Bear was with them now, and his strong words, together with those of Short Bull, warmed them. That was good, for with the way the weather was turning, they needed the warming. Cold gray storm clouds were rolling down from the Paha Sapa (Black Hills) to the northwest, and with them came a scattering of snowflakes and a thin, cutting, northwest wind that icily probed its way through their tattered clothing. But as the Indians pushed on toward their first goal—the clifflike side of a big mesa called Cuny Table, which they could see rising in the far distance—they thought about that new land they were going to where everybody was young and happy and all their relatives were alive again, and they forgot the cold and pressed on farther until darkness forced them to camp. The next day, in worsening weather, they wound their way up Cuny Table's south wall, then on for several miles across its top to the northern edge. There, they filed across a narrow land bridge a quarter-mile or so long and, in places, no wider than fifty feet to another and much smaller mesa. This second mesa was a flat grassland a little more than a mile long and about half as wide, and except for where the little land bridge connected it to the main mesa, it was entirely surrounded by almost sheer bluffs that dropped away for four hundred feet to the bottomland below. There were two springs on this mesa, and in the heads of the steep gullies in its roughly eroded sides, there was wood. This was the Stronghold—so remote that few white men even knew it existed, and accessible only by a land bridge so narrow that dozens could defend it against hundreds. And here, with the temperature now fallen to ten degrees above zero or lower, the Messiah's last true believers from Pine Ridge and Rosebud pitched their lodges on its flat unsheltered top in the blowing snow and settled down to dance and wait for the coming of Christ.

As soon as the first dramatic stories from Pine Ridge appeared in print, press correspondents were drawn to the agency like small boys to an unloading circus train. So many reporters arrived that in a very few days the demand for news had far outstripped the available supply. At that point (according to W. A. Birdsall, a Pine Ridge resident and guide for the army at the time) a group of shrewd local mixed-bloods and squaw-men, who recognized the potential profit in such a situation, set up a "news factory" to supply the shortage. The "factory" operated in one of Pine Ridge's favorite loafer hangouts—the back room of Asay Bro.'s Store—and was composed of Ott Means, Nick Janis, Doc Middleton, John Y. Nelson, and possibly others. The "outside" man of the enterprise was Tim Crimmins, who had been hired by the reporters to carry their dispatches to the telegraph at Rushville since Brooke was refusing to let the press use the Pine Ridge telegraph. Obviously, the more news there was, the more dispatches there were to be carried; and the more dispatches carried, the greater were Crimmins's profits. So with this incentive, he also functioned (in Birdsall's words) as a "camp scavenger"—gathering all the raw rumors and grapevine gossip possible and then taking them to the back room at Asay's for "processing." There, Means and Janis and the others tailored them into marketable form and then sold them to the correspondents. Birdsall later commented on the results of this operation saying that it provided "employment and pay to all concerned" and also that because of it, the country was "criminally misled." If such a news factory actually existed, it is certain that the local reporters would have been far less likely to use it than the "foreign" reporters. And the strong evidence that such a thing *did* exist lies in the fact that the discrepancy between the local and the "foreign" reporting of the Ghost Dance troubles at Pine Ridge must surely have been as great as in any event in American history. For instance, the *Chicago Daily Tribune* story datelined November 25 was headed:

GETTING READY TO FIGHT

The Indians Massing for a Stand
Against the Troops

Reds Ready for a Battle

And on the same day, Cressey of the *Omaha Daily Bee* wrote:

Things are just at that point today where the firing of a gun would undoubtedly precipitate a fight to the finish.

Whereas a reporter for the *Chadron* (Nebraska) *Advocate*, who had spent November 25 and 26 at Pine Ridge, wrote:

> It is hard, after visiting Pine Ridge Agency, to write with patience of the liars, big and little, who have filled the continent with scare headlines and inflammatory reports in the past two weeks. . . .
> We left Pine Ridge Agency Wednesday afternoon. It is a peaceful, orderly, well-behaved place. . . . Indian babies and children filled the streets. Soldiers were washing their garments and hanging them out to dry. The smoke of a thousand teepees rose in the still, hazy air; twice a thousand ponies grazed on the sunny hillsides. There was peace at Pine Ridge, whatever might be at the homes of frightened settlers and in the great newspaper offices.

The *Pierre* (South Dakota) *Free Press*, which had investigators out in the territory on and around the reservations at the time, also observed:

> If ever a stupendous fake was better faked . . . than this latest Sioux Indian hostility racket, please tell us about it! . . . it is when one approaches the alleged scenes of hostility that he begins to comprehend the dimensions of the grand farce. After getting into hostile country the visitor becomes so disgusted with the utter lack of signs of hostility that he becomes ugly himself, and a disposition to shoot something is almost irresistable.

But on November 27, Cressey of the *Bee* reported:

> The chances for blood and trouble generally are as good today as they were a week ago. . . . I, for one, of the correspondents here, propose to continue to warn the public that there is still grave danger from many thousands of Indians at Pine Ridge Agency. . . .
> . . . Will we ever get out of this with our hair? Or, will we get out of it at all? are the questions the latest news suggests. . . .

The *Rapid City* (South Dakota) *Journal* on the same day said:

> Everything was quiet today at the [Pine Ridge] agency and no trouble was expected.

Then, on November 28, the correspondents for both the *Chicago Daily Tribune* and the *New York Times* filed stories that sounded suspiciously like products of the news factory in the back room of Asay's store. The *Tribune* story was headlined:

ON THE EVE OF A BATTLE

. . . . . .
. . . . . .

Will Probably Be A Collision With
Hostiles This Morning

And the *Times* reporter announced:

> Couriers who have just reported to Gen. Brooke say that the redskins are
> dancing in circles . . . and their village has been so changed that the
> lodges form a circle. . . .
> When the couriers were before Gen. Brooke, the latter asked the
> significance of the circling Indians. One of the couriers, who is a
> half-breed, smiled and said: "The Sioux never dance that dance except for
> one purpose, and that is for war."

Also on November 28, Editor Charles Moody of the *Sturgis* (South
Dakota) *Weekly Record* loaded his pen, took aim at the sensation-
mongers, and opened fire:

> Isn't is about time some of these wild and wooly newspaper liars . . . be
> spanked and sent out of harm's way? . . . There never was any danger of
> an Indian outbreak, and none exists now, unless these silly sensational
> reports have scared people into acts that might properly be construed by
> an Indian into a desire to fight. Only a few days ago some damphool from
> Hot Springs sent out a report that a body of Indians were camped near
> that place, and that the citizens were organizing to defend themselves.
> That lie was actually telegraphed all over the United States. . . .
> It is a well known fact that Indians have been buying cartridges
> wherever they could for the last ten years. They all have guns and they love
> to shoot . . . firing off a gun is about the greatest form of dissipation they
> are acquainted with. Yet the mere fact of one of them asking for a
> cartridge is accepted as red-eyed proof of murder.
> It would pay the immigration department of South Dakota to lynch the
> majority of these liars . . . and stand the expense. . . . This ghost dance
> has been worked up into a very wonderful and exciting matter by
> pinheaded "war correspondents" and other irresponsible parties until they
> have succeeded in massing nearly half the United States army to be
> spectators to an Indian pow wow. . . .
> W. F. Steele, boss farmer at Pine Ridge, writes that he don't see
> anything to cause all this foolishness, although he is in a position to see it
> first. . . . Mr. Steele winds up by saying, "There has been no more
> excitement here than there would be in a fourth ward primary."

Then, while thoroughly warmed up and going strong, Mr. Moody also expressed himself on the subject of the settler panic in North Dakota:

> The *Mandan Pioneer* and the local correspondents of that place are entitled to an immense amount of credit for their success in having Ft. Lincoln reoccupied. The Indian scare was a shrewd scheme. . . . Now that a good trade at the fort is assured for the winter, and every desire has been gratified . . . it is hoped that the same industry and invention will be turned towards allaying apprehension, restoring confidence, and contributing to arrest the havoc caused by the insane fear so systematically worked up. . . .

On the other hand, however, there was at least one "foreign" reporter at Pine Ridge who did do his best to report accurately on affairs there. He was Carl Smith of the *Omaha World Herald*, and as a consequence of his diligence, he very quickly found himself unpopular with most of the other correspondents when his restrained dispatches almost invariably contradicted their more flamboyant ones. Even more quickly, he also found himself in trouble with Agent Royer. As Smith told it:

> My first dispatch was headed in such a way as to lead to the inference that he [Royer] was frightened. Mr. Royer . . . spoke to me about this and said that if the paper proposed any reflection of that sort he would expel me from the agency.

Smith then referred the Royer matter to his paper and immediately received a return wire saying,

> . . . the man who expels the representative of the *World Herald* because of adverse criticism will have to answer to the secretary in Washington. Show this to whomever you think should see it.

Although Smith was able to remain for a time on the basis of that strong response, from that moment his days at Pine Ridge were numbered. Shortly after his story of December 1, they ran out. The story was headlined (in part):

AGENT ROYER'S LACK OF EXPERIENCE AND
NERVE WAS RESPONSIBLE FOR ALL
THE SCARE THAT EXISTED

How He Treated The "World-Herald's"
Correspondent—Indians Have Not and
Do Not Want To Fight

and included in the story were the following observations;

> Mr. Royer seemed determined not to believe that there would not be
> carnage. After a time it became apparent to me and to every Army officer
> in the post—and most are Old Indian fighters—that Mr. Royer was trying
> to substantiate the fright which had caused him to call upon the troops. I
> do not wish to do anybody . . . an injustice, but there is not a
> circumstance which does not point to anything but a weak backbone, a
> vacillating spirit, and I may say from my own experience, a principle
> which would not cause him to hesitate to lie to a white man, to say nothing
> of an Indian. . . .
>   To hold his job Mr. Royer may succeed in aggravating these Indians
> into some sort of warlike demonstration, but it will be fighting against their
> will. . . .

As agent, Royer had the power to deny access to the reservation to
anyone who was not there on official government business. Moreover,
when it came to correspondents, he had the full cooperation of General
Brooke, who had no love for the press, himself. Hence, within three days
of the appearance of his story, Smith was evicted from Pine Ridge.
Interestingly, though, he was not expelled for "adverse criticism," nor
was he expelled by Royer. He was ordered from the agency by General
Brooke for the reason that Smith had been getting his news stories by
listening in on the army's Pine Ridge telegraph. (If true, this might very
well be the first case of wiretapping by the press.)

However, as upsetting as Carl Smith may have been to Royer during
the first days of December, he was no more than an incidental nuisance
to General Brooke, who had far weightier matters on his mind.
Specifically, he was trying to figure out how to get the Indians down off
the Stronghold and into the agency. On the first of December he had sent
some friendlies out to talk to them; on the second they returned to say
that the Messiah believers not only wouldn't talk, but instead, they had
fired bullets over the friendlies' heads. On December 3 Brooke tried to
get them off again, this time putting together a negotiating team of two
people so completely different from each other that between them there
just might be a chance of success. One was gentle, seventy-year-old
Father John Jutz, a Catholic priest in charge of Holy Rosary Mission
four miles north of the agency and a great favorite with the Indians. The

other was Jack Red Cloud, who had recently defected from the dance camp at the mouth of White Clay Creek.

That they were willing to start out for the Stronghold in the wretched weather of that afternoon of December 3 is clear testimony to their dedication to the mission. The day had warmed up somewhat from the morning low of near zero, but it was still well below freezing. Also, a light snow and a stiff wind had combined to produce a near-blizzard. The only favorable thing they could say for the weather was that the wind had swung to the southeast, so that as they headed their buggy down the White Clay Creek road, they had it at their backs.

By road it was forty miles from Pine Ridge to the south wall of Cuny Table, and they did not reach it until the following afternoon. When they did, they were stopped by a line of Indian pickets and were detained for hours while a messenger rode the additional ten miles to the Stronghold to see if they were to be permitted to proceed, then rode the ten miles back to tell them that they were. As a result, it was eleven o'clock at night when Jack Red Cloud and Father Jutz finally arrived at the Stronghold. They immediately went into council with the chiefs of the dance camp. Then, while the cold wind rippled and slapped at the canvas of the council lodge, they sat in a circle around a juniper fire and talked throughout the night. By dawn Father Jutz had finally persuaded six of the chiefs—the most important being old Two Strike—to come into the agency for a council with General Brooke.

It was still bitter cold and snowing the morning of December 5 when the old priest, who had had no rest for the past twenty-four hours, with Jack Red Cloud, the six chiefs, and an escort of twenty-five armed warriors set out. They camped at Holy Rosary Mission that night, and the next morning they went on in to the agency. When they entered Pine Ridge, they did so proudly. The tails of the young warriors' horses were tied up with ribbons, and there were eagle feathers in their manes. The warriors themselves were carrying Winchesters and were painted and dressed in the old way with fringed leggings and quilled moccasins. The only new thing they were wearing was their ghost shirts. They rode in as if in a parade. Leading them was a warrior prancing his horse and carrying a white flag. Next came a group of warriors, then five of the chiefs, and last a buggy flanked by four more warriors in which Father Jutz and Two Strike were riding together. The Indians had been hesitant about going into Pine Ridge with its thousand or more soldiers, and twice they had almost turned back. Both times they were prevented only by Father Jutz's insisting that if the whites hurt any of them, they were then free to kill him. And so, even though they were afraid, and even though the white men now ran their lives, they came in the old way, proudly, as if neither of these things were true.

In the long council that followed, Brooke had a strong new incentive to offer as he tried to talk the chiefs into bringing their people in. Only the day before he had been notified that the War Department would commence furnishing the additional food required to give the Sioux full rations as specified in the Agreement of 1876, to become effective immediately. Thus, Brooke was able to tell the chiefs that if their people would come in and camp at the agency, there would be plenty of food and nobody would have to go hungry anymore. There was a stir and murmuring as the chiefs heard these good words, for their people had lived too long with hunger. Furthermore, the soldier chief was now saying that if they came in he would also give the young men scouting jobs so they could have some money. The chiefs agreed that those were good words, too. But . . . maybe that was all they were, and if so, their people could neither eat good words nor get money for them. The chiefs were hesitant and noncommittal, first sounding as if they might come in, then as if they might not. Finally, Turning Bear suggested it would be a good thing if they were given something to eat right now. Agreeing readily, Brooke ordered the agent to make a special issue, and the council ended with a feast.

On the following day (December 7), the Indians, accompanied by thirty-two friendlies, returned to the Stronghold. Also with them was the mixed-blood scout, Louis Shangreau, carrying a special message from General Brooke. The weather had turned sunny and was warming up, and by the time they reached the Stronghold, everyone there was so involved in the Ghost Dancing that it was the following day before Shangreau could even get a council called to hear the general's message. When he finally did, he said to them,

> The agent will forgive you if you come in now, and he will also increase your rations. The only restriction is that you may not do the ghost dance.

Short Bull's reply was just as direct,

> If the Great Father would allow us to *continue* the dance, would give us more rations, and would quit taking away pieces of our reservation, I

would favor returning. . . . [But] if we return he will take away our guns and ponies, and put some of us in jail for stealing cattle and plundering houses. . . . We are free now and have plenty of beef, and can dance all the time in obedience to the command of Wakan Tanka. We tell you to return to your agent and say to him that the Lakotah in the Makoce Sica are not coming in.

With that the dancing began again and continued for two days. Then on December 10 there was another council at which Two Strike rose to his feet and announced that he was taking his people to Pine Ridge. Next, Crow Dog stood and said he was going to do the same. Instantly Short Bull leaped to his feet shouting,

At such a time we should stick together like brothers! These agency men are lying! They will take you to the agency and put you in jail! Louis [Shangreau] is at the bottom of this! He is a traitor! Kill him! Kill him!

Some of the dancers charged at Shangreau with clubbed rifles. Then the agency friendlies formed a defense around him; whereupon a big fight started with the men swinging stone-headed war clubs, shooting arrows, and firing guns. It was a big gravy-stirring—so hot that although it has never been known if any were killed, it is definite that many were hurt. When the medicine man chief, Crow Dog, saw what the people were doing to each other, he was greatly dismayed. Only nine years before he himself had murdered the great Brulé chief, Spotted Tail, after a quarrel between factions, and he knew well what such things could lead to. He made his way to the very center of the fighting, sat down, and pulled his blanket entirely over his head. At that, the warring suddenly stopped. When it did, Crow Dog rose, threw off the blanket, and extending his arms he cried out,

Brothers! Stop this! I cannot bear to see Lakotah shedding Lakotah blood! I am going now to the agency. You can kill me if you wish, [but] the great father's words are true. It is better to return than to stay here. I am not afraid to die.

After these words there was no more fighting. Instead, all but a few of the people hitched up their horses, loaded their lodges and lodge poles onto wagons, and began moving across the narrow land bridge and south toward the agency. At first Short Bull and Kicking Bear and a small group of hard-core faithful remained behind. Then they, too, struck their lodges, loaded their wagons, and drove away from the Stronghold. But five miles out on Cuny Table they stopped. A-h-h-h! This was too great a surrender to make! With the new world so soon to come for those who continued the dance, they would not give it up now. No! They would not! So the two high priests, Short Bull and Kicking Bear, turned back to the Stronghold accompanied by a few more than two hundred people—the last of their following among the Oglala and the Brulé.

Behind them, going in the other direction, the others—nearly a thousand people—followed Two Strike and Crow Dog slowly southward toward the agency. And with their going went the beautiful Indian dream that had so recently flamed across the Pine Ridge and Rosebud reservations. Nothing was left of it now but the one dim spark that Short Bull and Kicking Bear were trying to keep alive on the Stronghold mesa.

When General Miles learned that conditions at Pine Ridge and Rosebud were cooling down, he turned more of his attention to Cheyenne River and Standing Rock. Among the Indian believers on those reservations the Messiah dream was still bright and the dancing still strong, and Miles remained firmly convinced that only by stamping out the Ghost Dance faith on every one of the reservations could an Indian war be avoided.

CHAPTER
11
/\./\./\./\./\

Sitting Bull

ON NOVEMBER 24, when General Miles chose Buffalo Bill Cody to make the arrest of Sitting Bull, he did so because he believed the two men were friends and the arrest could therefore be made peacefully. Although he also believed that Cody was a master at the ways of the frontier, in that respect, Miles may have mistaken the reputation for the man. Undoubtedly, in bygone years Cody *had* been a competent frontiersman and scout (and possibly he still was), but when he later became a showman, he did so to the extent that he himself must have found it hard to tell when he was acting and when he was not. Furthermore, he had never been overafflicted with modesty. Those things, added to the fact that for a number of years he had been the hero of a wildly romantic dime-novel series, make it easy to understand why, by 1890, it was difficult to tell how much of Cody was talk and how much was talent, or to know how much about him was fact and how much fiction. One thing, however, emerges clear. To Buffalo Bill, publicity and adventure were the meat and bread of life; in the case of necessity he might have been able to subsist on only one of them, but in order to subsist well, he had to have both. General Miles's orders to arrest Sitting Bull gave him an opportunity to enjoy a glorious combination of the two. Hence, on November 24, the ink was hardly dry on his orders when he boarded a train at Chicago for the northwest. And being the kind of man who finds adventure the sweetest when shared, Cody stopped off in Wisconsin long enough to pick up three old cronies to join him. Then, proceeding on, he reached Bismarck on November 27, where his arrival was recorded in the *Bismarck Daily Tribune* thus:

> Among the distinguished people who alighted from yesterday morning's Pacific Express was Col. Cody—"Buffalo Bill"—, his old time friend, Dr. Frank Powell, better known as "White Beaver," John Keith, manager of Cody's ranch at North Platte, Neb., and R. H. Haslin, known as "Pony Bob," . . . Buffalo Bill bears an important commission from Gen. Miles and is on his way to Sitting Bull's camp on Grand River. The details of the commission cannot be made public at this present, but it may be surmised that Buffalo Bill will find out all there is to know of this Messiah humbug craze before he returns, or know the reason why. . . . A dangerous man to fool with is Buffalo Bill. . . .

The instant the "dangerous man to fool with" stepped off the Pacific Express in Bismarck, he went into action. Within hours he had hired two wagons and a wagon master named Con Malloy; he had bought a whole load of presents for Sitting Bull, including a huge amount of candy for the chief's insatiable sweet tooth; he had loaded the whole expedition—now increased by either four or five newspaper reporters—onto a special chartered train, and had then taken it across the Missouri River to Mandan, ten miles to the west. So swiftly was all this accomplished that by two-thirty that afternoon Cody and his entourage were heading their wagons south out of Mandan and toward Standing Rock.

After an overnight stop at Parkin's ranch, just north of the reservation, Buffalo Bill—clad in his Wild West Show dress suit, patent leather shoes, and silk stockings—and his troop of reporters and cronies rolled into Fort Yates, just across the road from Standing Rock agency. His arrival on November 28 brought no joy to either the post commandant, Lieutenant Colonel William F. Drum, nor to the agent, James McLaughlin. Drum had a true soldier's regard for military channels and procedures, and he resented being bypassed in such a critical matter by a civilian—especially one engaged in what so obviously seemed to be a publicity stunt. Although Whitehair McLaughlin was still of the opinion that Sitting Bull would have to be arrested eventually, he was also of the opinion that the only persons who could possibly arrest him peacefully were the Indian police, and even they would have to time it just right. But now, of all things, Sitting Bull was going to be arrested by this dapper dandy in comic-opera costume—this . . . this . . . *showman* with his ridiculous retinue of reporters and thrill-seekers. Impossible!

Drum and McLaughlin both agreed that the whole thing was a dangerous farce and that Cody could bungle it to the point of either getting somebody killed, or else starting a war, or possibly both. If only they had time, they might—just might—get his orders cancelled, and if the rumors of Cody's fondness for the bottle were true, they had a plan for making the time. Accordingly, they invited Cody to share a glass with some of the Fort Yates officers, then McLaughlin wired Washington:

> To Commissioner Indian Affairs:
>
> William F. Cody—Buffalo Bill—has arrived here with a commission from General Miles to arrest Sitting Bull. Such a step at present would be unnecessary and unwise, as it will precipitate a fight which can be averted. A few Indians still dancing, but it does not mean mischief at present. I have matters well in hand, and when proper time arrives can arrest Sitting Bull by Indian police without bloodshed. . . . Request Gen. Miles's order to Cody be rescinded and request immediate answer.
>
> *McLaughlin*, Agent

Contrary to the plan, however, as the evening wore on, Buffalo Bill displayed an exuberant alcoholic endurance seldom seen even at a frontier army post. The officers began working in shifts—the fresh replacing the casualties. The post Assistant Surgeon, Captain A. R. Chapman, reported, "Colonel Cody's *capacity* was such that it took practically all the officers, in details of two or three, to keep him interested and busy." Some people have said the party continued through the entire night and into the next day, and some have said otherwise. But whichever way it was, at midmorning on the twenty-ninth, having temporarily disabled most of the Fort Yates leadership, Cody mounted his wagonload of gifts ("a hundred dollars' worth for every pound the Old Bull weighs") and cheerily announced to the reporters, "I am off on the most dangerous assignment of my whole career." Then he started out.

Meanwhile, before Cody left, McLaughlin had sent carefully instructed scouts far to the south on each of the two roads leading to Sitting Bull's Grand River camp. That afternoon, twenty miles down the road at Oak Creek Crossing, Cody met Louis Primeau, who was one of them. Pretending to have just come from Sitting Bull's place, Primeau told Cody that the chief was headed north on the other road and was going to the agency. Cody and his troop, therefore, turned their wagons and started back for Standing Rock.

While Buffalo Bill had been traveling across Standing Rock reservation, McLaughlin's telegram had been traveling through the highest levels of government. Acting Commissioner Belt had referred it to the Secretary of the Interior, who referred it to Secretary of War Proctor, who referred it to the President himself. So swiftly had all this been done that by three o'clock in the afternoon McLaughlin had already received a reply. When Cody arrived back at the agency that evening, McLaughlin handed it to him:

Colonel William F. Cody, Fort Yates, N.D.

The order for the detention of Sitting Bull has been rescinded. You are hereby ordered to return to Chicago and report to General Miles.

Benjamin Harrison, President

Put out at having been deprived of the chance to score a great coup, Cody later wrote in his autobiography, "The result of the President's order was that the Ghost Dance War followed very shortly." In a huff, the showman gathered up his entourage the following morning and in the face of a gathering snowstorm set out for Mandan and the train back to Chicago. It was the last day of November.

Next came the Moon of Popping Trees, the month the *Wasicun* call December, and with it came the sharp cold of winter. One evening in the first days of the month, as the good-smelling woodsmoke lay over the camp in pungent, shifting wisps, and the pony herd cropped at the frost-crisped grass in the darkening draws, Sitting Bull was warming himself by the iron stove in his log cabin when a messenger came from Short Bull, who was on his way with a large band of people to dance at the Stronghold in the Makoce Sica (the Bad Lands). Short Bull sent word that he had spoken with some stars that had come to him as messengers from the Great Holy, Wakan Tanka. He had been told that the Wanikiye was coming very soon, down from heaven to the dancers in the Makoce Sica. Short Bull thought it would be proper if such a famous chief as Sitting Bull were there to greet Him. Sitting Bull pondered the matter for several days. He knew it was good for the people to believe in the message of the Indian Messiah because it led them back to the old ways and away from the road of the white man, but Sitting Bull was not at all sure that he believed in it himself. Besides, it was two hundred miles to the Stronghold and that was a long traveling in cold weather. On the other hand, Short Bull had acquired a great many followers, and perhaps Sitting Bull might learn from him how to use this dance to increase his own following beyond its present three or four hundred. Then, too, there was a chance that the Wanikiye really *was* coming, in which case He would surely be disappointed if Tatanka Iyotaka were not there to greet him.

It was too much to think about alone. Consequently, on the night of December 11, Sitting Bull held a council in his cabin to discuss it. Most of the council members were the old men who were what remained of the once-elite Midnight Stronghearts warrior society which they and Sitting Bull had belonged to since their youth. They were also the remaining ones of those who had arranged to have Sitting Bull appointed "chief of all the Sioux," back in 1867. To them, as well as to himself, he *was* chief of all the Sioux, even now. They, too, agreed that it would be a bad thing if Tatanka Iyotaka, the chief of the Lakotah, were not there to greet the Wanikiye. So it was decided. Sitting Bull would ask Whitehair McLaughlin for a pass to visit Pine Ridge. Summoning Andrew Fox, his educated nephew, the chief dictated the following letter (free rendering from Carlisle English):

> To the Major In Indian Office
>
> I want to write a few lines today to let you know something. I have had a meeting with my Indians today, and I am writing to tell you our thoughts.
> God made both the white race and the Red race, and gave them minds and hearts to both. Then the white race gained a high place over the Indians. However, today our Father is helping us Indians—that is what we believe.
> And so I think this way. I wish no one to come with guns or knives to interfere with my prayers. All we are doing is praying for life and to learn how to do good. . . .
> When you visited my camp you gave me good words about our prayers, but then you took your good words back again. And so I will let you know something. I got to go to [Pine Ridge] Agency and know this Pray [take part in the dance]: so I let you know that . . . I want answer back soon.
>
> Sitting Bull

On the following day, Bull Ghost, a member of the Stronghearts and one of the chief's bodyguards, carried the letter to the agency. While he was on his way, Colonel Drum received new orders:

Headquarters, Department of Dakota
St. Paul, Minn., December 12, 1890

To Commanding Officer
Fort Yates, N. Dak.

The division commander has directed that you make it your especial
duty to secure the person of Sitting Bull. Call on Indian agent to cooperate
and render such assistance as will best promote the purpose in view. . . .

M. Barber
Assistant Adjutant General

When Bull Ghost arrived with Sitting Bull's letter shortly after the new
order had come in, Drum and McLaughlin held a conference. Appar-
ently Sitting Bull's letter was both a request for a pass and an
announcement of his intention to go to Pine Ridge—whether he got the
pass or not. It was a touchy situation, but the two men agreed that any
attempt to arrest him at his camp in the midst of his old warrior cronies
and bodyguards was likely to be a bloody business. They decided,
therefore, to try to hold it off until the next ration day, which would be
December 20. The Old Bull didn't come in for rations anymore, but his
people did. Consequently, on ration day Sitting Bull's Grand River
settlement would be so nearly deserted that there should be little trouble.
Meanwhile, they would keep a sharp eye on the chief to make sure he
didn't run off before they could stop him. The best man they could get to
watch him, they agreed, was Lieutenant Bull Head, chief of the Indian
police.

Bull Head, called Afraid-of-Bear by the Indians, had a farm on the
south side of Grand River only three or four miles above Sitting Bull's
place. He was an industrious man and a good farmer, and as Indian
farms went, his was a showplace. One Fort Yates officer had admiringly
commented that not only was Bull Head's house "neat and tidy inside,"
but also his outbuildings and haystacks looked "more thrifty" than
"many a white man's." Knowing that Bull Head was at his farm,
McLaughlin sent him a message:

[Do not] come in here [to the agency] . . . You must watch Sitting Bull
closely. We learned sufficient news to lead us to believe that he (S. B.) is
going to leave the reservation. If he does you must stop him, and if he does
not listen to you . . . use your own discretion in the matter and it will be
alright. . . . Bull Ghost brought a letter to me, and it stated that he (S. B.)
wanted to go on a visit, and that is why I want you to keep a good watch

on him, and if he should insist on going you can do as you think best and it will be alright. . . .

As the courier, White Bird, was carrying Whitehair's message through the forty miles of wind and cold and moonless night to Bull Head's place, another council was being held in Sitting Bull's cabin. At this council it was decided that the chief should leave for the Stronghold as soon as possible. It would take two days to prepare for such a journey. Thus, he and a few others would start for the Stronghold on December 15. On the next day following the council, December 13, Bull Head's police seemed to find more than the usual number of reasons for riding the river road past the Sitting Bull settlement. As they rode by, casually but watching out of the sides of their eyes, they saw horses being corralled and wagons being greased and loaded with hay and tipi covers and lodge poles. Plainly, some of Sitting Bull's people were preparing to make a long traveling. But no matter how much the police visited with the people and listened to them, it was evening before the police finally found out *when* they were planning to leave. As soon as Bull Head did find out, he hurried to the school several miles below Sitting Bull's place and had the schoolmaster, Jack Carignan, write a letter telling Whitehair that Sitting Bull was planning to start south on the morning of the fifteenth.

On any of the Sioux reservations it was almost impossible to keep a secret for more than a day or so at most. Thus, even before Bull Head had discovered Sitting Bull's travel plans, the chief had learned that Colonel Drum and Whitehair McLaughlin were planning to arrest him. That evening during his customary smoking with old friends in his cabin, Sitting Bull made a complaining about it:

Why should the Indian police come against me? . . . We are all Sioux, we are relatives. . . . If the white men want me to die they ought not to put up the Indians to kill me. . . . Let the soldiers come and take me away and kill me, whatever they like. I am not afraid. I am a warrior. . . .

. . . I would not join his [McLaughlin's] church and ever since then he has had it in for me. Long ago I had two women in my lodge. One of them was jealous. Whitehair reminds me of that jealous woman.

Why does he keep trying to humble me? Can I be any lower than I am? Once I was a man, but now I am a pitiful wretch—no country, no fast horses, no guns worth having. . . . I was a fool ever to come down here. I should have stayed with the Red Coats in Grandmother's land.

I did not start this ghost dance. Kicking Bear came here of his own accord. . . .

On the next afternoon, December 14, when the sun was so near setting that the agency was covered by the long cold shadow of Proposal Hill just to the west, Hawk Man rode in with Bull Head's letter to McLaughlin. Almost before the agent had finished reading it, Colonel Drum stopped in. McLaughlin handed him the policeman's message. When the colonel had read it, the two men looked at each other in silent understanding. There could be no more delay—the time to arrest Sitting Bull had come. Moreover, regardless of the risk, there was now no choice but to arrest him at his camp, even in the presence of his warriors and bodyguards. Quickly Drum and McLaughlin planned their strategy. During the past twenty-four hours McLaughlin had assembled a substantial number of police on Grand River. Drum now agreed with the agent that these men would have a much better chance of making the arrest without a fight than the soldiers would. However, if things did get out of hand, the soldiers would be needed. Therefore, they agreed that while the Indian police would do the actual arresting, a military force would be sent far enough south to be able to support them if the need arose, but not be sent near enough to Sitting Bull's settlement to cause hostility and fear if they were not needed.

As Colonel Drum strode back to the fort to prepare the military part of the operation, McLaughlin called a lean, clean-cut-looking Yanktonais police sergeant and told him to make ready for a fast ride to Bull Head's place on Grand River. The agent then wrote the following to his two police lieutenants:

Lieut. Bull Head or Shave Head
Grand River

From reports brought by Scout "Hawk Man" I believe the time has arrived for the arrest of Sitting Bull and that it can be made by the Indian Police without much risk.—I therefore want you to make the arrest before daylight tomorrow morning. . . . The Cavalry will leave here tonight and will reach the Sitting Bull crossing on Oak Creek before daylight tomorrow [Monday] morning. . . .

I have ordered all the police at Oak Creek to proceed to Carignan's school to await your orders. This gives you a force of 42 Policemen for to use in the arrest.

Very Respectfully,
James McLaughlin
U. S. Ind. Agt.

P. S. You must not let him escape under any circumstances.

At half-past five Red Tomahawk (the Yanktonais) galloped out of the agency compound and headed south toward Grand River. Shortly thereafter, Colonel Drum completed drafting his orders for the military operation; then, as Captain Fechet recalled, ". . . about six P.M., as we were enjoying our after-dinner cigars by our comfortable firesides, 'Officers Call' rang out loud and shrill on the clear, frosty air. . . ."

Quickly, the officers left their quarters and trooped toward the lamp-lighted windows marking the square little commandant's office that stood alone in the middle of the parade ground. There, the colonel and McLaughlin described the mission. Then Drum handed Fechet his orders:

> Fort Yates, N. Dak., December 14, 1890
>
> Capt. E. G. Fechet, Eighth Cavalry, will proceed with Troops F and G, Eighth Cavalry, the Hotchkiss gun, and one Gatling gun, to the crossing of Oak Creek . . . for the purpose of preventing the escape or rescue of Sitting Bull, should the Indian police succeeded in arresting him.
>
> The command will move out at 12 o'clock midnight . . . and will be supplied with . . . 4,000 round of ammunition for Gatling gun, 25 rounds for Hotchkiss gun, cooked rations, and one days forage.
>
> . . . If, on arrival at Oak Creek, Capt. Fechet learns that the police are fighting or need assistance, he will push on, and if necessary, follow Sitting Bull as long as possible with his supplies, keeping the post commander informed by courier of his movements. . . .
>
> By order of Lieut. Col. W. F. Drum:
> E. C. Brooks
> Second Lieutenant, Eighth Cavalry, Post Adjutant

At eleven o'clock the men were given a hot, late supper. Just before midnight they were assembled on the parade ground: one hundred enlisted men, six officers, two Indian scouts, and the guide-interpreter, Louis Primeau. Then, in Fechet's words,

> Colonel Drum . . . stepped to the side of my horse, and, putting his hand on mine, said, "Captain, after you leave here use your own discretion. You know the object of the movement. Do your best to make it a success."

Promptly at midnight, the command moved out. It was a still, dark night, and cold—though not quite freezing; the sky had clouded over, and the air carried an icy smell of rain. The column moved through the darkness at a brisk trot and so rapidly that by half-past three it had already covered the twenty miles to Oak Creek Crossing. McLaughlin had told Fechet that when they reached the crossing, they would find a courier from Bull Head waiting for them. But no courier was there. Instead, the Oak Creek police post was deserted and dark. Fechet did some fast thinking. His orders called for him to hold at Oak Creek unless he learned that the police were "fighting or need assistance" . . . the courier's absence could hardly be taken as evidence that there was such trouble ahead, yet it *could* mean there was . . . And if there *was* trouble, even at a fast trot it was a three-hour ride from Oak Creek to Sitting Bull's place. . . . If the troops remained here at Oak Creek, they might as well be on the moon as far as helping the police was concerned. Adding up these things and disregarding his orders, Fechet made a field decision. He led the command forward, again at a fast trot, down the Sitting Bull road.

As fast as the army rode that night, however, Red Tomahawk rode faster. He had left the agency at five-thirty and was south of the river at Bull Head's by ten. That forty-mile ride in four and a half hours on a dark night required a pace that could kill a horse and was hard on a man, also. But Red Tomahawk, like the other police gathering at Bull Head's house, believed deeply in this thing he was doing. The Indian police—with their big, shiny badges—were called Ceska Maza (Metal Breasts) by their people, and Whitehair McLaughlin's Metal Breasts had long been impatient to arrest Sitting Bull. Some of the Blackfeet and Yanktonais among them had old grudges to settle with the Hunkpapa chief. Some of them who were Hunkpapa had old grudges, too, and all of them thought (like McLaughlin) that Sitting Bull was standing in the way of his people. Those whose hearts were not strong for this thing had been weeded out earlier, at another time that Whitehair had prepared to arrest Sitting Bull but was denied permission by the commissioner. That time the news had rippled through the Metal Breasts like the rings from a stone thrown into water. To be the police was one thing; to arrest a strong chief, that was something else. And for Yanktonais and Blackfeet to be among those seizing a Hunkpapa chief in his own camp—Ah-h-h! That was a bad thing—an insult that could spill much blood upon the grass. Many of them had not believed that the handsome uniform and the good pay-money were worth the shaming of their chief. Others felt they were not worth the risk of a big fight and maybe getting killed. Thus, Grasping Eagle, Big Mane, Standing Soldier, and others—even the police captain himself, Crazy Walking—had thrown their badges on Whitehair's table that day and were no longer Metal Breasts. Now, those who remained were eager to make the arrest.

Nevertheless, to be eager was one thing; to be facing doing it was another. So it was a long waiting night for the Metal Breasts gathered in Bull Head's well-kept house. They drank coffee, had a late-night supper, told old war stories, and talked and joked in the way men do when they are being brave and casual on top but are tense and frightened down underneath. As they talked, their minds were divided—the top part hearing the stories and jokes, the bottom part thinking about such hard things as the close relatives many of them had in Sitting Bull's camp and of such dangerous things as the old feud between Police Chief Bull Head and Sitting Bull's chief bodyguard, Catch-the-Bear. Once, when those two were in a foolish argument over the ownership of a flour sack, Bull Head had struck Catch-the-Bear on his back. Catch-the-Bear had taken that as such an insult that he had declared he would kill Bull Head for it someday. Now Catch-the-Bear, growing grouchier as he aged, had reached that time when old men remember long-ago things more vividly than those of yesterday. And one of the things he remembered best was Bull Head's insult. Ah-h-h! This could mean trouble.

Twenty-nine of the Metal Breasts had gathered at Bull Head's by the time they left, at about four o'clock in the morning, to ride the two miles or so downriver to the house of Sitting Bull's brother-in-law, Gray Eagle. There they were joined by ten more police. Gray Eagle had a deep sadness about this thing that was about to happen, yet he, too, supported it. Having failed to talk the Old Bull out of trying to lead the Indians back to a past that was forever gone, Gray Eagle had become convinced that for the good of the people the chief had to be removed from the reservation. For that reason he and three others now volunteered to help with the arrest. Thus, at half-past four when they mounted up to go, there were thirty-nine police and four volunteers who sat on their horses in Gray Eagle's yard and removed their hats while Bull Head made a prayer. He prayed to the white man's God, asking for help to do what they had to in such a manner that no blood would be on the ground when they were finished. Then, at Bull Head's quiet "Hopo!" they started out in a darkness in which horses and men were dim shapes that were heard more than seen; and with a cold misty drizzle now freezing on the naked cottonwoods and dripping from their hat brims, they rode down the river. Somewhere out on the bluffs there was a distant coyote howling, and from somewhere in the trees by the river came the voice of Hinhanska, the white owl, soft-echoing in the night-hushed bottoms. The owl made a grieving sound like a deep-voiced woman sobbing, and it was a bad thing to hear, for Hinhanska was the messenger of the Indians' God, who foretold of people dying.

At a little past five o'clock the police crossed the river just above the sleeping camp of Sitting Bull's Hunkpapas. As they reached the north bank, the morning stillness was shattered by the barking and yapping of the village dogs. Surprise now gone, Bull Head's police broke into a gallop, and charging among the dark houses and dancers' lodges, they surrounded Sitting Bull's cabin.

Swinging quickly off his horse, Bull Head knocked on the door, and from inside, the chief growled, "Hau! Timahel hiyuwo!" (Yes! Come in the house!) The door opened. A match hissed and flared, and a yellow flame ran across the wick of a kerosene lamp. The old chief sat up in his bed, naked. Ah-h! In answering the knock he had said "hiyuwo," which meant he had invited only one person to enter, not "hiyupo," which would have meant many. But in the flickering yellow light, he saw many people pushing and stamping into his house, and all of them white-scarved Metal Breasts. Then Bull Head said, "I come after you to take you to the agency. You are under arrest."

"Hau" (All right), responded the chief. "Let me put on my clothes and go with you." However, as Sitting Bull began dressing he also began thinking about what was happening, and he became annoyed. He started saying hard things to the police, then began to dawdle and hesitate in his dressing. But the Metal Breasts were in a hurry and they were afraid, so in their haste they tried to dress him themselves. Little Soldier said later, "Sitting Bull was not afraid, *we* were afraid."

Now although it was a great honor for a man to be dressed for an important occasion by friends whose hearts are good toward him, this was another thing, and during their rough jostling Sitting Bull said ironically, "You need not honor me like this. I can dress myself." When they finally thought he was dressed enough, Bull Head took one of Sitting Bull's arms, Shave Head took the other, and Red Tomahawk stepped behind him and held a pistol against his back. Then altogether they moved through the cabin door. When the police had first arrived at Sitting Bull's cabin, Bull Head had told Red Bear and White Bird to saddle Sitting Bull's horse and bring him to the front of the cabin. Buffalo Bill had given the chief this horse when he was in his Wild West

Show—an old gray horse that could do tricks. But Red Bear and White Bird hadn't returned with it yet, and the Metal Breasts and their prisoner had to wait.

By now a crowd of maybe a hundred and fifty people had gathered, milling angrily about in the light of lanterns and torches. Many of them had rifles under their blankets, and they were murmuring and buzzing like a freshly shaken wasps' nest. As they milled and buzzed, they kept pressing in and the police kept backing up, until pretty soon the line of police was holding only a small clearing in front of the cabin door. While this was going on, old Catch-the-Bear came shuffling and growling along the line of Metal Breasts, peering into each face and demanding, "Where is Afraid-of-Bear [Bull Head]?" as he sought his old enemy of the flour sack feud.

In a few more minutes the chief's horse was brought around and the police began moving Sitting Bull toward it. As they moved, familiar voices rose above the clamoring of the dark crowd behind the lanterns and seemed to swirl around the old chief in currents that pulled him first this way and then that.

He heard Crawler shouting, "Kill them! Kill them! Shoot the old policemen and the young ones will run."

The voice of Gray Eagle was pleading, "Brother-in-law, do as the agent says. Go with the police."

The sharp-tongued wife of Spotted Horn Bull was stridently cursing the police and calling them "jealous women."

Jumping Bull, whom Sitting Bull had captured from the Assiniboins as a small boy and then adopted as a brother, was urging, "Brother, let us break camp and move to the agency. You take your family and I will take mine. If you are to die there, I will die with you."

As a steady background to all the other voices was the eery, shrill chanting of one of the chief's wives as she sang,

> *Sitting Bull*
> *You have always been*
> *A brave man*
> *What is going*
> *To happen now?*

Then, from a figure silhouetted against the yellow lamplight of the cabin door came a cry, "You have always called yourself a brave chief, but now you are letting yourself be taken away by the Ceska Maza!" It was the voice of Sitting Bull's seventeen-year-old son, Crow Foot. Ah-h-h! To hear such shaming words from one's own son was too much to bear! Sitting Bull stiffened, pulled back against his captors, and roared, "All right! I will not go another step!"

Inflamed by their chief's defiance, as well as by the sight of him being pushed and pulled by a Yanktonais on one side of him and by another from behind, the Hunkpapas became a screaming, fist-shaking, police-cursing mob. Throwing off his blanket and raising his rifle, Catch-the-Bear shouted, "Come now! Let us protect our chief!"

Then it started. Catch-the-Bear shot Bull Head in the side. Falling, Bull Head fired upward into Sitting Bull's chest. Next, Red Tomahawk shot his pistol into the back of the chief's head. At the same moment Strikes-the-Kettle shot Shave Head. Shave Head and Sitting Bull fell together—Sitting Bull dead and Shave Head mortally wounded. When Sitting Bull fell, a wild melee erupted. The Indians attacked the police with guns, knives, and clubs. Private Lone Man snatched away Catch-the-Bear's rifle and beat him to the ground with it, then shot him. After that, the shooting came so fast it sounded like a string of firecrackers popping. Finally, the trained police were able to force their disorganized attackers to retreat to the cover of the trees by the river. Then, gathering up their dead and wounded, the police holed up in Sitting Bull's cabin. There, seeing a curtain move, Running Hawk ripped it away and exposed Crow Foot hiding behind it. The police asked their officers what to do with him. Bull Head, dying from four bullet wounds, answered bitterly, "Do what you like with him. He is one of them that has caused this!" One of the police then struck the boy a blow that sent him reeling through the door. Next, in a crash of rifle fire, Crow Foot spun and fell dead. Meanwhile, with all the shooting and commotion, Sitting Bull's old circus horse thought he was back in the Wild West Show. He sat down on his haunches and held up his forehooves as if he were praying. (Maybe he was.)

At some point during the fight, Hawk Man (one of the police) had ridden off at a full gallop to look for Captain Fechet and his soldiers and had found them about three miles away. Fechet immediately ordered his command forward at a gallop, and in a few minutes they arrived on a bench overlooking Sitting Bull's camp. From there, in the gray light of dawn he could see the cabin a half-mile ahead and a hundred and fifty feet below wreathed in rifle smoke as its occupants were exchanging fire

with riflemen in the trees. Not knowing which were the police and which
were Sitting Bull's Indians, Fechet ordered the Hotchkiss gunners to
commence dropping explosive shells in the clearing between them. After
three or four rounds had burst in the clearing, the Indians fled from the
trees and crossed the river into the hills and draws to the south. At the
cabin six Metal Breasts were dead or dying. Outside, eight Indians were
dead, including the great chief of the Hunkpapa Lakotah, Tatanka
Iyotaka—Sitting Bull.

Then most of the people fled—many of them to stop and return
peacefully after a short time, but about two-hundred kept on going until
they reached the camps of the Minneconjou on the Cheyenne River,
ninety miles to the south.

With the shooting now ended, Fechet's soldiers came down the hill
and occupied the camp. There they found Holy Medicine, a dancer who
was also the tailor that had made the ghost shirts. He was seeking his
kinsman, the policeman Strong Arm. When he found Strong Arm dead
behind the stable, Holy Medicine grabbed up a heavy neckyoke, and in a
burst of rage and grief began beating the body of Sitting Bull until he
was restrained and led wailing away.

As the troops paused for breakfast, a painted and ghost-shirted
warrior rode a big black horse out from the trees by the river, lowered his
lance and charged down on them. When their shooting forced him to
retreat to a distance, he rode across in front of them singing sadly,
"Father, I thought you said we were going to live." Then, turning his
horse, he vanished back into the trees.

At Sitting Bull's cabin his two wives, Seen-by-Her-Nation, and
Four-Times, made the keening death chant. *Iglastan* . . . It was finished.

CHAPTER

12

∧∧∧∧∧∧∧

The Flight of Big Foot

WHEN THE HUNKPAPAS fled south from the camp of the dead Sitting Bull, they did not all leave together, but went in scattered, straggling groups. Neither did they travel at the same speed. Some of them rode horses, some took the time to load their wagons with supplies so they could travel comfortably, and many took only the clothes they wore. All of them, however, had the same idea in mind—to seek refuge with their Minneconjou friends and relatives at Cheyenne River. Since the nearest of the large Minneconjou settlements that was well away from any soldier camps was Hump's, they had the same destination in mind, too—Hump's settlement at the mouth of Cherry Creek.

The ninety miles from Sitting Bull's camp to Hump's was hard traveling, especially for the wounded and for those who had nothing but the clothes they wore. The land between the two places was harsh and barren, and, in many places, such water as they could find was the kind that leaves white rings on the ground when it is drying and makes the bowels loose when it is drunk. Moreover, the settlements were so few and small and scattered in this part of the reservation that they offered little in the way of food or shelter. Because of this, if the Great Holy had not taken pity on the people and given them good weather, they would have left many bodies along the road. As it was, except for a raw facing wind and a few minutes' spatter of light rain the first day, the skies were clear and the winds light; the nights were hardly colder than freezing, and the daytime sun was bright and warm. Thus, although it was a hard and hungry journey, if anyone died on it, we have never been told.

For three days, beginning on December 17, the Hunkpapas straggled a few at a time down Cherry Creek to Hump's camp. On arriving there, however, they were shocked. Except for about eighty dancers, many of them young warriors, the camp was deserted. Furthermore, except for one white trader named Harry Angell, the white-man town of Cheyenne City across the river was also deserted. Confused, uncertain, and dull-eyed with grief and exhaustion, the Hunkpapas slowly gathered on Cherry Creek; then they hesitated there—not knowing where to go or what to do. While they were vacillating, the Hump people told them what had happened.

The first thing, why the whites had left, was a short story and one they could laugh about while telling. The newspapers, they recounted, had been saying how fierce and dangerous the Indians were becoming, and even the new agent, Palmer, was saying they were making ready for war. Then a white man (George McPherson, from west of the reservation at Bend) had visited the Ghost Dance and afterward had had it put in the paper that all it reminded him of was "a Methodist revival," and he couldn't see any cause in it for alarm. Nevertheless, even though the Cheyenne City people had been living right there where they could see that the things McPherson said were true, all of them except Mr. Angell had decided to believe what they heard instead of what they saw, and they had suddenly run away like chickens that see the shadow of a hawk.

When they told them of Hump, however, the Minneconjou did not laugh—for that was an angering thing. All through the fall and into the Moon of Popping Trees, they said, Hump had led his people in the dance, and everyone had been happily waiting for the new world to come. Then, on December 6, a white *Itancan* (captain) had come riding up the river through a snowstorm to see the chief. This captain, Ezra Ewers, was an old friend of Hump's from away back in 1877, when Hump had scouted for Bear Coat Miles against the Nez Percé. Hump had become good friends with Bear Coat at that time and had become almost *hunka* (brother-friends) with this Captain Ewers. Now, Ewers had come bearing a message from Bear Coat asking Hump to stop the dancing and to bring his people into Fort Bennett on the Missouri River. To the great disgust of some of his young warriors, Hump had unhesitatingly replied, "All right. If General Miles wants me, I will do as you say." Hence, on the following day Hump and all his people (except for the eighty or so here) had started for the fort. Then, the Minneconjous went on to say, an even worse thing had happened. As soon as Hump got to Bennett, he had again accepted the pay-money and the blue uniform of an army scout and was now helping the very soldiers who wanted to stop the dancing.

These were hard words for the Sitting Bull people to hear. They meant, no doubt, that Hump would soon be coming back up the river, bringing soldiers with him. Even so, the Hunkpapas were so tired from the hard and hungry running away that most of them were glad just to stay where they were—no matter what happened next.

A few of them, however, despite their fatigue turned westward and went on toward the camp of Big Foot, thirty-five miles farther up the Cheyenne. Fortunately, it turned out, they didn't have to go the entire distance. During the previous two days Big Foot's people had been traveling, also, and the Hunkpapas came upon them camped across the river from Cavanaugh's store, only twelve miles above Cherry Creek.

Big Foot's people, like those of Hump, had been so caught up in the dream of a beautiful new world that all through the fall and into December, they, too, had done little else but dance to its coming. During that time they had harmed no one, nor had they damaged any property. Nevertheless, again like Hump's band, in the public's mind they had become branded as extremely dangerous and likely to start a war. Looking back on it today, it seems likely that the public's fear was largely due to the statements of Palmer, the new agent. Then (as now), Sioux reservations were hotbeds of factional turmoil—one group always making strong and often highly exaggerated accusations against another. Thus, inexperienced agents, not knowing this (or which Indian reports to believe, either) were continually discovering frightening crises where none existed. This seems to have been the case with Palmer. He wrote the commissioner on the first of December that "according to friendly Indians" the bands of Hump and Big Foot "want to fight and will fight" and there was no doubt that they were "preparing for an outbreak." Palmer had made similar reports earlier, and because of this, by November General Miles had concluded that both Hump and Big Foot were so dangerous to the peace that both of them should be removed from the reservation. Consequently, by using Hump's friendship with both himself and Captain Ewers, in December Miles had removed him easily and peacefully. But having no access to Big Foot through friendship, the general decided that Big Foot must be arrested and his people captured, disarmed, and taken to a military fort. Thus, at the same time the Sitting Bull Hunkpapas were making their way up the river to Big Foot's camp, the order for Big Foot's arrest and the capture of his people had already been issued. Not knowing anything about it, however, Big Foot was under the impression that everything was fine between his band and the whites. Until recently he had known things were not right and had been worried; aware that the whites had become afraid of him, he had become afraid that their very fear might cause them to do something that would make trouble. For that reason, during the past few months he had regularly sent couriers riding the ninety miles to Pierre to pick up the latest newspapers so that he and his headmen could read them in council and know better what the whites were thinking.

Then, as November ended and the Moon of Popping Trees began, a new soldier chief had taken over command of Camp Cheyenne, ten miles southwest up the river from the Big Foot settlement. On December 4, Big Foot learned of his coming and that his name was Lieutenant Colonel E. V. Sumner. So despite a temperature below twenty degrees and a west wind that carried new snow as it gusted and whistled down the bluff-sided trench that is the Cheyenne River valley, on the next day Big Foot and his headmen had journeyed up the river to meet the new colonel. The chief took an immediate liking to Colonel Sumner who, it was plain to see, had a good heart for the Indians. In turn, Sumner liked Big Foot. As a result, the Indians remained at the army camp for two days while the two men spent much time together and became good friends. In their talks, Big Foot told the colonel that he and his people were not only willing, but were also anxious to obey the colonel's orders. Furthermore, Big Foot said, in the trouble presently going on he and his people were all on the side of the government. The chief did not tell Sumner, however, that in November he had told his Ghost Dancers to get all the guns and ammunition they could. After all, the guns were not intended for war, but only for their defense against anyone who might try to stop the dancing. Being the skilled diplomat and negotiator that he was (and also wishing to make a good impression on this new soldier chief), Big Foot did not find it necessary to tell him everything he knew—besides, it might easily be misunderstood. It would have been more accurate, as a matter of fact, had he said that whereas he, himself, was pretty much on the side of the government, some of his people were not, and he sometimes had a hard time controlling them. But it seemed better peacemaking to say it the other way, so he did.

On returning to their camp after the visit, Big Foot and his headmen felt easier than they had in a long time. They were sure Colonel Sumner would send their good words of peace to Bear Coat Miles . . . which, indeed, Sumner did. They were also sure the words would at last convince Bear Coat that Big Foot's people were friendly . . . which they did not. Nevertheless, because of that first good visit, as well as continued friendly visits with Sumner during the following week or so, Big Foot felt he could now stop worrying about trouble with the whites and could, instead, turn his attention to other pressing matters.

One of these was a message from Pine Ridge. Almost immediately after his return from Camp Cheyenne, three messengers had brought Big Foot a letter from some of the most important Pine Ridge chiefs, including Red Cloud, Knife, No Water, and Big Road. The letter said there was "a fire" of wrangling going on among the chiefs there and that the moment Big Foot, the peacemaker, got their letter they wanted him to come to Pine Ridge to help them put the fire out. Moreover, they said, if he would do this they would give him a hundred horses. Ah-h-h! This was a big thing to think about. There was great honor in being invited to make a peace among such big men as these—and to earn a hundred horses was to become prosperous. Unfortunately, though, the invitation conflicted with another pressing matter, that of making their annual journey to the agency at Fort Bennett to receive their treaty annuities. Inasmuch as these included new clothes for everybody and a little money besides, it would be too much to ask the people to give it up in order to go to Pine Ridge. Thus, Big Foot and his council decided to go to Bennett first and *then* go to Pine Ridge—hoping they could still get there in time for him to earn the hundred horses. On December 15, Big Foot went upriver to tell Colonel Sumner that he was saying goodbye for a while and was taking his people to Bennett.

Since it was eighty-five miles from the Big Foot settlement to Fort Bennett, the journey, including the camping and partying with old friends at the fort, would take about ten days. Therefore, the Indians spent the sixteenth loading up their wagons, fixing their fences, closing their gates, and shutting up their houses for the long absence. While they were going about their tasks, Colonel Sumner received the following message at Camp Cheyenne:

It is desirable that Big Foot be arrested, and had it been practicable to send you [Capt.] Wells with his two troops, orders would have been given that you try to get him. In case of arrest, he will be sent to Fort Meade to be securely kept prisoner.

By command of General Ruger.

This was a confusing message to Sumner. It was an arrest order, and yet it was not. And because he did not think Big Foot should be arrested, Sumner wanted no part of it. His reaction to the message, he later wrote, was, "I thought it best to allow him to go to Bennett a free man, and so informed the division commander by telegraph December 18. . . ." By delaying his response until then, Sumner gave Big Foot time to be well on his way to Bennett. Accordingly, his reply of December 18, directed to General Miles said:

> Ordered by division commander to arrest Big Foot; he has started with Big Foot [Indians] and other Cheyenne River Indians to Agency for annuities. If he should return I will try and get him; if he does not, he can be arrested at Bennett.

Meanwhile, unaware of his impending arrest, early on the seventeenth Big Foot began leading his Indians eastward, down the Cheyenne River. That night they made camp on its north bank across from Cavanaugh's store, twenty miles down. It was early the next morning when two Hunkpapa men came into camp from down the river, one of them limping from a leg wound. Saying nothing, they went directly into the chief's lodge. A few moments later Big Foot came out. In a loud voice so all could hear, he cried out that there had been a big fighting at Grand River and that Sitting Bull had been killed and his people, all scattered, were fleeing to the Minneconjou camps on the Cheyenne River.

When Big Foot's people heard the news of the fighting at Grand River and of Sitting Bull's death, they were first shocked and then frightened. On the two Hunkpapas' arrival, the Minneconjous had been preparing to break camp and go on toward Bennett. Now, not knowing what this news meant or what the white men were up to, they didn't know what to do—so they stayed where they were and did nothing. On the following morning, the nineteenth, they broke camp and moved, but only to the south side of the river by Cavanaugh's store where there was more grass for the pony herd. Then, because it was a warm sunny day, and because if ever they had needed the new world they needed it now, they began the dancing again. When they did, Cavanaugh and his two grown sons took fright and fled up the river toward Camp Cheyenne. Later that afternoon, a few more of Sitting Bull's Hunkpapas came straggling in. They told of a large number of people gathering at Hump's settlement and of how they were all hungry and without enough clothes for keeping warm. Hearing this, Big Foot's heart was touched, and he sent ten of his young men down the river to tell the Hunkpapas that any of them who wished to come to him would be welcomed, and he would see that they were fed and clothed.

Early the next day, on the morning of the twentieth, there was a great stir in the camp as someone cried out the news that Cavanaugh's store had been broken into and plundered. On investigation, Big Foot learned that the Hunkpapas had done it, but he wanted to make sure that none of his own people had been involved—for this was the kind of thing that could cause them bad trouble with the whites. He had the camp searched, but found none of the stolen goods. He did find, however, that five good Minneconjou horses and several saddles were missing, and that the Hunkpapas were missing, also. The chief realized that the fugitives he had befriended had done this thing (and had robbed their hosts as well), but that his own people would probably be blamed for it, and this was troubling to him. It was another of the bad things that were suddenly piling up so fast they set his mind to whirling. Knowing nothing else to do, he sent a messenger upriver with a letter for the soldier chief, Sumner. In the letter Big Foot declared that he was Sumner's friend and that he wanted to see him for a talk.

Meanwhile, also on the twentieth, Big Foot's young men arrived at Hump's camp on Cherry Creek. When they got there, they discovered that a great many Sitting Bull Indians were there now—more than two hundred. They also found Hump and a Lieutenant named H. E. Hale trying to talk the Hunkpapas and the eighty holdout Minneconjous into accompanying them to Fort Bennett. When the young men tried to tell the Hunkpapas of Big Foot's invitation, Hump's face grew dark with anger. He accused them not only of interfering, but also of trying to start a fight. And if it was a fight they wanted, Hump told them, he would make sure that they got it. Nonetheless, in spite of Hump, the young men managed to quietly circulate Big Foot's message among the Hunkpapas; then, since Hump was acting so fierce toward them, they started for home. Behind them was a tumult of arguing as the people tried to decide whether to go to Bennett or to join Big Foot. By midnight nearly all had gone to Lieutenant Hale and given him their guns and told him they would go to Bennett. But thirty-eight Hunkpapas and thirty young Hump warriors decided otherwise, and under cover of the first darkness, they slipped away and overtook Big Foot's ten young men and accompanied them to their camp.

When they arrived, Big Foot held another council, and as the talking went on, he became even more troubled. It had been bad enough when Hump had decided to become a scout. But now, according to the words these people brought, it sounded like Hump even wanted to fight the dancers. Moreover, Big Foot had been having trouble enough controlling his own young men, and these young Hump warriors who had joined him talked even wilder than his own did. Thus, as hard as it was to have his people give up their annuities, they would run too great a risk of getting into a shooting fight if they went on to Fort Bennett. For one thing he might run into Hump and have trouble, and for another he might not be able to control Hump's hot-blooded young warriors at the fort. The only safe thing to do now was to go home. So early the next morning, December 21, Big Foot's Indians struck their lodges, crossed to the north side of the river where the road was better, and started back west.

In the meantime, at Camp Cheyenne Colonel Sumner had received reports of Standing Rock Indians gathering along the Cheyenne, and on the twentieth he started downriver at the head of a force to intercept them. Big Foot knew of this, because the messenger carrying his letter to Sumner had found him camped at Narcelle's ranch a few miles west. Hence, as the Indians started moving that morning, Big Foot took two Sitting Bull Indians with him and went on ahead to find Sumner and have the talk that the chief now wanted so desperately. At the same time, it happened that Sumner had had the same idea and was now riding ahead of *his* force looking for Big Foot. When the two met very shortly, they sat on the winter-browned flats and smoked together and did a good deal of talking.

Big Foot started off by promptly—almost hastily—telling the colonel that he wanted to obey whatever orders the colonel had to give and that he promised to see that all his people obeyed them also. Then he told of the Hunkpapas that were with him. Sumner responded sternly to that, saying that the Standing Rock Indians were unlawfully away from their reservation and that Big Foot had no business taking them in and should have sent them to the soldier camp instead. The chief replied that although this might be so, these were their brothers and relations "who have come to us hungry and footsore and weary. We have taken them in and fed them, and no one with any heart could do any less." Though

Sumner continued to carry out his official role, he sympathized in his heart with Big Foot's statement, and in his official report of the meeting he commented:

> The Standing Rock Indians with Big Foot answered his description perfectly, and were, in fact, so pitiable a sight that I at once dropped all thought of their being hostile or even worthy of capture. Still, my instructions were to take them and I intended doing so.

There is no record of Sumner's having told Big Foot at this point that he had orders to take him and his band to Fort Meade on the edge of the Black Hills. He did, however, tell the chief that he and all his people were not to be allowed to stop at their own settlement, but were to accompany the troops on to Camp Cheyenne and to camp there. Big Foot agreed, and with that settled, those Indians who had no horses or wagons were given rides in the army wagons, and the soldiers and Indians began moving west together. When they camped at Narcelle's for the night, Sumner counted 333 Indians in the group—most of them hungry—and had eight beeves killed. Then there was feasting, and with the feasting (for the night at least) there was good feeling between the soldiers and the Indians.

On the following morning, the twenty-second, they resumed their journey under a sky that was clear, but that held the drifting cloud-rags which tell of bad weather coming. As the day wore on, the wind gradually shifted from the southwest to the north; then high gray clouds slid over the sun, the sky turned the color of an old steel knife, and the temperature fell.

By midafternoon the long column of wagons and horses was splashing through the river shallows where the road crossed to the south bank just below Big Foot's camp. By this time the north wind had developed a cheek-stinging bite, and under the dull sky the river bluffs, with their sharp gray ridges rough-grooved by gullies of dark, rusty, plum brush, looked as chilled and cheerless as old broken iron. It seemed as if the whole world had turned bleak and cold. In a few more minutes the shivering travelers began passing among the settlement of cabins that lay scattered over the grassy delta where Deep Creek joins the Cheyenne. To the troopers, these gray little Indian cabins with their littered yards and sod roofs bristling with the dead stalks of the past summer's weeds looked as bleak and cold as the day itself. But to the Indians these little cabins were *home*, and inside them there were stoves for warming. Seeing them (even though they had agreed not to stop, but to go on to Camp Cheyenne with the soldiers), the Indians suddenly stampeded—each family to its own house.

Quickly, before the soldiers could do anything rash, Big Foot went to Sumner and said,

> If you wish it, I myself will go with you to your camp; but if you try now to make these cold and hungry people leave their own houses they will probably make a fight. Besides, this is their home where the Government told them to stay, and they have not done a single thing to give anybody the right to make them go away from here.

Sumner saw Big Foot's point immediately, but now he was in a bind—forced to choose between following his orders or following his good judgment. He explained his decision in his official report thus:

> I concluded that one of two things must happen—I must either consent to their going into their village, or bring on a fight; and if the latter, must be the aggressor, and if the aggressor, what possible reason could I produce for making an attack on peaceable, quiet Indians on their reservation, at their homes, killing perhaps many of them. . . . I confess that my ambition was very great, but it was not sufficient to justify me in making an unprovoked attack on the Indians. . . .

Having come to this decision, the colonel then secured Big Foot's solemn promise that on the following day he would come to Camp Cheyenne for a council and, also, that he would bring the thirty-eight Standing Rock Indians with him and surrender them to Sumner. Then Sumner made another decision, one that was to cause him a great deal of trouble and, for a time, threatened to severely damage his military career. Under the circumstances, military prudence dictated that he should either leave one or two troops at the camp for surveillance, or else that he should camp the whole command nearby. However, he did neither. Instead, he led his entire force back to Camp Cheyenne. He explained this later by saying that since Big Foot had been fair and cooperative and had kept his word in all things, he felt the army should demonstrate similar good faith. The outcome was that shortly after Sumner arrived back at Camp Cheyenne his troubles began. Just after his meeting with Big Foot on the morning of the previous day, he had informed General Miles:

On the march to Big Foot's camp this morning met him and several Standing Rock Indians. They were willing to do anything I wish. . . . Tomorrow I will take the whole crowd . . . to my home camp, and unless otherwise ordered, will send them to Fort Meade. . . . This clears up all Indians on Cheyenne River as far as Cherry Creek, and if any other Standing Rock Indians are out they must be few.

At about midnight on the twenty-second, he received Miles's reply:

I think you had better push on rapidly with your prisoners to Meade, and be careful that they do not escape, and look out for other Indians. When will you be at Meade?

This put Sumner in the awkward position of being ordered to bring in Indians which he had told Miles he had, but which now he had not. Sumner answered:

Did not succeed in getting Indians to come into my camp on account of want of shelter for women and children. Did not feel authorized to compel them by force to leave their reservation.

Standing Rock Indians are at Big Foot's village, with their friends, and Big Foot has agreed to hold them there or bring them here, either. [The Standing Rock Indians] seem a harmless lot, principally women and children. There is little danger of their going toward the Bad Lands, having very little transportation.

While Sumner's troubles were piling up, things weren't going very well for Big Foot either. During the past few weeks there had been an epidemic of either severe colds or else some sort of influenza among the Cheyenne River Indians, and now, whichever it was, Big Foot had caught it. During the cold day's travel back to camp from Narcelle's, he had felt weak and sick and that night had gone to bed with a fever. On the following morning, he was supposed to have been taking the Standing Rock Indians to Camp Cheyenne, but was still in bed feeling no better when a messenger came to tell him that the Standing Rock Indians were no longer in camp, but had fled during the night. Nor was that all the bad news. Also, he was told, Yellow Bird and some of the others were agitating the people by saying it was foolish to stay here where they were at the mercy of Sumner's soldiers when they could all run away to the Bad Lands. Thus, both because he was ill and because he was embarrassed by not being able to deliver the Standing Rock

Hunkpapas as he had promised, Big Foot failed to keep his word to go to council with Sumner at Camp Cheyenne and, instead, remained fretting in his bed.

At Camp Cheyenne, Sumner was fretting also. From the exchange of messages with General Miles, it was becoming clear to the colonel that more of his military career than he cared to think about might now depend on Big Foot's cooperating with him and keeping his promises. So on December 23, Colonel Sumner spent a very long morning waiting for the chief to come in with the Standing Rock Indians as he had promised. Finally, when noon came and Big Foot had still not appeared, Sumner ordered his troops to prepare for a march on the Indian village.

Just as they finished their preparations and were ready to move out, a farmer named John Dunn came to the camp to sell butter, and with his arrival Sumner hit upon still another plan for avoiding a possible fight with the Indians. John "Red Beard" Dunn was known to be well acquainted with Big Foot and was able to speak fluent Lakotah, also. Because of that, Sumner hired him to go to the village ahead of the advancing troops and to deliver a message to the chief. He was to tell Big Foot that Sumner was now ordering him to take his people and start immediately for Fort Bennett (which is hard to understand, considering that Miles had ordered Sumner to take the Indians to Fort Meade) and that he (Sumner) expected Big Foot to obey his orders promptly and peacefully and that, furthermore, he was bringing troops down the river to make sure that he did. While he was delivering the message, Sumner told Dunn, the command would pause several miles short of the village and wait for him to return with the chief's reply.

Accompanied by Felix Benoit, a half-breed scout, Red Beard Dunn arrived at the settlement about three o'clock. While Benoit stopped to visit with some of the people, Dunn went on to Big Foot's house alone.

The effect of what Red Beard told Big Foot and his council was so explosive and the ultimate result was so fatal that it is unfortunate it is not known for sure what he said. According to Dunn himself, he told the Indians exactly what he had been instructed to, and after an investigation, the army accepted his account.

According to the Indians, however, Red Beard told them things that were both frightening and (it later turned out) false. As the Indians related it, Red Beard told them he had overheard the officers at Camp Cheyenne saying that they were going to send a thousand soldiers into Big Foot's camp in the night when everyone was asleep. The soldiers were then going to seize all the Indian men and take them to Fort Meade, and from there the men would be sent away and kept on an island in the eastern sea. Red Beard said the only way they could prevent this from happening, and also prevent a fight in which much blood would be spilled, was to run away that very night to Pine Ridge. Big Foot objected to Red Beard's advice. He declared that this was his home and that if he must die, he would die right here. But Red Beard persisted, saying they must run away and that they must go to Pine Ridge. He went on to say he was bringing the Indians this news because he was their good friend, and he was also doing it because he had many cattle nearby which he could lose if there was a war. He concluded by telling the Indians that Colonel Sumner would be very angry if he knew that Red Beard was revealing the army's secrets, and he hoped, therefore, that his Indian friends wouldn't tell anyone he had done so.

Although Dunn's own account of what he told the Indians at Big Foot's cabin seems to be the more generally accepted, there are good reasons for believing the Indian version to be much closer to the truth. For one thing, it is hard to see how Sumner's actual message could have caused the Indians to react so violently. For another, although Dunn claimed to be a good friend of the Indians, he was also a signer of that September petition in which the settlers pleaded for more army protection against the Indians. Furthermore (as the Indians *said* Dunn had told them), he *did* have a good many cattle on the range not far from the reservation, and there is little doubt that he would have felt more secure about them if the meat-loving Indians could have been either forced or frightened into living somewhere else.

Whatever Dunn actually did tell the Indians, it disturbed them so much that when he and Benoit rode out of the camp just before four o'clock, the Indians were already gathering in their horses. In Big Foot's cabin a heated council began the moment Dunn left. Some of the headmen were determined that the people start for Pine Ridge at once. Others insisted they should all go up Deep Creek and camp at the big cedar grove; then if no soldiers had come in three days, they would return home again. Big Foot declared they should do neither, but should go to Bennett and get their annuities. Then he changed his mind and said he thought they should move up on the ridge east of Deep Creek to a place where there was water and wood. They would be in a flexible position there. If no soldiers came, they could return home. If soldiers did come, they would be in a position to get away by going either east toward Bennett or south toward Pine Ridge. The council agreed to that, and immediately the Indians saddled and hitched their horses and loaded their wagons. By five o'clock all of Big Foot's people, along with the thirty Hump warriors, were streaming south in the gathering darkness on Deep Creek road. A short distance up the creek they came to a hogback sweeping upward in a long smooth curve from the valley floor to the eastern rim of the Deep Creek gorge. Following the hogback, they climbed to the plains above and there held another council. It was a short one. Scouts had come with the report that they had found Sumner's men in camp only five miles above the village. To most of the headmen this was proof that Red Beard had spoken straight and that the soldiers *were* coming to take the men away to that distant island. They should, therefore, head immediately south to Pine Ridge. Besides, the headmen argued, had they not already been invited there, and could not Big Foot also earn a hundred horses by going there? Coughing now, and flushed with fever, Big Foot felt himself forced to agree. At that, the ragged caravan began moving as fast as a mixed column of wagons and pedestrians possibly could, heading toward Pine Ridge, a hundred miles to the southwest.

About this same time two scouts rode into Sumner's camp and reported to the chagrined colonel that Big Foot's village was deserted and that they thought the Indians had fled to the south. Sumner therefore dispatched two other scouts to follow the Indians and to report their location. Then he ruefully reported to General Miles that, instead of coming in as he had promised, Big Foot had broken his word and run away.

Around midnight His Horse Looking, one of Sumner's scouts, overtook the Big Foot people near Davidson's ranch far down Deep Creek road. As he rode up to them, some of the young warriors surrounded him and shouted that they were going to kill him because he was working for the soldiers. But Big Foot intervened and spoke to His Horse Looking in a friendly way, asking him to tell Colonel Sumner that his friend Big Foot was sorry about the broken promise and that he had really intended to go to Fort Bennett, but that his headmen had overruled him and were forcing him to take his people to Pine Ridge.

Continuing on their journey, the Indians had hard traveling that night. It had been a cold and cloudy day, and the night was even colder. Moreover, it was so dark that a lantern man had to walk ahead to show the road, and other lanterns had to be used along the line so the people would have something to follow. And later in the night a snow flurry made things miserable. In spite of these difficulties, however, the Indians traveled so rapidly that long before daylight they had already covered nearly thirty miles and had found a sheltered, hidden place on the north fork of Bad River where they camped for a few hours' sleep.

Shortly after daybreak, under clearing skies, but in a bitterly cold wind, they started off again—traveling hard. By midafternoon they were at the Bad Lands Wall laboriously working their rattling wagons down the dangerous, crumbling slopes of what would afterward be known as Big Foot Pass. Just before dark they crossed White River and although still fifty miles from the agency, they were at last on Pine Ridge reservation. They made camp on the White River that evening.

Behind them, north of the Bad Lands Wall, Colonel E. A. Carr and four troops of the Sixth Cavalry (one of them commanded by a young lieutenant named John J. Pershing) were also making camp. Having moved in from the west, they had been sweeping the country all day in a fruitless search for Big Foot. Tomorrow they would sweep again. But not believing it possible for the Indians to have come so far so fast and to be already south of them, they erroneously planned to continue tomorrow's search to the north.

In Rapid City, where General Miles was now headquartered, the general was pacing the terrazzo floor of the Harney Hotel lobby looking as fierce as the stuffed buffalo heads that glared down from the panelled walls. He was furious with Sumner and had sent him a sharp reprimand. He was also furious with Big Foot, whom he thought was trying to join forces with the dancers on the Stronghold. In his dispatches to his commanders, Miles was saying that "Big Foot has been defiant to both the troops and to the authorities, and is now harboring outlaws and renegades from other bands. . . ." and he was determined to round up this defiant Indian and his band if it was the last thing he ever did.

Also at the Harney Hotel, the artist-writer Frederic Remington had just come in from a stay with Colonel Carr's cavalry at the mouth of Rapid Creek and was now preparing his latest article and sketch of the Indian troubles for *Harper's Weekly*.

Upon the windswept Stronghold, a delegation of five hundred "friendlies" headed by Little Wound, Big Road, and Fast Thunder were trying to persuade Short Bull and Kicking Bear and their dancers to give up and come into the agency.

At Chicago, the *Daily Tribune*—just now coming off the presses—carried the following story:

SITTING BULL'S RENEGADES ESCAPE

They Object to Being Disarmed and Fly to
the Bad Lands

. . . Col. Sumner mourns the loss of his Christmas present. Big Foot and Sitting Bull's renegades object to being disarmed and fled in the night. . . .

In the Indian camp on White River, Big Foot's illness was turning into pneumonia.

And everywhere, it was Christmas Eve . . .

By Christmas day Big Foot was so ill that the Indians moved only eight miles before camping at a place called Cedar Spring (now known as Big Foot Spring). From there the sick chief sent three riders to Pine Ridge to inform the Indian chiefs there that he was on his way to see them, that he was coming in peace, and that he was very ill.

Late that night a strong wind began building up, and the Indians arose in a wild roaring dawn with the clouds scudding across the sky so fast that looking up at them gave the feeling that the earth itself was moving. As the gale tore at the lodges, the thin agency-issue canvas whipped and slatted against the poles, and a few of the lodges that hadn't been tied down to an inside anchor stake in the old way were lifted up and overturned. Breaking camp, the Indians faced eye-stinging clouds of alkali dust as they fought their way against the wind for four miles to the shelter of steep bluffs along Medicine Root Creek; then camped to wait it out.

By the following morning the wind had died to a gentle westerly breeze. The sky was cloudless, and the sun held a promise of warmth to come. Before the Indians could break camp and take advantage of the good traveling weather, however, Big Foot's messengers returned from Pine Ridge. They brought word from the Pine Ridge chiefs that Short Bull and Kicking Bear had agreed to surrender, and they planned to come into the agency on the twenty-ninth. They wanted Big Foot to time his travel so that he would arrive at the same time. They also wanted Big Foot to know that there were now soldiers camped on Wounded Knee Creek looking for him, and the chiefs thought he should make a big swing to the south and then to the west in order to avoid them. The news of soldiers ahead caused Big Foot and his headmen to hold another council. Most of them were in favor of making a big southward swing around the soldiers, but this time Big Foot prevailed. He was too sick for all that extra traveling, he said; they would go on straight ahead and take their chances with the soldiers. Because of all the talking, it was noon when the Indians finally started moving, and since Big Foot was anxious to get to Pine Ridge before he became any sicker, and since later there was a bright moon to guide them, they traveled on into the night. When they finally camped near the deserted settlement of American Horse, they were only one long day's travel from the agency.

At sunrise on the twenty-eighth, the Indians broke camp once more and began following American Horse Road southwestward over the next divide to Porcupine Creek. At noon, while they were stopped for lunch on Porcupine Creek, the advance guard came in bringing four captured Indian army scouts. The scouts said they were from the camp on Wounded Knee, just ahead over the next divide. Detaining two of the scouts, Big Foot sent the other two back to report to the soldier chief, Major Whitside, that the Minneconjous of Big Foot were coming to his camp in peace. Two hours later the Indians and the soldiers met. Major Whitside said, "Big Foot, I want you to come to the camp with me." "All right," replied the chief, "I was going there anyway."

CHAPTER
13

AAAAAAA

Wounded Knee

IT WAS GROWING dusk when Major Whitside led his column of cavalry and captured Indians down the long slope to Wounded Knee. Light was fading fast from the hilltops, and the dimming valley was filling with the blue-gray shadows of the gathering night. The windows of Mousseau's trading post shone square and yellow with lamplight, and the still air was tangy with woodsmoke from the fires of the cavalry camp and held the first brisk touch of evening chill. Hooves and wagon wheels clattered and rumbled hollowly on the wooden planking of the Wounded Knee bridge as the column crossed and passed between the Wounded Knee post office on the right and Mousseau's store on the left. Suddenly, Mousseau found himself doing a lively business as Indians pushed and crowded up to the crude plank counter of his little store to buy sugar, candles, coffee, and other supplies. After this little flurry of shopping, Whitside kept the column moving. Turning sharply to the left at the store, he led the Indians southwest down Agency Road for about a quarter of a mile to the edge of a shallow, sheer-sided ravine that ran from the creek on the east up into the ridge on the west. Here, along the north edge of the ravine and about a hundred yards to the south of the cavalry's tents, Whitside ordered the Indians to set up their camp. Then, in the open space between the two camps, closer to the cavalry than to the Indians, he ordered a row of five big Sibley tents erected. The three on the east were for Indians who had no shelter of their own, the one on the west was for the interpreter-scouts, and the one between them was for the ailing Big Foot himself. After ordering the chief's tent to be equipped with a stove and the regimental assistant surgeon, Dr. James Glennan, to

178

attend him and to make him as comfortable as possible, Whitside had rations of bacon and hardtack distributed to the captive Indians. Meanwhile, he stationed troops so as to entirely surround the Indian camp, and on a low hill to the west of the cavalry tents and to the north of the Indian camp, he set his two little fast-firing Hotchkiss guns— which the Indians called "twice-shooting guns" because of their explosive shells. He aimed them directly into the Indian camp.

About half-past eight, the soft thunder of hundreds of shod hooves could be heard to the west, and the light of the low-hanging full moon revealed a long line of horsemen riding in. Earlier, just after he took the Indians into custody, Whitside had flashed a heliograph message to Pine Ridge in which he had announced the capture of Big Foot and, also, had requested that the commanding officer of the Seventh Cavalry, Colonel James W. Forsyth, bring the rest of the regiment out to assist in disarming the Indians. Now, accompanied by the remaining four troops of the Seventh, a troop of Indian scouts, and two more Hotchkiss guns, Colonel Forsyth arrived. He carried further orders from General Miles through General Brooke that read:

> Disarm the Indians. Take every precaution to prevent their escape. If they choose to fight, destroy them.

Assuming command, Forsyth deployed more troops around the Indian camp and stationed the troop of Indian scouts south of the ravine and a little distance back from it. He added his Hotchkiss guns to the two already in position on the low rise that would later become known as Cemetery Hill. Also accompanying Colonel Forsyth to Wounded Knee was the Pine Ridge storekeeper, James Asay, who had brought along a small keg of whiskey to toast the capture of Big Foot. Thus, after making the necessary dispositions of their troops and completing their other official chores, the officers celebrated. According to all reports, the celebration was neither lengthy nor particularly boisterous, and before long cavalry tents went dark as lanterns were extinguished; and, as lodge fires burned low, the lighted cones of the Indian tipis also darkened. Then, in the still, clear moonlight of a night that was not quite freezing (and therefore gentle for December) in the valley of Wounded Knee, both soldiers and Indians slept peacefully.

Early the next morning, as the sound of the army bugle echoed and died against the naked hills, the camp awoke in the gray, fresh-smelling dawn of a day that promised to be even more springlike than the day before had been. As yet there was no sign of the storm the medicine man had predicted and which the Indians were expecting. When they had been back in the camp on Medicine Root Creek, Yellow Bird had heard the owl hoot three times at sunset, which he said meant a big blizzard was coming in three days. This was the third day, but no matter. It was being said that the soldiers were taking them to Pine Ridge, so even if a storm did come, they would be there in just a few hours and well ahead of it. The women were happy this morning that their long journey was almost finished, and after a breakfast of bacon and hardtack, they sang and visited as they began loading their wagons. The youngsters, also, were enjoying the morning and were running and playing among the lodges (as one witness put it) "like children in a country schoolyard."

While the Indians were breakfasting, Colonel Forsyth was mulling over the approaching business of disarming the Indians. In the orders he had received from General Brooke, two points stood out as clearly as if chiseled in stone: one, he *must* disarm the Indians promptly and completely, and two, he *must not* allow any Indians to escape. Earlier, when he was in conference with his officers, the colonel had devised a plan whereby he hoped to execute those orders quickly and with a minimum of trouble. If sheer manpower were all he needed to make the operation successful, he could see at a glance there would be no problem. According to Major Whitside's count, the Indian strength was:

Men	120
Women and children	230
	350

On the other hand, the army strength was:

	Officers	Enlisted	Total
Seventh Cavalry, Headquarters	5	3	8
Seventh Cavalry, 1st Squadron	10	229	239
Seventh Cavalry, 2nd Squadron	10	181	191
Battery E, 1st Artillery	2	20	22
Scouts—Army officers	2		2
Scouts—Oglala Indians		30	30
	29	463	492

Artillery: Four Hotchkiss guns firing explosive shells 1.65 inches in diameter and weighing slightly over 2½ pounds. The four guns together capable of firing at the rate of not quite one shell per second.

Soldiers' weapons: Single-shot Remington rifles and Colt revolvers.

How many guns the Indians had, the colonel did not know; in fact, no one has ever known. Nonetheless, judging by the rifles Whitside saw when he intercepted Big Foot's band, and also by the fact that a rifle was a male necessity worth almost any sacrifice to most of the reservation Sioux, he could assume that well over half of the men had them. Furthermore, he could expect most of them to be Winchester twelve-shot repeaters—which would give the Indians a per-man firepower far superior to that of the soldiers with their single-shot Remingtons.

Finally, the colonel reflected, he would be in a better position if he had a more experienced force. A few of his officers were seasoned in Indian matters, but most of them, like the colonel himself, were not. Among the enlisted men there were a few well-seasoned noncommissioned officers, but aside from them almost none of his troops had ever been under fire or had ever faced any military danger—Indian or otherwise. Moreover, eighty of the men—about twenty percent of his enlisted force—were raw recruits, mostly from Eastern city slums, and of these about forty had been in the army hardly more than a month. Thus, he had a number of cavalrymen in his outfit who barely even knew how to ride a horse. Still, considering that he had the artillery and also had the Indian fighting men outnumbered four to one, he couldn't see that his disadvantages were very serious. Besides, the troops were not at Wounded Knee to fight, but actually only to make a show of strength sufficient enough to convince the Indians that their only choice was to submit peacefully to military orders.

Satisfied that his plans could now be executed successfully, at seven that morning Forsyth ordered the trumpeter to sound Officers Call, then instructed his commanders to deploy their troops thus:

The Indian men and grown boys were to be assembled near Big Foot's tent in the open area between the Indian and the cavalry camps. There they could be kept in a compact enough group to be easily managed and at the same time be surrounded with troops, thereby discouraging any attempts at resistance.

The four troops of the first squadron—Troops A, B, I, and K—were to provide close-in support and, rather than being mounted, would serve on foot in the following arrangement:

B Troop, commanded by Captain Varnum, was to form a line approximately two hundred feet long (making a space about four feet between each man) along the northwest side of the disarmament council area.

K Troop, under Captain Wallace, was to form a similar line along the southwest side of the council area, at a right angle to the B Troop line. Together, B and K Troops should be able to effectively seal the council area off from the Indian camp.

About forty men of A and I Troops were to form an east-west line between the cavalry tents and the foot of Cemetery Hill. This line would be roughly at a right angle to the B Troop line and just to the north of it, and it would be in position to protect the artillery on the hill. The remaining seventy-five or so men of A and I Troops were to form a long, widely-spaced line (approximately twenty feet between the men) around the west and south sides of the Indian village and well back away from it.

The troops of the second squadron—Troops C, D, E, and G—were to serve mounted, as were the Indian scouts, and were to form an outside perimeter of secondary support as follows:

Troop G, commanded by Captain Edgerly, was to establish a hundred-yard-long line along the southeast side of the council area, but well back from it—about two hundred yards to the east across Agency Road.

Troop E, under Lieutenant Sickel, was to take up a position on a small knoll immediately west of Cemetery Hill. From there it could give protection to the artillery and also prevent the Indians from escaping to the northwest.

Lieutenant Taylor was ordered to deploy his Oglala scouts in an east-west line about two hundred yards long and a hundred yards south of the ravine.

Finally, C and D Troops, commanded respectively by Captains Jackson and Godfrey, were ordered to stand in reserve in a second east-west line a little to the south of the line of Indian scouts.

As it turned out, Forsyth's troop arrangement later caused him to be court-martialed. In fact, about the most positive thing that could be said for it was that it clearly demonstrated that (despite countless later accusations to the contrary) the army did not have the slightest intention of getting into a fight with the Indians that day at Wounded Knee. At any rate, no matter how unfortunate its later consequences, the arrangement seemed all right to Forsyth at the time, and if any of his commanders thought otherwise, there is no record of their having said so. Therefore, at seven-thirty, just as the sun was climbing above the eastern ridge, the trumpeter sounded Assembly and the troops gathered and were given their orders.

While the soldiers were going to their assigned positions, Forsyth sent interpreter Philip Wells to tell the Indian men to assemble at Big Foot's tent for a council. In a few moments the musical call of the camp crier, Wounded Hand, could be heard singing out a message among the lodges, and shortly thereafter Indians began streaming into the council square around the chief's tent.

Inside the tent the regimental medical director, Dr. Hoff, was attending the ailing Big Foot. The chief's condition had worsened to the point where he was now barely able to sit up. He lay wrapped in his old gray overcoat with a blanket around that, and had a scarf pulled down over his head and knotted under his chin. Yet in spite of all the wrapping and the springlike morning, he was shivering with cold. Outside, the gathering Indians stood and sat in scattered groups, talking and smoking and telling jokes and waiting for the meeting to begin. At the tent, Forsyth and a few of his officers visited with Father Francis Craft, a Catholic priest, and with one or two news reporters. Lanky, good-natured Captain George Wallace was mingling with the Indians. There were only five officers left in the regiment who were veterans of the Custer fight at the Little Big Horn, and Wallace was one of them. The Custer fight notwithstanding, Wallace liked the Indians and they liked him. Moving among them now, the soft accents of South Carolina strong in his speech, he and the Minneconjous were joking and laughing together.

Omaha World Herald reporter T. H. Tibbles wandered up to the gun battery on Cemetery Hill. While Tibbles was visiting with Captain Charles Ilsley, the commander of the second squadron, Lieutenant Harry Hawthorne was looking out over the deployment of troops around the square. It appeared to him that their arrangement was such that if a fight did break out, they wouldn't be able to shoot at the Indians without also shooting at each other. He commented on this to Captain Ilsley, and then asked the question which, in one form or another, was asked countless times afterward (including at Forsyth's court-martial) and which haunted Forsyth for the rest of his life. He asked, "Isn't that a rather strange formation of troops in case there is any trouble?" Captain Ilsley laughed and replied, "There's no possibility of trouble that I can see. Big Foot wants to go to the agency, and we're a guard of honor to escort him."

At a little past eight, when it appeared that most of the men and grown boys had come into the council square, interpreter John Shangreau called for their attention and got them seated in a rough semi-circle to the south of Big Foot's tent, with the tent as its hub. Then, as Shangreau repeated the words in Lakotah, Forsyth made a little speech. It was a pleasant speech in which he used no stern words and made no threats. He simply said that the Indians were safe now, that the soldiers were their friends, and that their rations had been increased so that no one would have to go hungry anymore. However, the colonel added, there had recently been much trouble and, although there had been no fighting, there had been great danger of it. Therefore, he said, to prevent some accidental fight getting started he must ask them to give him their guns.

Ah-h-h! Now there was a rustling and murmuring among the Indians in the square. They had known since yesterday that the soldiers wanted their guns, but as it was not their custom to worry much about a thing until it was actually upon them, they hadn't been too concerned about it and had hoped the soldier chief would maybe even forget about the guns. Now they had to face it. He still wanted their guns even though they had already agreed to submit to him and to do all that he asked of them. Surely the soldier chief knew that meekly to surrender one's gun was to be something less than a man—it was almost to be like one who runs away when there is trouble. Besides, there had been some bad stories of how white men had disarmed Indians and then had shot them. Uncertain what to do, the Indians chose two of their men to confer with Big Foot. When they asked for his advice, he whispered, "Give them some of the bad guns, but keep the good ones." John Shangreau, who had followed the men into Big Foot's tent, then suggested to the chief that it would be well to give the guns up altogether; they could easily be replaced, he said, whereas "if you lose a man you cannot replace him." But Big Foot stuck to his decision and replied, "No! We will keep our good guns."

When the two men returned to the group outside, Forsyth and Whitside, not knowing what had taken place in Big Foot's tent, counted off twenty Indians from one end of the semi-circle and sent them to the Indian camp with instructions to bring back all the guns that were there. When they finally returned, they handed over only two rifles, both so broken and battered that Lieutenant Gresham of B Troop was moved to comment that they had been "long used, no doubt, as toys by the children." Irritated now, Whitside flatly told the Indians that he knew they had plenty of guns, and good ones, because he had seen them. The Indians denied it, saying these two were the only guns in the entire camp. At this, Whitside, who was as experienced in Indian dealings as Forsyth was inexperienced, advised the colonel that Big Foot should be brought outside and ordered to tell his people to cooperate. Bleeding from the nose now, Big Foot was carried out and laid in front of his tent, where Dr. Hoff remained beside him. Through interpreter Philip Wells, Forsyth asked the chief to tell his men to surrender their guns. "We have no guns," replied Big Foot. "The soldiers at Cheyenne River took them all away from us and burned them." This was not true and Forsyth knew it. He said to Wells, "You tell Big Foot that yesterday at the time of surrender his Indians were well armed, and that I am sure he is deceiving me." But again, having started his lie, Big Foot stuck to it and responded, "No! I gathered up all my guns at Cheyenne River agency and gave them to the soldiers and they burned them all up."

Forsyth and Whitside held a quick, quiet conference. Obviously they were going to get no help from the chief. The only thing to do, they decided, was to search the whole Indian camp. They established two search groups. Captain Wallace and Lieutenant Mann, taking fifteen men from their K Troop and Shangreau as interpreter, went to the east end of the camp. Captain Varnum and fifteen men from his B Troop, accompanied by squadron adjutant Lieutenant Garlington and interpreter Wells, went to the northwest end. Then the two details began working toward each other.

The search was a ticklish operation at best. The Indians were understandably jumpy, and incidents could easily occur. To minimize the hazard, Forsyth ordered that only officers were to enter the tents and that they were to use the utmost tact. The enlisted troops, who were to search only the outside areas, clearly overreacted. They unloaded wagons and dumped their contents on the ground, ripped open packs and took axes, hatchets, butcher knives, even the women's quilling awls—everything, in fact, that could conceivably be considered a weapon. The most delicate part of all, searching the women, had to be done, too; for the Indians had long ago learned the trick of concealing guns beneath the skirts and blankets of their women. But it was accomplished and it produced results. "The first rifle I found," said Captain Varnum, "was under a squaw who was moaning and so indisposed to the search that I had her displaced, and under her was a beautiful Winchester rifle." Reporter Charles Allen described watching the soldiers roll a woman over who was lying on the ground in front of a tent and thereby "exposing a gun handsomely concealed." Nevertheless, the searching of the women (which could so easily have been mishandled) seems to have been done with surprising tact. Lieutenant Mann wrote of it:

> The squaws were sitting on bundles concealing guns and other weapons.
> We lifted them up as tenderly and treated them as nicely as possible . . .
> they could not have been treated with more consideration. The squaws
> made no resistance. . . .

The most serious complaint from among the numerous survivor accounts given by the Indian women who were subjected to the search was that of Medicine Woman, who said,

> One white man with a Roman nose seemed to have a whole lot to do with
> me. Every now and then he felt around my waist to see if I had any knives.
> I threw my blanket back and showed them I didn't have anything.

All in all, considering the rummaging through and the scattering around of their belongings, and the searching of the women as well as the general indignity of being subjected to a search in the first place, the people of the camp accepted it with a remarkably small show of resentment. Much of the credit for that belongs to the genial Captain Wallace. A warm, easygoing man, he tried to put as good a face as possible on the operation, and while the troopers were rummaging through the camp, he was talking and joking with the women, playing with the youngsters, and chucking toddlers under the chin.

However, though the temper of the Indian camp remained easier than might have been expected as the long search went on, the mood of the hundred and six Indian men in the council square grew steadily worse. In the beginning they were fairly relaxed and compliant. Not because they did not resent what was happening; they did resent it—particularly the young men. But twenty-five years of being herded about by soldiers had given the Sioux a sort of fatalistic acceptance of such situations, and besides, it was hard to get too upset on such a beautiful day.

On December 29, 1890, Pine Ridge reservation was enjoying its best weather of the month and almost of the entire winter. It was a day so gentle and clear that the distant brown hills looked as warm and soft as rumpled deerskin, and it was so still that the faraway sounds could be heard clearly, and the thin brown haze of smoke rising from Mousseau's kitchen chimney stood straight as a sunflower stalk against the blue sky. So at first the Minneconjous around Big Foot's tent sat calmly enjoying the friendly sun as they smoked and talked. But as they continued to speak about this thing that was happening and about their lodges being searched, they looked around and saw how tightly they were encased in a box of soldiers who stood watching them with loaded guns, and a feeling of cold uneasiness began to build. As it did, more and more of them—especially the young men—began to mill about in rapidly increasing agitation. Big Foot, lying between his brothers-in-law, Iron Eyes and Horned Cloud, asked them to raise him so that he might quiet the commotion. His voice was too weak to be heard, however, and the restlessness continued to grow. About this time Yellow Bird, the medicine man, moved to the west side of the Indian circle, stretched his arms west toward the Messiah, and began to pray that the people's ghost shirts be made strong enough to protect them. When he finished praying, he began dancing around the circle and chanting and pausing periodically to throw handfuls of dust into the air. He also kept blowing an eagle-bone whistle, calling Wanbli Gleska, the spotted eagle that was the protector of the Nation. After completing the circle, Yellow Bird turned to the young men (more or less gathered together now) and exclaimed, *"Ahan!"* a warning word that means "Look out! Something bad is about to happen!" Then he cried out, "I have lived long enough!" It was a saying warriors often shouted before charging into a fight. Next he spoke to the young men:

> Do not be afraid! Let your hearts be strong to meet what is before you! There are lots of soldiers and they have lots of bullets, but the prairie is large and the bullets will not go toward you, but over the large prairies. . . . As you saw me throw up the dust and it floated away, so will the bullets float harmlessly away over the prairie.

At this the young men responded enthusiastically, *"Hau! Hau!"* That was a word of many meanings, but in this case it meant "Amen!" or "We believe!"

Hearing Yellow Bird's speech, Philip Wells told Forsyth, "That man is making mischief."

"Tell him to sit down," the colonel ordered. Wells did so, and after the medicine man continued to make "silent maneuvers or incantations" for a short time, he sat down and was temporarily silent. His damage, however, was already done. He had aroused a strong fear among all the men that they might be shot by the soldiers, and he had reminded the young men of the invulnerability of their ghost shirts. Moreover, he had talked to them as if he expected them to go to war. Altogether, he had created a bad atmosphere for what came next—the return of the search parties.

When the search details returned at half-past nine, they had collected a whole mountain of butcher knives, crowbars, axes, quilling awls, and other such things. They had uncovered only thirty-eight rifles, however, and only a few of them were good Winchesters. The rest were old and next to useless. They laid the guns in a pile on the north side of the square, where Lieutenant Preston guarded them by sitting on them while the officers discussed their next move. Yesterday, when the Indians met Whitside's troops, they had made no secret of their many good Winchesters. On the contrary, they had flourished them. So if those guns weren't in the lodges or on the wagons, the officers concluded, they had to be on the Indians themselves, concealed in their blankets. Just as they were saying this, Wells exclaimed to Forsyth, "There goes one with a rifle under his blanket!" Forsyth ordered a sergeant to seize the rifle, then, through Wells, he announced to the Indians that he knew some of them were carrying weapons and that now they must give them up. He did not wish to subject them to the indignity of a personal search, the colonel said. Therefore, he hoped they would come forward like men and surrender such weapons as they had and open their blankets to show they had no more. Whitside, Wallace, Varnum, and six troopers formed two facing inspection lines just west of Big Foot's tent. As they did, about twenty of the older men walked forward and opened their blankets. All were unarmed.

Yellow Bird, meanwhile, had begun chanting again and making speeches to the young men, none of whom had come forward. Now, Whitside ordered them to start doing so, and—amid growing tension—a few sullenly complied. Two of the first three of them who passed through the inspection line had rifles hidden in their blankets.

(Up to this point the record of the day's events is clear. Thereafter it is cloudy. Although there are many eyewitness accounts and a great deal of sworn testimony in existence, the excitement and confusion of the moment, the considerable emotional bias of the observers from both sides, and the inevitable distortions of memory have combined to produce a set of stories so varied they are often completely contradictory. The following account has been derived from the more consistent and more reasonable of those stories, and is—hopefully—a fair approximation of what actually happened.)

On seeing their guns being taken away, a young Indian leaped angrily to his feet. Some Indian witnesses said his name was Black Coyote and that he was deaf, others said his name was Hosi Yanka, which means (roughly) Deaf. All of them, however, agreed that he was a troublemaker. But whatever his name, the young man hauled a good Winchester from his blanket and began waving it over his head while parading around and shouting that it was his gun, that he had given much money for it, and that he would not give it up without being paid for it. At the same time this was going on, Yellow Bird was chanting, another medicine man was singing a ghost song, and all the young men who had not been disarmed were on their feet, drifting away from the disarmament line and toward the east side of the square.

Meanwhile, the tension in the square became something larger—a feeling of peril that was ominous and growing. The Indians felt it. They remembered that this was the Seventh Cavalry. At the Battle on the Greasy Grass (Little Big Horn) it had suffered the bloodiest defeat ever given white soldiers by Indians. It had lost Long Hair Custer and two hundred sixty-four men, whereas the Indians had lost only a handful. There were some who claimed that the Seventh had been thirsting for revenge ever since. Their sense of danger was quickened even more by Yellow Bird as he continued to dance among them chanting, "Don't be frightened—let your hearts be strong to meet what is before you—the Great Holy is with you—your ghost shirts will keep the bullets from you." Nerves tightened like drying bowstrings, and there was a feeling in the air like the cold wind that runs ahead of a thunderstorm.

The young troopers were as nervous as the Indians. They were green and unseasoned, and the greatest military danger most of them had experienced so far was learning to ride a horse. Now, suddenly, they were facing the Sioux. They knew from their dime novels that the Sioux were treacherous, butchering savages. On top of that, there was a fierce-looking old man wearing a painted and feathered nightshirt hopping around out there, chanting and blowing a whistle and throwing dirt at them. Their palms moistened and their fingers curled around the triggers of their old Remingtons.

The officers smelled danger, too. Lieutenant Mann recalled, "I had a peculiar feeling come over me—some presentiment of trouble." He passed the word quietly through K Troop, "Be ready. There is going to be trouble."

Colonel Forsyth called to Philip Wells, who was trying to persuade the influential Horned Cloud to quiet the medicine man and the young Indians, "You'd better get out of there. It's looking dangerous."

"Just a minute, Colonel," replied Wells, "I'm trying to get this fellow to quiet them." Even as he spoke, however, Wells saw a powerful young warrior stalking toward him from behind. Turning, Wells cautiously began to back out of the square.

Meanwhile, Black Coyote (or Hosi Yanka) had torn a strip of paper from an old brown bag and had moved off to the side. Holding his beloved rifle in the crook of his arm, he was trying to roll a big cigarette in the paper. As he did so, two sergeants who were after his gun slipped up from behind and seized him. There was a quick, fierce scuffle. The gun pointed skyward and fired. Then all in the same instant Yellow Bird threw a cloud of dust into the air, and half a dozen young Indians threw off their blankets and aimed their Winchesters at K Troop.

Lieutenant Robinson yelled, "Look out! They are going to fire!"

Varnum looked up from the search line and cried, "By God! They have broken!"

Philip Wells whirled around to find his Indian stalker lunging at him with a knife.

Lieutenant Mann remembered thinking, "The pity of it! What can they be thinking of!"

A split second later the Indian volley ripped into K troop, and Mann heard himself screaming, "Fire! Fire on them!"

Instantly, both B and K Troops fired volleys into the Indians, and the square exploded into a roar of gunfire and disappeared under swirling clouds of yellow-gray powder smoke.

"There was an awful roar." (Dog Chief)

"It sounded much like the tearing of canvas." (Rough Feather)

"Everything was smoking from then on." (Peter Stand)

"The smoke was so dense I couldn't see anything." (White Lance)

"People were lying all about where formerly they were all sitting or standing." (Richard Afraid-of-Hawk)

Philip Wells partially deflected his attacker's knife—it sliced through the end of his nose, which dangled over his mouth, held on by only two strips of skin.

Captain Wallace was running to rejoin K Troop when the second Indian volley tore away the top of his skull.

Big Foot struggled to sit up, caught a bullet in his head, and fell back beside the body of Horned Cloud. Seeing her father fall, Big Foot's daughter ran screaming toward him, was shot in the back, and fell dead across him.

As Father Craft moved through the smoke attending to the dying, an Indian plunged a knife deep into his back, collapsing a lung. Ignoring the wound, the priest went on with his work.

With the troops deployed as they were, any bullets from B Troop volleys that failed to strike Indians flew in the direction of G Troop— three hundred fifty yards to the east and across the road. Likewise, when both B and K Troops were shooting at the Indians from certain angles, they were also shooting at each other. The Indians were in a similar situation at their location; any of their bullets that missed the soldiers sped directly into the Indian camp. Thus, it is probable that some of the army casualties were caused by the soldiers' own guns, and that some of the Indian casualties among the women and children were caused by the Indians' own guns.

In a few moments the fighting in the square became hand to hand, and the struggling figures were indistinct in the dust and smoke as the Indians fought to break through the soldiers' lines. Within two or three minutes they had done so, a few fleeing toward the east, but most of them toward the Indian camp. To cover their retreat, those Indians who had guns turned even as they ran and fired at the troops behind them.

Once the Indians had broken free of the square, Colonel Forsyth spurred his horse up Cemetery Hill to the Hotchkiss battery, and Troops B and K fell back to the cover of the cavalry tents. Behind them the bloody dust of the council square was littered with the bodies of around thirty dead and wounded soldiers and about the same number of dead and wounded Indians.

Until then the troops stationed outside the square had only been able to look on in stunned disbelief. One moment the square had been silent. The next it had exploded in gunfire and disappeared beneath a pall of smoke that hung unmoving in the still air. They knew only that a fight had broken out. Nothing more. The guns on Cemetery Hill had been silent, also—unable to fire without slaughtering their own men.

Now that the fleeing Indians had separated themselves from the troops, however, the guns could be used. Hence, under the direction of Captain Capron, they began dropping shells into any of the Indian groups they saw firing at soldiers. In a few minutes, when most of the Indian riflemen were shooting from the camp itself, the Hotchkiss fire followed them, and shells began exploding among the lodges at the rate of almost fifty per minute. Now there was pandemonium. Lodges blazed up and burned. Shrapnel whirred and whistled and people screamed and fled—or fell. Many of the wagons had been hitched up for travel, and now the horses reared and squealed, some of them falling tangled in their harness, some of them running away with packs and other possessions flying from wagons that bounced and bounded over the rough prairie behind them. Suddenly, a few wagons loaded with women and children erupted out of the upper corner of the camp and raced northwest in a cloud of dust up Fast Horse Road—a path that led them directly under the guns of E Troop. Seeing that they were women and children, Lieutenants Sickel and Rice ordered their men not to fire. Then an old woman who was galloping alongside the wagons on a horse raised a rifle and fired at the troopers. "There's a buck!" one shouted and raised his gun.

"No! It's a squaw! Don't shoot on her!" commanded Rice.

"Well, by God, Lootenant, she's shootin' at us!" the trooper retorted. Nevertheless, E Troop held its fire and allowed the wagons to escape.

When the Hotchkiss shells began exploding in the camp, the women and children poured out and into the ravine, closely followed by the men. Facing them from the south bank was the wide-spaced line of men from A and I Troops commanded by Captain Nowlan. As the first wave rushed toward them, Nowlan called out, "Don't fire! They are squaws!" Then came the wave of men and he shouted, "Here come the bucks! Give it to them!"

Once in the ravine, most of the Indians started running up it to the west. One group of men, women, and children, however, went on across it and tried to escape to the south down Agency Road. There they ran into the lines of C and D Troops. "Commence firing!" ordered Captain

Godfrey. He remarked later that ". . . it seemed to me only a few seconds until there was not a living thing before us; warriors, squaws, children, ponies, dogs . . . went down before that unaimed fire." A number of women did escape, though, and ran toward Lieutenant Donaldson of C Troop. He sent them to safety behind the lines and ordered the troop's horse-holders to look after them.

Now, except for those who had either successfully fled the battle area or else were immobilized by their wounds, nearly all of the surviving Indians were in the ravine. If there actually ever were any justification for calling Wounded Knee a massacre, it is at this point that it occurred. Until now the action had been so furious, shifting, and confused that once the fighting erupted, it is most unlikely it could have been stopped by anyone. However, now that the Indians had become confined to the ravine, it seems likely that if the cavalry had withdrawn to a safe distance and then made overtures of peace, the outnumbered and outgunned Indians would almost certainly have stopped shooting. By the same token, it seems just as likely that if the Indians had ceased firing the army would have ceased also. But as it was, the Indians had little reason to trust the army's intentions, and in defense of themselves and their families, so long as they were being shot at and so long as their ammunition lasted, they could see no choice but to shoot back. Peter McFarland, a civilian packmaster who observed the fight, but took no part in it, remarked that the Indian sniping was so accurate that "it was almost certain death to advance along the gulch." Similarly, not knowing how the fight started, the soldiers naturally assumed it resulted from the "Sioux treachery" they had read and heard so much about. What's more, they knew they were being shot at and that some of them were being killed. Thus, like the Indians, they shot back also. The result was that both the Indians and the soldiers were caught up in one of those too often repeated tragedies of history wherein each side goes on fighting for the sole reason that the other side is; thus the senseless carnage continued.

On gaining the shelter of the ravine, the Indians were protected from direct fire by its sheer earthen walls. However, when their sniping from it drew the attention of the Hotchkiss guns, it became another matter. The walls gave no protection from the singing shrapnel of shell bursts, and as the ravine became murky with the dust and smoke of exploding rounds, more people died.

Back in the supposedly secure, body-littered council square, two

closely spaced shots rang out and two troopers grunted and fell.
Standing nearby, Packmaster McFarland saw a wisp of smoke curling
from a fresh-cut slit in the scout tent just to the west of Big Foot's and
immediately reported it to K Troop. A young private charged at the tent
with a knife, exclaiming, "I'll get the son of a bitch out of there!"

"Come back!" commanded Lieutenant Mann. But he was too late.
Before anything could be done, there was another shot and the trooper
cried out, "My God! I'm killed!" He spun around, ran a few steps, and
fell dead. Infuriated, the men of K Troop raked the tent with a hail of
gunfire, then rolled a burning bale of hay against it. As the flaming
canvas fell away, it revealed the body of Yellow Bird. The medicine man
was still clutching his rifle and was still fierce—even in death.

In the ravine, the Indians continued to flee westward, some of them
keeping on until the troopers shot them down farther along, some until
they escaped over the ridge to the west. Many, however, stopped at a
sheltered corner created by a sharp bend in the gulley about three
hundred yards west of the Indian camp and subsequently called "the
pocket." Not only did the women and children take refuge in the pocket,
but the remaining Indian riflemen collected there, also. One of them was
a twenty-five-year-old warrior named Iron Hail, who was later called
Dewey Beard. His father, Horned Cloud, had died beside Big Foot. His
wife had died among the lodges. According to his own account
afterward, Iron Hail had killed one soldier in the square and another one
while fleeing to the ravine. Running up the ravine, he overtook his
mother. She was weaving along badly wounded, with a pistol swinging
loosely in one hand. Seeing Iron Hail, she cried out, "My dear son, pass
me by! I am going to fall down now!" Just as she spoke, another bullet
struck her, and she died. Grieving and bitter, on reaching the pocket Iron
Hail led the men there in making it the last remaining center of Indian
resistance. Their fire immediately drew a response from the Hotchkiss
guns; but although the shell bursts made the pocket a hell of dust and
smoke, as well as wild with the wailing sound of frightened people
singing their death songs, the angle of the pocket was such that the
Hotchkiss guns weren't very effective. The Indians were pouring out a
deadly fire, and according to his brother, Joseph Horned Cloud, Iron
Hail himself killed four more soldiers from there. One of the Indian
rounds struck artillery Lieutenant Hawthorne, who was up on Cemetery
Hill. It hit him in his watch-pocket, and (as one soldier put it) "the works
[of the watch] were scattered through his anatomy," later requiring five

operations to remove it. Corporal Weinert heard Hawthorne cry out "Oh my God!" and saw him go down. Weinert later told investigators:

> I said, by God! I'll make them pay for that! and ran the gun [off the hill and] fairly into the opening of the ravine . . . they kept yelling at me to come back . . . I kept yelling for a cool gun. . . . Bullets were coming like hail from the Indians' Winchesters. . . . Once a cartridge was knocked out of my hand just as I was about to put it in the gun, and it's a wonder it didn't explode. I kept going in and pretty soon everything was quiet at the other end of the line.

With the resistance in the pocket ended, the firing died away. What followed seemed to be a great stillness, although it was not. There were still the cries of the wounded, the officers' shouted commands, and the wailing of the death songs. Then Philip Wells, his nose still dangling, started up the ravine calling, "All of you who are still alive, get up and come on over, you will not be molested or shot any more." Rough Feather remembered Wells in the ravine and said, "His face was all covered with blood . . . and of course he looked horrible."

Slowly at first, and fearfully and still in shock, the Indians who could come out did so. Troopers went in behind them to carry out the more seriously wounded. While this was going on, there followed one more tragic, senseless act. Up in the ravine a wounded man raised himself up and was bracing himself with his hands when a mounted platoon that didn't know the fighting had ended swept over a knoll to the west. There was a burst of gunfire, and the man went down. At this, Forsyth, already at the breaking point because of the storm that had erupted around him, screamed, "For God's sake! Stop shooting at them!"

And then it was over.

Wells walked back to the council square where lay the bodies of about twenty Indian dead and many wounded. In the breast pocket of one was a religious tract which had been perforated by the bullet that had killed its owner. On the cover was printed, "The Kingdom Of God Has Come Nigh Unto Thee."

Wells called out, "Those of you who are alive, raise your heads." A dozen or so heads were lifted. Then, from among the wounded, Big Foot's brother, Frog, raised himself up on his elbow, pointed with his chin toward Yellow Bird, and asked, "Who is that lying burned there?" When Wells told him, Frog lifted his closed fist and shot out his fingers toward the body in a gesture of deadly insult which meant "Nothing I could do to you would be as bad as what you deserve." Then in a voice trembling with grief and rage, he said to the scout, "He is our murderer. Only for him inciting our young men we would have been alive and happy."

Next the grim aftermath began. A field hospital was set up for emergency treatment of the wounded. When they were finally all gathered up, there were thirty-seven soldiers, two civilians (Philip Wells and Father Craft), and fifty-one Indians. Unquestionably there were many more Indian wounded who had escaped and either had been or would be picked up by other Indians and taken to their camps. How many will never be known.

The wounded Lieutenants Hawthorne and Garlington were loaded into one of the army ambulances, and Father Craft and a seriously hurt sergeant were loaded into the other. The rest of the army and Indian wounded were loaded into freight wagons whose beds had been softened by sacks of grain covered by a layer of straw. In still other wagons, the bodies of the twenty-five army dead were placed, including Captain Wallace, who had survived the Little Big Horn and become a friend of the Indians only to die at Indian hands in a battle he had tried to prevent.

About three-thirty that afternoon the sad caravan started for Pine Ridge. Behind it—littered over a wide area—lay the bodies of eighty-four Indian men, forty-four Indian women, and eighteen of their children; one hundred forty-six altogether. There were more. Some were dead in hidden places. Some of the escaped wounded would die later, as would seven of the fifty-one taken to Pine Ridge by the army. By making an accounting of the known survivors and the known dead, one can reasonably guess that the total number of Indians who died in the battle of Wounded Knee that day was no fewer than one hundred seventy and no more than one hundred ninety. But no one will ever know for sure.

By comparison to the Indians, the army had suffered little—but only by comparison. One out of every eight soldiers at Wounded Knee had been killed or wounded; a casualty rate which, in any ordinary engagement, would have been considered high indeed.

Unaware of the events unfolding at Wounded Knee, Pine Ridge agency began that day as placidly as any other. In the vast sprawl of camps surrounding the agency the Indians were passing the time in perfunctory chores, in visiting, or simply in warming themselves in the sun. On the porch of the dispensary was the usual line of Indians waiting to be treated by Dr. Eastman. At the boarding school, classes were in session. Of the army of reporters at Pine Ridge, only three had thought it worth the bother to go with Colonel Forsyth to Wounded Knee and now the rest of them were either idling around Jim Finley's hotel, or were at Asay's store waiting for the latest invention of the "news machine." At the Episcopal Church of the Holy Cross, Elaine Goodale and the Indian women from various church women's societies were sacking candy, because, as schoolteacher Thisba Huston Morgan later explained,

> on . . . Christmas Eve, there had been set up in . . . the Church of the Holy Cross, a huge cedar tree reaching to the ceiling. It was lighted by candles and (had a) large star at the top. It was festooned with yards and yards of strung popcorn and laden with little bags of fruit, candy, and nuts. . . .
>
> . . . Each day during the Christmas octave, the tree was to be redecorated and each night the Indians from the various outlying districts where the church had sub-missions, were coming in their turn to the Mother Church for Christmas gifts. . . .
>
> Five times the tree had been laden with gifts. Four times the beautiful Christmas service had been given in the Sioux language. . . .

The women now were preparing for the sixth of the eight Christmas parties when, just before ten o'clock, a muttering rumble of cannon fire could be heard coming from the distant northeast, and the serenity at Pine Ridge was shattered by the knowledge that something had gone terribly wrong at Wounded Knee.

A little past noon Indian runners came in with the first news of the battle. The moment their story was told, two rumors developed—both of them causing uproar and panic. According to the rumor flashing through the Indian camps, the white men had lined up Big Foot's people and then shot them down; now they were going to do the same to all the other Indians. In panic, a great many struck their lodges and soon, according to Elaine Goodale,

> . . . their white camps melted away like snow-banks in April. The brown hills were instantly alive with galloping horsemen and a long line of loaded wagons disappeared in the distance.

The news reached Short Bull and Kicking Bear a few miles down White Clay Creek where they were leading the last of the dancers into the agency. Upon hearing it, they immediately turned around and headed for the Bad Lands. Among the whites, the rumor spread that the Indians were rising, that they had cut off the cavalry, and that they were now moving to kill all the whites they could find. Terrified, the white women and children of the agency staff crowded into the big combination dispensary-council room-police headquarters where Dr. Eastman tried to calm them down.

Outside, a ghost-shirted warrior rode slowly down the main street calling out, "Prepare to fight! We are going to shoot into the agency!"

On the ridge just southwest of the agency, a line of mounted warriors appeared. Seeing this, Dr. Eastman became concerned for Elaine Goodale. On Christmas day this full-blood Sioux physican, who had been raised in a tipi and had gone from there to earn an M.D. at Boston University, had asked the teacher-writer-poet from Massachusetts to marry him and she had consented. Now he sent a messenger to the church with a saddle horse and instructions that she was to ride to Rushville to safety. She refused and instead stayed to help quiet the frightened people. Later she wrote,

> Soon the chapel and mission house were swamped by a crowd of sobbing, terrified women and children—church members. . . . The solid outside shutters were slammed to and the oil lamps lit, and an effort made to calm the excitement with the help of hot coffee and sandwiches.

Outside, it was beginning to look as if the warriors on the ridge were planning to attack the boarding school. To prevent them, American Horse and a body of his warriors moved to occupy the school grounds. At that, the warriors turned their attention away from the school and began a scattered, long-range firing at the agency buildings. Some of Brooke's officers asked permission to shoot back at them with the Hotchkiss gun. Showing both great restraint and understanding of the Indians' panic, Brooke not only refused permission for *any* firing at the Indians, but also wired Miles that "the Indians belonging to this agency are excited but not hostile." The result of Brooke's wisdom and forbearance was that no fighting broke out at the agency. Instead, about dusk the warriors withdrew and rode off to join the people fleeing toward the Bad Lands.

Near evening a cloud cover drifted in and darkness came early. By that time nearly half of the six thousand Indians camped about the agency had fled. The rest of them huddled in their lodges, quiet and frightened. The news of the Grand River fight and the death of Sitting Bull had caused hardly a ripple among the Brulés and the Oglalas. The killing of Big Foot and his people, however, had them shocked and stunned. In the agency buildings and in the church and school, whites and Indians sat by lamplight behind barred doors and shuttered windows, waiting for what would happen next.

At half-past nine the Seventh Cavalry rode in from Wounded Knee. This time it did not come proudly as was its custom, with guidons flying and the band playing "Garry Owen," but soberly and shocked as it escorted the wagons of dead and wounded. They took the wounded to the military hospital, but after receiving the army's wounded and thirteen of the injured Indians, the hospital was filled. The remaining thirty-eight Indians were then taken to the Church of the Holy Cross where the Sioux pastor, Thomas Cook, made a place for them by removing the pews and altar and covering the floor with straw and blankets. There, in the dim lamplight of the Christmas-decorated chapel, Dr. Eastman, Elaine Goodale, army physicians, and Indian church women cared for these final casualties of the Indians' dream of a new world.

Outside, a cold northwest wind sprang up and with it came a light, sifting snow. In the dark deserted valley of Wounded Knee, the bodies began to freeze where they lay, and the blood began to freeze where it had been spilled. When dawn came the bodies and the battlefield were blended together under a blanket of white. And so it was ended—not only a battle, but an age. The Industrial Age avalanche that had ground over the Sioux for so long had finally come to rest.

The settlers could go onward uninterrupted now—to build their fences, plow their fields, settle the land, and develop industries. And so, even though for many the future would turn out to be less bright than they expected, for most of them it was the beginning of an age of hope and promise.

And, although the Indians' ancient way of life had never been as rich as they now remembered it, that life had been one they understood. And it had been a free life, and therefore good. But now that life was gone forever; they must learn new ways, and for them the age of hope was ended.

Later, in looking back on Wounded Knee and the life that was lost, the Oglala medicine man, Black Elk, said:

I did not know then how much was ended. As I look back from the high hill of my old age . . . I can see that something else died there in the bloody mud and was covered up by the blizzard. A people's dream died there. It was a beautiful dream . . . [Now] the nation's hoop is broken and scattered. There is no center any longer, and the sacred tree is dead.

And in far-away Nevada, when the prophet Wovoka was told of Wounded Knee, he pulled his blanket over his head and mourned. Then, for perhaps the last time, he spoke not as Wovoka but as the voice of the Great Holy speaking through Wovoka, and he told his people of the Indians' life to come:

Hoo-oo! My children! My children! In days behind, many times I called you to travel the hunting trail or to follow the war trail. Now those trails are choked with sand; they are covered with grass, the young men cannot find them. My children, today I call upon you to travel a new trail, the only trail now open—the White Man's Road.

Epilogue

WITH THE STILLING of the guns at Wounded Knee, the subjugation of the American Indians was complete and the Indian wars were ended, even though there was a brief aftermath of violence. During the next several days angry warriors made scattered attacks on army units and a few more people died. White casualties were one civilian and three soldiers killed (one being Lieutenant Mann) and five soldiers wounded. Indian casualties numbered about the same. These skirmishes, however, were minor, like the last scattered stones that fall in the silence after an avalanche has run its course. While striving to avoid more bloodshed, Miles gradually tightened his noose of troops around the troubled area until, on January 15, the warrior Kicking Bear voluntarily placed his rifle at the feet of the warrior Miles. Then it was truly ended.

To head off any renewal of Indian agitation, Miles promptly arrested the twenty-five principal Ghost Dance leaders, with the intention of sending them to be confined at a military post. Meanwhile, however, Buffalo Bill Cody had persuaded the Secretary of War to allow him to hire them for a foreign tour with his Wild West Show. Thus—like some modern agitators whose activities have led to highly paid appearance tours rather than to jail—throughout the following year Kicking Bear, Short Bull and the others found themselves earning (for those days) big money while touring Europe with Buffalo Bill.

As for some of the others involved in the story of the Ghost Dance and Wounded Knee:

Philip Wells' much abused nose was taped back where it belonged and where it healed, leaving only a hairline scar.

201

Elaine Goodale and Dr. Eastman were married in New York City and then settled in Amherst, Massachusetts. He practiced medicine there, and both of them wrote articles and books in support of Indian causes.

Before leaving Sitting Bull's camp in October, Catherine Weldon had been told by the Indians that her attacks on the Messiah faith would bring tragedy upon her, and, coincidentally or otherwise, it came almost immediately. Within three weeks her son died of an infection contracted while they were traveling by riverboat to Kansas City. Also, on that same trip, the cases containing her silver, paintings, and other possessions were lost. After arriving in Kansas City, the now bereaved, impoverished and embittered Mrs. Weldon wrote a stream of letters to Sitting Bull, and became even more embittered when he answered none of them.

General Miles removed Forsyth from his command six days after Wounded Knee. Accusing the colonel of having permitted the massacre of non-combatants and also of deploying his troops so that they suffered casualties from their own cross-fire, Miles appointed a court of inquiry that, he was certain, would confirm these charges. In the subsequent intensive investigation, the court amassed a body of evidence too impressive to be ignored by any objective historian. From it the court concluded that only in isolated instances had non-combatants been deliberately killed. According to the evidence, most casualties among the women and children had resulted from the confusion of battle, from the warriors' firing from the midst of non-combatant groups and thus drawing rifle and cannon fire upon them, and from the inability of inexperienced and excited young troops to distinguish between blanket-clad men and blanket-clad women. Furthermore, the court reported, although some troops had been so positioned that they *could* have taken casualties from their own cross-fire, it could prove no instance in which they actually had. Accordingly, the court found Forsyth innocent of both charges.

Nevertheless, as previously revealed by his attitude toward Sitting Bull and Big Foot, once Miles made up his mind about a man it stayed made up. Therefore, and in a way that told the investigators they'd better find Forsyth guilty of *something,* he ordered the investigation repeated. The court's second findings differed from its first only in that it now charged Forsyth with unwise deployment of B and K Troops. Adding a stinging endorsement in which he accused Forsyth of both disobedience and incompetence, Miles forwarded the report to Washington. To his disgust, the endorsement failed to influence either Secretary Noble or Commanding General Schofield, and Miles was ordered to restore Forsyth to his command.

Prior to Wounded Knee most of the press had been, as one correspondent said, "hollering for more blood!" And there is substantial evidence indicating that without the newspapers' distortion of the facts and continual agitation of both whites and Indians, there would not have been a Battle of Wounded Knee. According to prominent journalist-historian Professor Elmo Scott Watson of Northwestern University, "The seeds of newspaper jingoism . . . had borne bitter fruit in an 'Indian massacre' in which red men were the victims . . ." But once it had obtained the blood it had been "hollering for," much of the press faced about and began working the other side of the street. Consequently, the Indians they had been calling "treacherous" and "murderous" were now "innocent victims," and the soldiers they had been picturing as heroic defenders of the frontier were now murderers and were guilty of "slaughter without provocation." This was especially true of the Democratic papers, for in Wounded Knee they saw a chance to brand the Republican administration with the guilt of a brutal bloodletting. However, Republican and Democratic papers alike resurrected the ghost of George Armstrong Custer and joined in promoting the grimly romantic notion that the Seventh Cavalry had somehow arranged the killing at Wounded Knee in revenge for Custer's defeat at the Battle of the Little Big Horn.

Although more than eighty years have passed now since that bloody morning at Wounded Knee Creek, neither the accusations nor the evidence concerning it have changed very much. Today as in the past, the accusations are, more often than not, emotional, factional, sensational, and dramatic. On the other hand, the evidence is more prosaic, matter-of-fact, and less dramatic. This may be why we have generally come to know and accept the story of Wounded Knee more in terms of the accusations than of the evidence, and have come to understand it as a simple confrontation between Good and Evil rather than as the complex tragedy of errors that the evidence indicates it actually was.

The truth is, the facts of Wounded Knee have been so long obscured by the dust of controversy and the evidence is so incomplete and so often contradictory that we will never know just how the blame should be distributed. But it is time we stopped concerning ourselves with the blame anyhow, because what's done is done, and knowing the details wouldn't change it. In their relationships with each other it is high time both whites and Indians ceased to dwell upon "the guilt of our grandfathers" and upon the injustices, both real and fancied, of long ago. Instead, it is now time that we get on with the business of achieving equality and justice for both Indians and whites in the future, for that is where all of us and our children will spend our lives.

Bibliography

1. BOOKS

Andrist, Ralph K., *The Long Death*. New York: The Macmillan Company, 1964.

Armstrong, Virginia Irving, *I Have Spoken —American History Through the Voices of the Indians*. Swallow Press, June 1971.

Boyd, James P., *Recent Indian Wars*. Philadelphia, 1891.

Brown, Dee, *Bury My Heart at Wounded Knee*. Holt, Rinehart & Winston, 1970.

Brown, Joseph Epes, *The Sacred Pipe— Black Elk's Account of the Seven Rites of the Oglalla Sioux*. Norman: University of Oklahoma Press, 1953.

Chief Eagle, D., *Winter Count*. Johnson Publishing Co., 1967.

Cody, W. F., *An Autobiography of Buffalo Bill*. New York: Cosmopolitan Book Corp., 1920.

Cook, James H., *Fifty Years on the Old Frontier*. Norman: University of Oklahoma Press, 1957. Original copyright, New Haven: Yale University Press, 1923.

Deloria, Vine, Jr., *In Utmost Good Faith*. Straight Arrow Books, 1971.

Eastman, Charles A. (Ohiyesa), *The Soul of the Indian*. Boston and New York: Houghton Mifflin Co., 1911.

Frink, Maurice M., *Photographer on an Army Mule*. Norman: University of Oklahoma Press, 1965.

Hamilton, Henry W. and Hamilton, Jean Tyree, *The Sioux of the Rosebud, A History in Pictures*. Norman: University of Oklahoma Press, 1971.

Hassrick, Royal B., *The Sioux—Life and Customs of a Warrior Society*. Norman: University of Oklahoma Press, 1964.

Hyde, George E., *Red Cloud's Folk*. Norman: University of Oklahoma Press, 1937.

——, *A Sioux Chronicle*. Norman: University of Oklahoma Press, 1956.

Jackson, Donald, *Custer's Gold—The United States Cavalry Expedition of 1874*. New Haven: Yale University Press, 1966.

McGillycuddy, Julia B., *McGillycuddy: Agent*. Palo Alto: Stanford University Press, 1941.

McGregor, James H., *The Wounded Knee Massacre*. Baltimore: Wirth Bros., 1940.

McLaughlin, James, *My Friend the Indian*. Boston and New York: Houghton Mifflin Company, 1910.

MacLeod, William Christie, *The American Indian Frontier*. New York: Alfred A. Knopf, 1928.

Miles, Gen. Nelson A., *Serving the Republic*. New York: Harper & Brothers, 1911.

Morison, Samuel Eliot, *The Oxford History of the American People*. New York: Oxford University Press, 1965.

Neihardt, John G., *Black Elk Speaks.* Lincoln: University of Nebraska Press, 1961.

Nelson, Bruce, *Land of the Dakotahs.* Minneapolis: University of Minnesota Press, 1946.

Olson, James C., *Red Cloud and the Sioux Problem.* Lincoln: University of Nebraska Press, 1965.

Putney, Effie Florence, *In the South Dakota Country.* Educator Supply Co., 1922.

Russell, Don, *The Lives and Legends of Buffalo Bill.* Norman: University of Oklahoma Press, 1960.

Sandoz, Mari, *Old Jules.* Boston: Little, Brown & Co., 1935.

Schell, Herbert S., *History of South Dakota.* Lincoln: University of Nebraska Press, 1961.

Sell, Henry, and Weybright, Victor, *Buffalo Bill and the Wild West.* New York: Oxford University Press, 1955.

Standing Rock Sioux Tribal Council, *Treaties and Agreements, and the Proceedings of the Treaties and Agreements of the Tribes and Bands of the Sioux Nation.* Compiled and published by the Standing Rock Sioux Tribe, Fort Yates, North Dakota, 1973.

Tebbel, John, and Jennison, Keith, *The American Indian Wars.* New York: Bonanza Books, 1960.

Tibbles, Thomas Henry, *Buckskin and Blanket Days.* Garden City: Doubleday & Co., 1957.

Time-Life Books Editors, "Old West Series": *The Expressmen,* 1974; *The Forty-Niners,* 1974; *The Indians,* 1973; *The Pioneers,* 1974; *The Railroaders,* 1973; *The Soldiers,* 1973; *The Trailblazers,* 1973. New York: Time-Life Books.

Utley, Robert M., *Frontier Regulars, the United States Army and the Indian, 1866–1890.* New York: The Macmillan Company, 1973.

———, *Last Days of the Sioux Nation.* New Haven: Yale University Press, 1963.

Vestal, Stanley, *New Sources of Indian History.* Norman: University of Oklahoma Press, 1934.

———, *Sitting Bull—Champion of the Sioux.* Boston and New York: Houghton Mifflin Company, 1932.

Walsh, Richard J., *The Making of Buffalo Bill.* Indianapolis: Bobbs-Merrill Co., 1928.

2. GOVERNMENT PUBLICATIONS

Cohen, Felix S., *Handbook of Federal Indian Law,* U.S. Government Printing Office, Washington, 1945.

Commissioner of Indian Affairs, *Annual Reports,* 1890–91.

Densmore, Frances, *Teton Sioux Music,* Bureau of American Ethnology Bulletin 61, Washington, 1918.

Mooney, James M., *The Ghost-Dance Religion and the Sioux Outbreak of 1890,* 14th Annual Report of the Bureau of American Ethnology, 1892–93, Pt. II, Washington, 1896.

Secretary of War, *Annual Report,* 1891.

3. MANUSCRIPT MATERIAL

Nebraska State Historical Society. The Judge Eli S. Ricker Collection. The McLaughlin Papers (assembled by Reverend Louis Pfaller).

4. NEWSPAPERS

Bismarck Tribune
Black Hills Daily Times (Deadwood)
Black Hills Union (Rapid City)
Buffalo Gap Republican
Chadron Advocate
Chicago Daily Tribune
Custer Chronicle
London Times
Mandan Daily Pioneer

New York Times
New York Tribune
Omaha Daily Bee
Omaha World Herald
Pierre Daily Free Press
Rapid City Journal
The Republican (Valentine)
Sioux Falls Leader
Sturgis Weekly Record

5. Periodicals and Articles

Eastman, Elaine Goodale, "The Ghost Dance War and Wounded Knee Massacre of 1890–91," *Nebraska History*, 26 (1945).

Fechet, Col. E. G., "The Capture of Sitting Bull," *South Dakota Historical Collections*, 4 (1908).

Goodale, Elaine, "On the Indian Question," *Hartford Courant* (Oct. 16, 1885).

Greene, Jerome A., "The Sioux Land Commission of 1889: Prelude to Wounded Knee," *South Dakota History*, Vol. 1, #1 (Winter 1970).

Harper's Weekly, 1890–91.

Jacobsen, Ethel, "Life in an Indian Village," *North Dakota History*, Vol. 26, #2 (Spring 1959).

Jordan, William Red Cloud, "80 Years on the Rosebud," *South Dakota Historical Collections*, 35 (1970).

Lee, Bob, "Indian Leaders," *Wi-Iyohi*, Bulletin of *South Dakota Historical Society* (May 1, 1957).

———, "Messiah Craze—Wounded Knee," *Wi-Iyohi*, Bulletin of *South Dakota Historical Society* (May 1, 1955).

———, "Messiah War on Cheyenne River," *Wi-Iyohi*, Bulletin of *South Dakota Historical Society* (Nov. 1, 1963).

Morgan, Thisba Huston, "Reminiscences of My Days in the Land of the Ogalalla Sioux," *South Dakota Historical Collections*, 19 (1958).

North American Review, "The Future of the Indian Question" (January 1891).

Olson, Louise P., "Mary Clementine Collins, Dakotah Missionary," *North Dakota History*, Vol. 19, #1 (January 1959).

Palais, Dr. Hyman, "A Survey of Early Black Hills History," *The Black Hills Engineer*, Vol. 27, #1 (Rapid City: South Dakota School of Mines, April 1941).

Parker, Mrs. Z. A., "Ghost Dance at Pine Ridge," *Journal of American Folk-Lore*, 4 (1891).

Pfaller, Father Louis, "Indian Scare of 1890," *North Dakota History*, Vol. 39, #2 (Spring 1972).

Pound, Louise, "The John G. Maher Hoaxes," *Nebraska History*, 33 (1952).

Remington, Fredric, "Chasing a Major-General," *Harper's Weekly*, 34 (Dec. 6, 1890).

———, "The Art of War and Newspaper Men," *Harper's Weekly*, 34 (Dec. 6, 1890).

———, "The Sioux Outbreak in South Dakota," *Harper's Weekly*, 35 (Jan. 24, 1891).

———, "Lieutenant Casey's Last Scout," *Harper's Weekly*, 35 (Jan. 31, 1891).

Riggs, Theodore F., M.D., "Sitting Bull and the Ghost Dance," *South Dakota Historical Collections*, 29 (1958).

Robinson, Doane, "The Education of Red Cloud," *South Dakota Historical Collections*, 12 (1924).

Steel, Maj. M. F., "Buffalo Bill's Bluff," *South Dakota Historical Collections*, 9 (1918).

Sweeney, Mary Hopkins, "Indian Land Policy Since 1887 with Special Reference to South Dakota," *South Dakota Historical Collections*, 13 (1926).

Watson, Elmo Scott, "The Last Indian War, 1890–91—A Study of Newspaper Jingoism," *Journalism Quarterly* (1943).

Wells, Philip, "Ninety-Six Years Among the Indians," *North Dakota History*, Vol. 15, #4 (October 1948).

Williamson, John, "Paul Highback's Version of the Disaster of Wounded Knee," *Wi-Iyohi*, Bulletin of *South Dakota Historical Society* (June 1, 1956).

Index